Re-Centring the City

FRINGE

Series Editors
Alena Ledeneva and Peter Zusi, School of Slavonic and
East European Studies, UCL

The FRINGE series explores the roles that complexity, ambivalence and immeasurability play in social and cultural phenomena. A cross-disciplinary initiative bringing together researchers from the humanities, social sciences and area studies, the series examines how seemingly opposed notions such as centrality and marginality, clarity and ambiguity, can shift and converge when embedded in everyday practices.

Alena Ledeneva is Professor of Politics and Society at the School of Slavonic and East European Studies of UCL.

Peter Zusi is Associate Professor of Czech and Comparative Literature at the School of Slavonic and East European Studies of UCL.

Re-Centring the City

Global Mutations of Socialist Modernity

Edited by Jonathan Bach and Michał Murawski

First published in 2020 by
UCL Press
University College London
Gower Street
London WC1E 6BT

Available to download free: www.uclpress.co.uk

ISBN: 978-1-78735-413-5 (Hbk.)
ISBN: 978-1-78735-412-8 (Pbk.)
ISBN: 978-1-78735-411-1 (PDF)
ISBN: 978-1-78735-414-2 (epub)
ISBN: 978-1-78735-415-9 (mobi)
DOI: https://doi.org/10.14324/111.9781787354111

Contents

List of figures

List of contributors

Pushpa Arabindoo is an associate professor in Geography & Urban Design at UCL, Department of Geography.

Jonathan Bach is a professor of Global Studies, at The New School, New York.

Yevgenia Belorusets is an artist working in Kyiv and Berlin.

Khadija von Zinnenburg Carroll is Professor and Chair of Global Art History at the University of Birmingham, Department of Art History, Curating and Visual Studies.

Clementine Cecil is the executive director of Pushkin House, London.

Izabela Cichońska is an architect based in Poland.

Joy Gerrard is a multimedia artist working between London and Belfast.

Stephen Graham is a professor of Cities and Society at Newcastle University, School of Architecture, Planning and Landscape.

Owen Hatherley is a journalist working in London.

Adam Kaasa is a senior tutor at the Royal College of Art, London, School of Architecture.

Jennifer Mack is a lecturer at KTH Royal Institute of Technology, Stockholm, School of Architecture.

Michał Murawski is a lecturer in Critical Area Studies at UCL, in the School of Slavonic and East European Studies.

Patrick Neveling is a researcher at the University of Bergen, Department of Social Anthropology.

Vladimir Paperny is a professor at the University of California at Los Angeles, Department of Slavic, East European and Eurasian Languages and Cultures.

Daria Paramonova is the CEO of Strelka Architects.

Karolina Popera is an architect based in Poland.

Oleksiy Radynski is a filmmaker and author based in Kyiv, Ukraine.

Natalia Romik is an independent researcher currently carrying out a postdoctoral project on Jewish architectural heritage in Eastern Europe supported by the Gerda Henkel Foundation.

Andreas Schönle is a professor of Russian at the University of Bristol, School of Modern Languages.

Kuba Snopek is an architect and researcher, and the BA Programme Director at the Kharkiv School of Architecture.

Jonas Tinius is a postdoctoral research fellow at the Humboldt University of Berlin, Department of European Ethnology, Centre for Anthropological Research on Museums and Heritage.

Vyjayanthi Venuturupalli Rao is the director of the Terreform Center for Advanced Urban Research in New York City.

Tom Wolseley is an artist and filmmaker living in London.

Preface

The UCL Press FRINGE series presents work related to the themes of the UCL FRINGE Centre for the Study of Social and Cultural Complexity.

The FRINGE series is a platform for cross-disciplinary analysis and the development of 'area studies without borders'. 'FRINGE' is an acronym for Fluidity, Resistance, Invisibility, Neutrality, Grey zones and Elusiveness – categories fundamental to the themes that the Centre support. The oxymoron in the notion of a 'fringe centre' expresses our interest in (1) the tensions between 'area studies' and more traditional academic disciplines, and (2) social, political and cultural trajectories from 'centres to fringes', and inversely from 'fringes to centres'.

The series pursues an innovative understanding of the significance of fringes: rather than taking 'fringe areas' to designate the world's peripheries or non-mainstream subject matters (as in 'fringe politics' or 'fringe theatre'), we are committed to exploring the patterns of social and cultural complexity characteristic of fringes and emerging from the areas we research. We aim to develop forms of analysis of those elements of complexity that are resistant to articulation, visualisation or measurement.

The present volume re-examines architectural and urban modernity by projecting the topic through the prism of what was once called the 'second world'. In Cold War terminology, the 'second world' bore distinct connotations of second-class, and thus in some sense of peripherality. But this volume understands 'second world' as a central pivot between what that older schema called the 'first' and 'third' worlds. By replacing the obsolete term 'second world' with the conception of a 'Global East', this volume de-anchors the East from any specifiable geographical space, produces a novel genealogy of its architecture, and reveals its pattern: re-centring the city.

Alena Ledeneva and Peter Zusi,
School of Slavonic and East European Studies, UCL

Acknowledgements

Re-Centring the City is the product of several years of collaborative thinking and talking. The project started off as a panel at the American Anthropological Association convention in Washington, DC in November 2014, then ballooned into a mammoth international conference held at London's Calvert 22 in June 2016, the first of the many international events organised under the auspices of UCL's FRINGE Centre. A great many people contributed to both of these first two events, as well as to the process through which the book gathered shape and coherence during subsequent years. In particular, the authors would like to thank Alena Ledeneva, the founding director of the (delightfully oxymoronically named) FRINGE Centre, for her enthusiasm for our endeavour (which at first sight may seem somewhat contradictory to the goals and styles of FRINGE, but – as her and Peter Zusi's Preface explains – is entirely symbiotic with them). We would also like to thank Jan Kubik, the Director of the School of Slavonic and East European Studies, UCL, at the time of the conference, for the energy and support which he gave to our project, and Akosua Bonsu for her indispensable participation and support on intellectual as well as organisational fronts. Several other UCL students, and colleagues from UCL (and beyond), also made an active contribution to the conference, whether on stage or behind the scenes, among them Uilleam Blacker, Wendy Bracewell, Victor Buchli, Xinyu Guan, Andrew Harris, Claire Melhuish, David Mountain, Claudia Roland, Jordan Rowe, Rūta Valaitytė, Leyla Williams and Peter Zusi. Douglas Murphy took most of the participants on a surreal journey around what was then and probably still is London's most spectacular site of zombie monumentality, the Olympic Park. At Calvert 22, Will Strong, Elizaveta Butakova-Kilgariff, Lesya Myata, Ruxandra Mateiu and Anastasia Nikitina produced the Power and Architecture exhibition and programme, under the auspices of which our conference took place, and Sam Goff and Anastasiia Fedorova of the *Calvert Journal* gave our ideas and several of our authors exposure to a wider audience. Apart from FRINGE, the UCL Mellon Programme, the Grand Challenge for Sustainable Cities, the UCL Urban Lab and the New School Global Studies Program provided generous funding and institutional support. In the later stages of the project, UCL Press's Chris Penfold has been a supremely patient and understanding editor, while the three anonymous peer reviewers who took the time to read the manuscript closely provided extensive and engaged feedback, without which the present manuscript (and our own contributions to the volume) would have taken on a much more discombobulated form. Finally, we would like to express particularly heartfelt, existential gratitude for the efficient, thoughtful and confident editorial work of Erin Simmons, who provided a saviour-like centripetal impulse during the final several months of work on pulling together the final version of this manuscript and to Julia Ballester for her invaluable assistance with the index.

Introduction: Notes towards a political morphology of undead urban forms

Jonathan Bach and Michał Murawski

Towards a political morphology of the centre

The idea of the city dominated by a soaring landmark or a grand epicentre – whether a sacred temple, a secular monument, or a single central business district – has allegedly been buried along with high modernity and replaced with the polycentric, distributed and purportedly 'smart' city. In the same crypt, we are told, lies the socialist city, leaving a legacy of ruin, relic, failure and obsolescence. This book argues that not only are such characterisations empirically inaccurate, but they contain contestable normative assumptions about how urban form relates to ideology. Instead, we wish to draw attention back towards the centre to better understand the relation between power, architecture, planning and politics, and to invite new theoretical understandings of cities in relation to state processes and sociocultural structures left incomplete by neoliberal explanations of urban transformation. In so doing, we question the linear grand narrative in which a discrete high modern epoch, dominated by central ensembles, is transformed into a twenty-first-century epoch of political, economic and spatial decentralisation. We do this not to embrace some kind of reactionary valorisation of centrality, but rather to signal a discomfort with the way that polycentricity, when viewed as inevitable and unquestionably laudable, has become a kind of urban 'end of history' that risks obscuring its own politics and potential for transformation. How, the book asks, can we empirically understand the continued and powerful influence of centrality on the formerly socialist and late-capitalist cities of today, both as a metaphorical position from which political or economic power emanates, and as an actual architectural form or urban morphology?

Centrality is generally considered an exemplary high modern urban concept, practice, ideology, form and aesthetic. Sometime during the second half of the twentieth century, between the horizontal vernacularism of Denise Scott Brown, Robert Venturi and Steven Izenour's *Learning from Las Vegas* and Google's plans for 'smart cities' (with the collapse of the Soviet Union in between), politicians, planners and scholars rallied around a new urban age said to be taking shape in its place. This age promised to be humbler, more sustainable, polycentric and periphery-oriented: brownfield eco-cities instead of monumental axes or skyscraper forests; relational-aesthetic 'micro-utopias' instead of heaven-storming atheist ziggurats; pop-up innovation hubs rather than palaces of culture; fleeting anti-statues in place of equestrian heroes and triumphal arches; Amazon, Airbnb and WeWork on the relics of the Galeries Lafayette, the Grand Hotel, and Lord & Taylor.

Ideologically, then, from the late twentieth century on, the centre began to be associated with authoritarian polities and command economies, exemplified by grandiose central ensembles and architectural monumentality. Meanwhile, liberal democracies and late capitalism became increasingly associated with architectural asceticism or decentralisation, moving away from classic capitalism's love affair with monumentality and verticality. In this vein, the world's most influential planning theorists, economists and political scientists – from Jane Jacobs to Economics Nobel laureates Paul Krugman and Elinor Ostrom – described and celebrated the dismemberment of 'inflexible' and 'authoritarian' urban monocentricity.[1] In its place the de-centred or 'polycentric' city has come to consolidate itself as today's hegemonic spatial form of neoliberal urbanism, promising a more efficient distribution of work, residence and government. We have nothing against efficiency, yet we wonder about the ways in which the discourses of democracy are being used to make discourses of neoliberalism seem self-evident.

Is this decentralising, centrifugal tendency really as absolute, inevitable, or even desirable, as its prophets claim? Metaphorically, it is the centre that holds things together, providing the right balance for the alignment of political, spatial and social forces. When the centre cannot hold, as in Yeats's poem 'The second coming', things famously fall apart. It is no coincidence that this poem trended sharply on Twitter in the days following the Brexit referendum in June 2016, and again following Donald Trump's election victory in November of that year ('what rough beast, its hour come round at last / Slouches towards Bethlehem to be born?').[2] By contrast, when centrist saviour of the established order Emmanuel Macron defeated revamped neo-fascist Marine Le Pen in the

French presidential elections in April 2017, the Tweets and headlines read – surprise, surprise – 'the centre holds'.

Yet the city centre is a metaphor written in stone and streets – it is the exertion of power through the symbolic representation of the built environment. As such, the city centre provides a conundrum for political power as part of the age-old struggle between the decentralisation and re-centralisation of power. Power changes its shape with the rise and fall of regimes, ideologies and economies, but the shape of the built environment is harder to change with elections and revolutions. Rather, new forms of power appropriate the centre in new ways, repositioning (sometimes literally) its monumentality. Today, when the global political and economic order is increasingly subject to both the centrifugal impulses of neoliberalism and the centripetal tendencies of neo-populism, the time is right to revisit the very concept of the 'centre' in thinking through the morphology of the urban today.

The de-centred, polycentric city, much in vogue over the last few decades, relies on a binary of urban centrality and peripherality that is constantly threatening to fold in on itself, and for that reason remains the focus of sustained and often violent efforts to police and reinforce its boundaries, as well as of creative attempts to confuse and confound them. We can speak, guardedly perhaps, of a 'crisis' of centrality and its attendant forms of monumentality and verticality which gives rise to skyscrapers distributed like shards across the cityscape, to inverted cities, ghost cities, anti-cities, instant cities and ex-cities.[3] This crisis of centrality gives rise equally to morphologically confusing political trends that centralise power as they move 'from the extreme fringe to centre stage',[4] mixing up fringe and centre in what anthropologist Michael Taussig has called 'the new normal, in which Trump Tower displaces the White House' (although, as he notes, 'there is no normal anymore').[5]

The essays collected here are part of a conversation stretching over the past hundred years, during which a great deal of scholarly energy has been expended on interrogating the permutations of the back-and-forth between concentration and dispersal – the 'ceaseless battle between centrifugal forces that seek to keep things apart, and centripetal forces that strive to make things cohere', as Michael Holquist puts it with reference to Mikhail Bakhtin's philosophy of language.[6] To name a few prominent, canon-forming instances, these have included explorations into fission and fusion,[7] charisma and kingship[8] in political anthropology, centre–periphery relations in political sociology and international relations,[9] Marxist political economy,[10] ancient archaeology[11] and broadly defined urban studies,[12] studies of polycentric organisation in science and government,[13] theories of morphology and period in art and architectural history,[14] modes of arborescence versus rhizomaticity or linearity and non-linearity in continental philosophy,[15] and models of centrifugality and centripetality in urban economic geography.[16]

From its vantage point of the experience of the 'Second World' (discussed more fully below), this volume continues this interrogation, questioning the established 'political morphologies' (commonly held linkages between style and shape, aesthetics and geometry) and examining the ongoing play of de- and re-centring. There has never been an immutable relationship between liberal democracy and decentralisation, but the current, Yeats-trending crisis of centrality is doing a particularly vivid job of laying bare the inadequacies of our established categories and laying the ground for our attempt at a political-morphological rethinking.

This presents us with a rich array of questions and contradictions. What is the difference between 'centrism' (in the Blair or Macron mode) and 'centralism' (in the semi-authoritarian, Leninist sense)? How are these geometric, volumetric or aesthetic connotations attached to different modes of doing politics? On an urban terrain, the odds in the 'ceaseless battle' have, it seems, been tilting decidedly in favour of the centrifugal side. This anti-centric political geometry coheres well with what Clifford Geertz (crediting Alfred Kroeber) has characterised as the long-standing 'centrifugal impulse' of disciplines such as anthropology.[17] And indeed urban scholars today – not only anthropologists, but also those in neighbouring social science and humanities disciplines – are committed to rendering the 'irreducibility' of urban life, to analytically 'de-centring' the city. At the same time, there is certainly something centre-fetishising about the neo-populists, the neo-rightists and the alt-rightists, who hark after 'traditional' value, appeal to qualities like 'authority' and 'leadership', and express their dissatisfaction with the rhetorics and aesthetics of the old liberal order. And there is a lot of monumentality and verticality wrapped up in the palatial, Trumpitectural 'Capitalist Realist' politics and aesthetics, which Trumpism and Putinism have in common.[18]

We are interested, then, in exploring how these sorts of alignments are made and remade between ideas pertaining to geometry, morphology and aesthetics, and those pertaining to politics, economy, culture and social organisation. How are urban centrality and peripherality linked to particular ways of doing and imagining politics and economics, from totalitarianism to democracy, (neo)liberalism to (neo-)populism, state socialism to high capitalism, production-line Keynesianism to flexible accumulation, sacredness to secularism, protest to repression? What are the 'elective affinities' between the politics of centrality, and other styles, shapes and geometries, on the level of architectural style as well as city planning? How do various forms of monumentality (sculptural, palatial or domestic), verticality and horizontality crystallise on urban centres and fringes? How do these connections, in turn, map onto our understandings of epochal transformations, within which the politics and morphologies we examine are caught up? Can we imagine (and perhaps implement) counter-intuitive, paradoxical and subversive forms of monumentality, verticality and centrality, whether the type of intimate, domestic, modernist monumentality discussed by Adam Kaasa in his contribution to this volume or the forms of feminist, counter-patriarchal monumentality and centrality explored by artists, among them Sanja Iveković and Zofia Kulik?[19] On a historical level, what is the relationship between high centrality, monumentality and high modernity, especially in the state socialist incarnation (broadly understood) of the first-named? Have this morphology and that epoch died together, and, if so, what are their posthumous lingerings, afterlives and reincarnations?

Cultures One, Two and Free

The end of Soviet-led state socialism constituted a great de-centring of power, and the cities that took shape under the tutelage of epicentric socialist modernity swiftly found themselves de-centred, subjected to the centrifugal, disordering impulses of laissez-faire late capitalism (now better known as 'neoliberalism').[20] Post-socialist urbanism gives us perhaps the clearest example of twentieth-century centrality as it encounters the newly forged, reconfigured, reincarnated mutant and zombie centralities and peripheralities of the twenty-first century. It reflects the global impact of socialist modernism far beyond the Soviet bloc, which made its mark on contemporary cityscapes from Mexico to India, China, Nigeria, Iraq, Vietnam, Mongolia, Cuba, Tanzania and beyond.[21] The socialist incarnation of high modern epicentricity has a lasting legacy not only on post-socialist cities but on world urbanism as a whole, with planetary implications for theorising the urban in the t wenty-first century.

Thus, to rethink centrality, and with it the genealogy of the contemporary global city, this volume starts from the experience of the 'Second World' during and after socialism.[22] Arguably, it is there that modernity witnessed its furthest-reaching and most radical realisation.[23] And yet post-socialist cities are often doubly excluded in urban scholarship and theory building because, as Tauri Tuvikene puts it, they appear neither central nor peripheral enough, 'neither mainstream nor part of the critique',[24] especially in the context of post-colonial urbanism. To rethink centrality is thus also a way to better understand the changing valence of post-socialist cities in thinking about urban theory. This does not mean some kind of redemptive re-centring of the socialist city, but rather using the lens of socialist urbanism to open up discussion about centrality as a theme across much urban discourse, from geographical discussions of centre and periphery to planning discussions of polycentric and 'smart' cities. Thus, it seeks to be part of that larger set of 'conversations open[ing] up among the many subjects of urban theoretical endeavour in cities around the world', as Jennifer Robinson has put it, that are moving away from 'an authoritative voice emanating from some putative centre of urban scholarship'.[25]

One of the key points of departure behind this volume is a highly influential analysis by architectural historian Vladimir Paperny, according to which modern Russian architectural culture oscillates endlessly between two fundamental variants: Culture One (centrifugal, horizontal, constantly in motion, aesthetically sparse), which can be most straightforwardly identified with the Soviet avant-garde of the 1920s, and Culture Two (centripetal, vertical, static, aesthetically opulent), which achieved its most extravagant flowering during the Stalin years.[26] Paperny has expressed doubt about whether these categories can be applied in their purity to post-socialist Russia, but he has also – in exemplary high structuralist fashion – expressed scepticism about whether it is possible to go beyond them and arrive at something like a 'Culture Three'.[27]

The contributions in this book raise the possibility that this binary opposition can be strategically redeployed, if not dialectically sublimated, in order to make sense of the late-capitalist political-morphological common sense of the Euro-American world. This common sense, in simplified form, is that the West and the North are moving towards an emancipated new urban culture – let us call it Culture *Free* – that is possessed of all of the dynamism, fringiness and horizontality of Culture One, but liberated of its grandiose modernist narratives and centralities. The 'rest' of the world – the Global East and the Global South – meanwhile, are often cast as if they were languishing within an obsolete variant of Culture Two, whose contours are dictated by the whims of gold-plating, column-proliferating dictators and parvenu oligarchs.[28] Yet the centripetal morphologies of Culture Two – allegedly obsolete, or consigned to the peripheries – continue to hold sway over cities far beyond the realm of wherever it is that the Global East begins and ends.

In (re-)centring the experience of socialist urban modernity, then, this book represents urban stories from a small selection of the former Soviet-bloc 'Second World' – Russia, Poland, East Germany and Ukraine – and juxtaposes them with select tales from beyond – Sweden, India, the United Kingdom and Mexico. Without any aspiration to comprehensiveness, and with a keen awareness that greater coverage would always be desirable (China, for example, deserves its own treatment in this regard), the book theorises the urban planet through the afterlife of socialist high-modern urbanism. To this end we cautiously find the term Global East useful, not as a replacement for the notion of 'post-socialism' (although we find that term wanting), but because it allows us to operationalise Zsuzsa Gille's argument that there is a global context for post-socialism – a 'global post-socialist condition'.[29] As we use it here, the term Global East is also consciously derivative of the concept of the Global South; indeed it seeks to engage the (former) socialist (urban) world in a conversation started by post-colonial and de-colonial studies. The project of provincialising the West and the North, we would like to suggest, can be a project of centring not only the South, but also the East.[30]

One of our reservations about the term 'Global East', however, is that, while centring a particular compass point broadly associated with actually existing socialism, it also, paradoxically, runs the risk of eliding (or provincialising) socialism's centrality to the construction (as well as the deconstruction) of modernity. For this reason, we would like to use this opportunity to flag the usefulness of concepts such as 'zombie socialism' and 'still-socialism' which seek to overcome the fatalistic Fukuyamian overtones of *post*-socialism.[31] We actively call for the development of new concepts along these lines – the term 'trans-socialism' springs to mind here as one possibility – that can account for both socialism's afterlives and enduring legacies as well as its spatial and temporal global reach.

Fanning out from Moscow

Starting from the Global East, then, and extending beyond, this volume asks what it means, in practice, to explore the tension between forces of de-centring and re-centring as they reshape the political, economic and social fabric of the urban. Emerging out of an interdisciplinary conference on power and architecture held in London 2016, the essays are purposely eclectic.[32] They represent a medley of narrative styles and methodological orientations, from grounded academic essays, to reflections on artistic practice, to political interventions. They draw from urban studies, social anthropology and architectural and artistic theory and practice to explore empirically how cities, mostly but by no means exclusively in the Global East, are dealing with the inheritance of older models of centrality and how they appropriate, reinvent and repurpose the centre – both the built environment itself and the attendant political discourses about the centre as the location of power. Because architecture and power are inextricably intertwined, the cases provide insights into the changing nature of modern power as a function of the shifting imaginaries of centrality.

Re-Centring the City consists of six thematic parts radiating out, as it were, from the legacy of high socialist modernity in its metropolitan centre of Moscow, the capital of the state socialist cosmos, which forms the first part. 'Moscow, point of departure' begins with a personal account of the flight from Moscow's centripetal force by Vladimir Paperny (chapter 1), whose notions of Culture One and Culture Two form a conceptual waltz throughout this volume. From there it moves to accounts of Moscow's ongoing struggle with its varying conceptions of centrality by contrasting the Kremlin itself, in Clementine Cecil's account of its hegemonic status (chapter 2), with the sprawling Stalinist-era park known as VDNKh, which Andreas Schönle (chapter 3) presents as exemplary of what he calls the post-post-socialist condition. The next two chapters draw our attention to the absences and interstices in and around these oddly mimetic monumental spaces, first in Owen Hatherley's (chapter 4) alternative genealogy of today's decentralising fantasies in the Soviet Constructivist's 'disurbanism' movement of the 1930s, and then through Daria Paramonova's (chapter 5) explanation of contemporary Moscow's focus on space as an organising principle for new architecture in the post-Soviet era.

In the second part, 'Off-centre: palatial peripheries', the book fans out from Moscow to explore the styles, shapes and ideologies of palatial monumentality – in its pre-socialist, socialist, post-socialist and *still-socialist* incarnations – in Berlin and Warsaw, cities on the socialist world's privileged fringes, or second-order centres. Jonathan Bach's essay (chapter 6) examines a structuring absence at the centre of East Berlin that lasted for twenty-three post-war years between the destruction of Berlin's imperial castle and the building of the socialist Palace of the Republic (which, in turn, was torn down after reunification and replaced by a reconstruction of the imperial castle, bearing the name Humboldt Forum). The imperial castle's reappearance is the subject for Khadija von Zinnenburg Carroll and Jonas Tinius (chapter 7), who take today's Humboldt Forum as a case study for understanding centrality along the intersecting axes of 'spatial horizontality' and 'vertical temporality'. Rounding out this part, Michał Murawski (chapter 8) presents Warsaw's assertively vertical Palace of

Culture and Science as a socialist-era edifice alive with subversive public spirit, one that leads us back to Stalinist Warsaw's leading architectural ideologue, Edmund Goldzamt, and his strikingly prescient theories, formulated in the 1950s, about architectural power and centrality.

The third part, 'Looking inward: re-centring the sacred', shifts perspective to examine the social centrality of sacred spaces and their changing architecture emerging from confrontations between secular and sacred forms of modernity. Kuba Snopek with Izabela Chichońska and Karolina Popera (chapter 9) provide an intriguing look at how parish churches in post-war Poland emerged as vernacular and communal architecture alongside, and against, the rigid modernism of the central state. If, in post-war Poland, many parish churches were built with the implicit tolerance of the Polish socialist state, Jewish temples and community buildings, especially in former shtetls, were explicitly allowed to deteriorate, and Natalia Romik (chapter 10) explores interventions into the spectral architecture of abandoned Jewish property through the work of the Nomadic Shtetl Archive. The last essay in the part, by Jennifer Mack (chapter 11), focuses on the pressing question of how centrality constitutes community through the construction of mosques in Sweden today, exploring how plans for their construction become part of a redefinition of what counts as the centre of Swedish public life and urban space.

A discussion of centrality would not be complete without verticality, which has haunted socialist modernism, from its obsessions with the never-built Tatlin Tower and Palace of the Soviets, to the legacy of Moscow's seven tall buildings in the immediate post-war period and its Warsaw spin-off. The fourth part, 'Looking upward: power verticals', examines how verticality reorients our ideas of centre and periphery. Stephen Graham (chapter 12) connects the metaphysics of reaching for the sky with the politics of ever-higher skyscrapers as a marker of global centrality. Vyjayanthi Venuturupalli Rao's following essay (chapter 13) brings the politics of skyscrapers down to earth, as it were, by examining the politics of air rights in Mumbai, where the high-rise apartment building becomes decidedly anti-monumental (in contrast to Graham's examples of trophy towers), mired in an 'air rights game' that ultimately challenges the very idea of urban development. We end the part with a photo essay by Tom Wolseley (chapter 14), based on his film, *Vertical Horizons*, about living in the shadow of London's infamous Shard skyscraper.

The penultimate part, 'Looking outward: hinterlands, diffusions, explosions', moves from the heights of our modern Icarian fantasies to reconceptualise the urban 'edge' beyond the binary of centrifugal and centripetal forces. Pushpa Arabindoo (chapter 15) argues that the salient distinction for understanding (capitalist) urbanisation is less the classic 'urban vs rural' than 'urban vs non-urban'. Arabindoo uses the case of Chennai to supplant the 'periphery' with the concept of the 'hinterland' as an interpretive vocabulary for understanding a wide range of morphological forms and settlement typologies ranging from the urban to the wilderness. On a planetary scale, Patrick Neveling (chapter 16) argues that special economic zones, as distributed centres for capitalist production, also produce new hierarchies and, therewith, new mythologies of the centre. Building on the latent sense of rupture in the recombinations of capitalist urban modernity of the previous chapters, Irish multimedia artist Joy Gerrard (chapter 17) provides a visual coda to the analytical explorations of centre and periphery. Through a series of prints that range from the 2011 Arab uprisings to anti-Trump and Black Lives Matter protests, her images explore the explosive potential inherent in the relation between crowds, architecture and the built environment.

In the final part, 'Things fall: (after)lives of monumentality', the book ends with an extended reflection on what is perhaps the most common-sense understanding of the centre: as the location of monuments and monumentality around which the city is oriented, physically and symbolically. In a seemingly counter-intuitive move, Adam Kaasa (chapter 18) shows how what he calls 'domestic monumentality' was foundational to the Mexican revolutionary state's pursuit of scalar urban monumentality, an argument he develops through the case of a famous modernist housing estate project in Mexico City and the work of 'technicians' in the urban research studio Taller de Urbanismo. The final two pieces, both from Ukraine, confront the infamous cases of what has been called 'Leninoclasm', the destruction of Lenin monuments which swept through the country after 2013. Oleksiy Radynski (chapter 19) examines the limits of Leninoclasm after 2014 in Crimea, where a well-known activist and a film director were falsely accused of trying to blow up a monument to Lenin as a kind of symbolic revenge for the fragments of Lenin now found throughout Ukraine. These fragments form the centre of Yevgenia Belorusets' concluding piece (chapter 20), where they circulate as tenuous relics of a semiotics of centrality, ultimately unable to offer either effective ritual absolution or the foundations for a new national myth.

Taken together, the typologically and descriptively rich contri-butions to this volume challenge readers to rethink perceived affinities between despotism and grandiosity, democracy and polycentricity, high modernity and creative destruction. By including scholars from both within and outside of the former socialist world, architects, activists, journalists and artists, we hope for cross-boundary dialogues that speak to all readers interested in the relation between power, urbanism and architecture. The empirical contributions illustrate how epicentric spaces continue to radiate over the everyday lives of cities and their inhabitants on aesthetic, political-economic and everyday levels. The centre, this book shows, remains a moving target that both sutures and sunders our elusive understanding of the urban.

Notes

1. Jacobs, 1961; Ostrom, 1972; Fujita, Krugman and Venables, 1999.
2. See Taylor, 2016; also Parini, 2016.
3. On how 'crisis' is epistemologically constituted and historically mobilised, see Roitman, 2013.
4. 'From extreme fringe to the centre stage: the rise of Breitbart News', *Irish Times*, 15 November 2016; 'For a Trump advisor, an odyssey from the fringes of Washington to the centre of power', *Washington Post*, 20 February 2017; 'How the so-called "alt-right" went from the fringe to the White House', *Mother Jones*, 22 November 2016; Matthew Garrahan, 'Breitbart News: from populist fringe to the White House and beyond', *Financial Times*, 7 December 2016.
5. Taussig, 2017.
6. Bakhtin, 1981: xviii.
7. Evans-Pritchard, 1940.
8. Geertz, 1993.
9. Shils, 1975.
10. Wallerstein, 1979; Wolf, 1982.
11. Rowlands, Larsen and Kristiansen, 1987.
12. Park, Burgess, McKenzie and Wirth, 1925; Harris and Ullman, 1945: 7–17; Jacobs, 1961; Gottmann, 1980, vol. 19; Lefebvre, 1991, 2003; Sassen, 1991; Hall, 1997; Soja, 2000.
13. Polanyi, 1951; Ostrom, 1972.
14. Wölfflin, 1950; Vidler, 2000; Paperny, 2002.
15. Deleuze and Guattari, 1987; De Landa, 1997.
16. Fujita et al., 1999.
17. Clifford Geertz, 2000: 284.
18. For more on the politics and aesthetics of Trumpitecture in East and West, see Michał Murawski, 2017.
19. Sanja Iveković has been concerned with feminist and radical forms of counter-monumentality for several decades. Her 2001 project *Lady Rosa of Luxembourg* is documented in Lunghi and Pejic, 2012. Her 2017 project, exhibited at Documenta 14 in Athens and Kassel, is documented in Latimer and Szymczyk, 2017. For an analysis of Zofia Kulik's experiments with the centrality, symmetry and monumentality of 'closed form' see Murawski, 2019. See also Kowalczyk, 1999; Wilson, 2001: 233.
20. Cf. Stenning, Smith, Rochovská and Świąte, 2010.
21. Cf. Stanek, 2012: 299–307.
22. We are indebted and sympathetic to the idea that 'Second World' urbanity can function as a corollary term to post-socialism, as systematically and convincingly put forward in Bocharnikova and Harris, 2018.
23. Rogers, 2010. In critical engagement with Jean and John Comaroff's idea of 'theory from the south', Don Kalb formulated the idea of 'theory from the east' during the keynote speech of the Society for European Anthropology at the annual meeting of the American Anthropological Association in Denver, Colorado, in November 2015.
24. Tuvikene, 2016: 139.
25. Robinson, 2016: 196.
26. Paperny, 2002. The author revisits his considerations from the 'genealogical morphological' vantage point of his own family story in his contribution to this volume.
27. Paperny, 2013. See also Martinez's critical exploration of the idea of the 'New East' in Martinez, 2019: 201–220.

28. In this sense, our arguments here – a critique of the West's idea of everyone else's obsoles-cence – are in correspondence with the agendas of the Former West project. See Hlavajova and Sheikh, 2017. Directly linked is the EECASWOB Project (Eastern European Critical Area Studies Without Borders), currently in development by Wendy Bracewell, Tim Beasley-Murray and Michał Murawski.
29. Gille, 2010.
30. The term 'Global East' is used in Murawski, 2018. This concept is also theorised in a comple-mentary but distinct way – as a corollary or even replacement for the idea of 'post-socialism' – by urban geographers Martin Müller and Elena Trubina. See Müller, 2018 and 2019.
31. See Chelcea and Druţă, 2016; Murawski, 2018.
32. The conference was organised by the School of Slavonic and East European Studies and the FRINGE Centre for the Study of Social and Cultural Complexity at University College London together with the Global Studies Program at The New School (New York) and the Calvert 22 Foundation.

Bibliography

Bakhtin, M. M. *The Dialogic Imagination: Four Essays*, edited by Michael Holquist, translated by Caryl Emerson and Michael Holquist. Austin: University of Texas Press, 1981.
Bocharnikova, Daria and Steve E. Harris. 'Second World urbanity: infrastructures of utopia and really existing socialism', *Journal of Urban History* 44, no. 1 (2018): 3–8.
Chelcea, Liviu and Oana Druţă. 'Zombie socialism and the rise of neoliberalism in post-socialist Central and Eastern Europe', *Eurasian Geography and Economics* 57, no. 4/5 (2016): 521–44.
De Landa, Manuel. *A Thousand Years of Nonlinear History*. New York: Zone Books, 1997.
Deleuze, Gilles and Félix Guattari. *A Thousand Plateaus: Capitalism and Schizophrenia*, translated by Brian Massumi. Minneapolis: University of Minnesota Press, 1987.
Evans-Pritchard, E. E. *The Nuer: A Description of the Modes of Livelihood and Political Institutions of a Nilotic People*. Oxford: Clarendon Press, 1940.
Fujita, Masahisa, Paul Krugman and Anthony J. Venables. *The Spatial Economy: Cities, Regions, and International Trade*. Cambridge, MA: MIT Press, 1999.
Geertz, Clifford. 'Centers, kings, and charisma: reflections on the symbolics of power'. In *Local Knowledge: Further Essays in Interpretive Anthropology*, by Clifford Geertz, 121–46. London: Fontana Press, 1993.
Geertz, Clifford. *Available Light: Anthropological Reflections on Philosophical Topics*. Princeton, NJ: Princeton University Press, 2000.
Gille, Zsuzsa. 'Is there a global postsocialist condition?', *Global Society* 24, no. 1 (2010): 9–30.
Gottmann, Jean, ed. *Centre and Periphery: Spatial Variation in Politics*. Beverly Hills, CA: SAGE Pub-lications, 1980.
Hall, Peter. *Cities of Tomorrow: An Intellectual History of Urban Planning and Design in the Twentieth Century*. Oxford: Blackwell, 1997.
Harris, Chauncy D. and Edward L. Ullman. 'The nature of cities', *Annals of the American Academy of Political and Social Science* 242 (November 1945): 7–17.
Hlavajova, Maria and Simon Sheikh, eds. *Former West: Art and the Contemporary after 1989*. Cam-bridge, MA: MIT Press, 2017.
Jacobs, Jane. *The Death and Life of Great American Cities*. New York: Random House, 1961.
Kowalczyk, Izabela, 'The geometry of power in Zofia Kulik's work', *n.paradoxa* 11 (1999): 19–25.
Latimer, Quinn and Adam Szymczyk (eds), *Documenta 14: Daybook*. New York and London: Prestel, 2017.
Lefebvre, Henri. *The Production of Space*, translated by Donald Nicholson-Smith. Oxford: Black-well, 1991.
Lefebvre, Henri. *The Urban Revolution*, translated by Robert Bononno. Minneapolis: University of Minnesota Press, 2003.
Lunghi, Enrico and Bojana Pejic. *Sanja Iveković: Lady Rosa of Luxembourg*. Luxembourg: Edition Mudam and Casion Luxembourg, 2012.
Martínez, Francisco. *Remains of the Soviet Past in Estonia*. London: UCL Press, 2019.
Müller, Martin. 'In search of the Global East: thinking between North and South', *Geopolitics* (2018): 1–22. Accessed 21 July 2019. https://doi.org/10.1080/14650045.2018.1477757.

Müller, Martin. 'Goodbye, postsocialism!', *Europe-Asia Studies* 71, no. 4 (2019): 533–50.

Murawski, Michał. 'Odessa: what happens when you mix politics and real estate on the Black Sea coast?', *Calvert Journal*, 3 January 2017. Accessed 28 May 2017. http://www.calvertjournal.com/articles/show/7379/trump-odessa-batumi-mikheil-saakashvili-real-estate.

Murawski, Michał. 'Actually-existing success: economics, aesthetics, and the specificity of (still) socialist urbanism', *Comparative Studies in Society and History* 60, no. 4 (2018): 907–37.

Murawski, Michał, 'Zofia Kulik's palace complex: revealing the complexity of closed form (filling it with her own madness)'. In *Zofia Kulik: Methodology, My Love*, edited by Agata Jakubowska, Warsaw: Museum of Modern Art/Chicago: University of Chicago Press, 2019.

Ostrom, Vincent. *Water and Politics: A Study of Water Policies and Administration in the Development of Los Angeles*. Los Angeles: Haynes Foundation, 1972.

Paperny, Vladimir. *Architecture in the Age of Stalin: Culture Two*, translated by John Hill and Roann Barris. New York: Cambridge University Press, 2002.

Paperny, Vladimir. *Культура три. Как остановить маятник?* ('Culture three: how to stop the pendulum?'). Moscow: Strelka Press, 2013.

Parini, Jay. 'Was Yeats' "The Second Coming" really about Donald Trump? How poetry transcends political crises through time', *Literary Hub*, 18 April 2016. Accessed 28 May 2017. http://lithub.com/was-yeats-poem-the-second-coming-really-about-donald-trump/.

Park, Robert E., Ernest W. Burgess, Roderick D. McKenzie and Louis Wirth. *The City*. Chicago: University of Chicago Press, 1925.

Polanyi, Michael. *The Logic of Liberty: Reflections and Rejoinders*. Chicago: University of Chicago Press, 1951.

Robinson, Jennifer. 'Comparative urbanism: new geographies and cultures of theorizing the urban', *International Journal of Urban and Regional Research* 40, no. 1 (2016): 187–99.

Rogers, Douglas. 'Postsocialisms unbound: connections, critiques, comparisons', *Slavic Review* 69, no. 1 (2010): 1–15.

Roitman, Janet. *Anti-Crisis*. Durham, NC: Duke University Press, 2013.

Rowlands, M., Mogens Larsen and Kristian Kristiansen, eds. *Centre and Periphery in the Ancient World*. Cambridge: Cambridge University Press, 1987.

Sassen, Saskia. *The Global City: New York, London, Tokyo*. Princeton, NJ: Princeton University Press, 1991.

Shils, Edward. *Center and Periphery: Essays in Macrosociology*. Chicago: University of Chicago Press, 1975.

Soja, Edward W. *Postmetropolis: Critical Studies of Cities and Regions*. Oxford: Blackwell, 2000.

Stanek, Łukasz. 'Introduction: the "Second World's" architecture and planning in the "Third World"', *Journal of Architecture* 17, no. 3 (2012): 299–307.

Stenning, Alison, Adrian Smith, Alena Rochovská and Dariusz Świąte. *Domesticating Neo-Liberalism: Spaces of Economic Practice and Social Reproduction in Post-Socialist Cities*. Oxford: Wiley-Blackwell, 2010.

Taussig, Michael T. 'Trump studies', *Cultural Anthropology*, 18 January 2017. Accessed 21 July 2019. https://culanth.org/fieldsights/trump-studies.

Taylor, Ashley Phillips. 'The Second Coming: why people are tweeting Yeats in days following Trump's election', *Medium*, 16 November 2016. Accessed 28 May 2017. https://medium.com/@ashleyphillipstaylor/the-second-coming-why-people-are-tweeting-yeats-in-days-following-trumps-election-75e006949c61.

Tuvikene, Tauri. 'Strategies for comparative urbanism: post-socialism as a de-territorialized concept', *International Journal of Urban and Regional Research* 40, no. 1 (2016): 132–46.

Vidler, Anthony. *Warped Space: Art, Architecture, and Anxiety in Modern Culture*. Cambridge, MA: MIT Press, 2000.

Wallerstein, Immanuel. *The Capitalist World-Economy: Essays*. Cambridge: Cambridge University Press, 1979.

Wilson, Sarah G. 'Zofia Kulik: from Warsaw to Cyberia', *Centropa* 1, no. 3 (Sept. 2001), 233–44.

Wolf, Eric R. *Europe and the People without History*. Berkeley: University of California Press, 1982.

Wölfflin, Heinrich. *Principles of Art History: The Problem of the Development of Style in Later Art*, translated by M. D. Hottinger. New York: Dover Publications, 1950.

Part I
Moscow, point of departure

1
Centre and periphery: a personal journey

Vladimir Paperny

I am going to address the theme of centre and periphery from an unusual angle, through the history of my family as related to the changing values and places of residence of its members.

I

My paternal grandfather, Samuil Paperny, was born in 1888 in a Jewish shtetl, Glusk (Hlusk, now in Belarus), into a poor family. He received a standard religious education, attended *cheder* and *yeshiva*, studied the Torah and the Talmud – and hated it all. He lived at the periphery of the Russian empire: its centre was in St Petersburg and later in Moscow. Samuil's dream was Russia, Russian language and Russian literature, just as for urban teenagers of my generation the dream was America and the English language. His first stop on the way to the centre was a Russian gymnasium in Kyiv, which was set up specifically for the 're-education' of Jewish boys in the spirit of Sergey Uvarov's famous triad, Orthodoxy, Autocracy and Nationality. Jewish boys were buying none of this and behaved rather naughtily. During the mandatory performance of a hymn for the emperor, in the line 'Let God give him power', they replaced 'power' with 'hernia'.[1] Later, Samuil entered the Teachers' Institute in Kyiv. Eventually, he got a job in Moscow teaching Russian literature in the Navy academy.

In the late 1940s, when state-supported anti-Semitism was on the rise, his barely noticeable Yiddish accent became objectionable, and he could no longer teach language and literature. Through a tightly knit

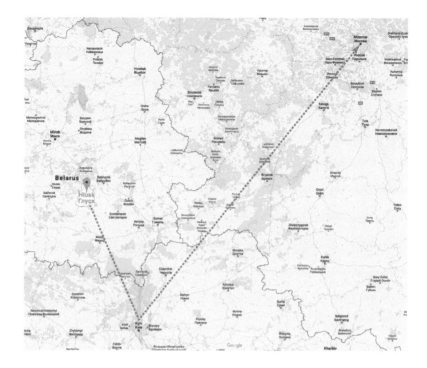

Figure 1.1 Samuil Paperny's path from Hlusk to Moscow. Map data: Vladimir Paperny.

circle of friends and relatives, he got a job as curriculum director at the Children of Railroad Employees Club. Railways under Stalin were militarised. Samuil received the rank of major and a uniform, which he had to wear to work. In the 1970s, my grandfather became disillusioned with the Soviet system and started listening to the Voice of Israel. He considered emigrating to Israel but felt he was too old for such a dramatic move.

Samuil's older brother Lev Paperny resisted the 'oppressive' Jewish education by secretly reading Marx and then joining the underground Bolshevik party in 1915. As a Civil War fighter, Lev travelled all over the former Russian empire and for a while settled in Kustanaj.[2] A true Marxist, he proudly declared in official forms, 'No personal property'. In 1917 Lev became a delegate to the second All-Russian Congress of the Soviets in Moscow and then moved to Moscow permanently. He was sent to the US to study English and demography and brought back two wooden tennis rackets, Antelope brand, for his nephews Boris and Zinovy (my father). In 1937, Stalin appointed Lev People's Commissar for Agriculture of Ukraine,

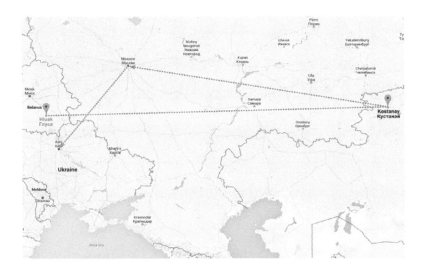

Figure 1.2 Lev Paperny's path from Hlusk to Kyiv. Map data: Vladimir Paperny.

in Kyiv. A year later, he was arrested and executed – like the majority of the old Bolsheviks. Because Lev's case was handled by the local Ukrainian People's Commissariat for Internal Affairs (NKVD)[3] the family in Moscow did not suffer the usual repercussions. The nephews were told their uncle had died in a mountaineering accident. Zinovy learned the truth only in the 1960s. The two tennis rackets survived in our apartment in Moscow for many years.

My paternal grandmother, Ita Maizil, was born in 1893, also in a shtetl, into the family of a rabbi. She had three sisters, Rachel, Gitl and Munia, and two brothers, Nachman and Yekhiel. Ita married my grandfather in 1918 in Kyiv. In 1919 they ran from the infamous Kyiv pogrom on foot holding newborn twins Boris and Zinovy (my father). The pogroms of the first post-revolutionary years were a manifestation of a backlash against an influx of Jews and other minorities, which became possible after the lifting of the Pale of Settlements (created by Catherine the Great in 1791 and abolished by the Provisional Government in 1917). Because of pogroms, between 1918 and 1921 half a million Jews were left homeless, and many perished. In 1923, Ita's parents left for Palestine, and Gitl and Nachman accompanied them. The others, with the help of the omnipotent Bolshevik Lev, moved to Moscow.

Nachman Maizil (a.k.a. Meisel), who in the early days published a Yiddish newspaper, *Kultur-Liga*, in Kyiv, later went to Warsaw to publish *Literarische Bleter*, and then to New York, where he started

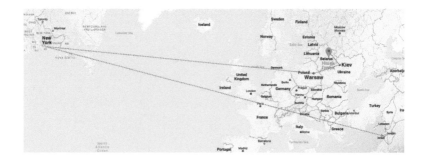

Figure 1.3 Nachman Maizil's path from Hlusk to Tel Aviv. Map data: Vladimir Paperny.

Yidische Kultur. He finally moved to Israel in 1965 and died there a year later.

In 1965 there was an event that deeply affected me and my worldview. Gitl Maizil, my grandmother's younger sister, suddenly showed up in Moscow. A small party was arranged in my parents' apartment. There were Ita, Munia, Samuil and Yekhiel, who had not seen Gitl for forty-two years, my parents, and, of course my younger sister and I. It was my first year at the Stroganov Art Academy. I had my first TTL camera and took many photos.

Gitl brought small gifts for everyone. Mine was a roll of Scotch Magic tape, something I had never seen before.

'This is a special kind', explained Gitl in flawless Russian. 'You can write on it. My brother Nachman uses it for editing. He came this year and now lives in a kibbutz.'

'What's a kibbutz?' I asked.

'Why should I tell you?' said Gitl. 'Come to visit and you'll find out.'

'Come to visit?' I exclaimed. 'Are you kidding? You know what kind of people are allowed to travel to foreign countries? My father has a PhD and he is a party member, and he still could go nowhere but to Bulgaria and the GDR.'

'Look,' said Gitl calmly, 'you don't need to lecture me on life in the USSR. I probably know more about it than you do. The times are changing. People are coming to visit their relatives in Israel; I know quite a few of them. You are my blood relatives; I'll send you and your sister an invitation and you'll know everything about kibbutzim. You can even earn some money working there.'

It never happened. Our parents panicked and talked my 13-year-old sister and a 21-year-old me into waiting. But it did not matter; the

Figure 1.4 Gitl Maizil's visit to the Papernys' apartment in Moscow, 1965. Source: Vladimir Paperny.

genie was already out of the bottle. From that day on, I knew that I could escape. I also started wondering how it had happened that the borders of my country had become impenetrable. I vividly remembered Gitl's stories about how, in the 1920s, everybody was shuttling between Moscow, Berlin and Paris. Why did it stop? What happened?

II

My mother, Kaleria Ozerova, was born into a patriarchal Russian Orthodox family of third-generation Muscovites. Both her parents attended the Moscow Conservatory. Kaleria's father, Nikolai Ozerov, with help from his teacher and mentor, the conductor and composer Nikolai Golovanov, was accepted by the Bolshoi Theatre as a singer. He also composed liturgical music and worked as a choir conductor in Moscow churches. In the late 1920s, Golovanov was fired from the Bolshoi for his outspoken anti-Semitism. My grandfather was arrested as Golovanov's most active supporter. He was offered a return to the Bolshoi in exchange for becoming an NKVD informer. He refused and was exiled to Kasnoyarsk, Siberia. Whether he shared Golovanov's anti-Semitism is not clear.

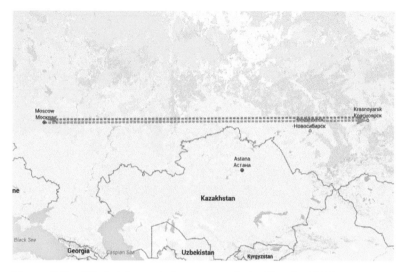

Figure 1.5   Nikolai Ozerov's four-year exile in Siberia, 1920s.
Map data: Vladimir Paperny.

Nikolai Ozerov spent four years in exile, working as musical director in a workers' club. My mother, still a schoolgirl, visited him in Siberia
twice. Both my mother and my grandfather later recalled the time away
from Moscow as very happy.

My parents met in 1937 at the Institute of Philosophy, Literature
and History (IFLI). Established in 1934, when some elements of the
Russian empire were beginning to reappear, this institution represented
a shift from Marxism to nationalism. The decree of 1934 required history
to be taught 'in a lively, absorbing form' rather than as 'abstract defini-
tions of social-economic formations' – an obvious jab at Marxism. Pre-
revolutionary university professors, who had been barely surviving in
Soviet Russia, were hunted and recruited to join the new institute. These
professors belonged to the same cohort of prominent writers, scholars
and intellectuals who, in 1922, were arrested and sent to Germany on
the so-called 'philosophers' ship'. 'There was no reason to shoot them',
explained Leon Trotsky, 'but to tolerate their presence was impossible.'
Twelve years later, their presence was not only tolerable but highly
desirable.

When my parents announced their plans to get married, it shocked
both sets of parents. No one said 'Couldn't you find somebody of your own
kind?', but such a thought may have flashed through somebody's mind.
They got married on 15 March 1941. They passed their final exam at IFLI

on 21 June 1941, the night before the German invasion. During the war, my father was mobilised to dig anti-tank trenches around Moscow, while the rest of the family was evacuated to Bashkiria in the foothills of the Ural Mountains.

III

In 1964, I entered the design department of the Stroganov Art Academy. The school was established by Count Sergei Stroganov in 1825.[4] In 1920 it became one of the centres of the Russian avant-garde and was renamed VKhUTEMAS (Higher Art and Technical Studios). Among the faculty and guest teachers were Alexander Rodchenko, Kazimir Malevich, Lyubov Popova, El Lissitzky, Aleksandra Ekster, Gustav Klutsis and other avant-gardists.

In 1964 Khrushchev's 'thaw' was still in progress, although Khrushchev himself was ousted on 14 October. The rector of the Academy was Rodchenko's former student, Zakhar Bykov, who was trying to preserve some avant-garde themes and concepts, even if in a watered-down form. In 1967 the 'thaw' was slightly 'refrozen', and Bykov was ousted and replaced by one of the worst Stalinist architects, Grigory Zakharov.

Industrial design was a new concept imported from the West. For me and some other design students, the creative and intellectual centre was the Hochschule für Gestaltung in Ulm. Needless to say, we were not able to visit it, but we could follow its news via international magazines, some of which were available at the Stroganov library. Working on my graduation project, a home electronics kit, I was having an imagined dialogue with the famous designer Dieter Rams and his Braun design minimalism. My teachers liked the project and wanted to give me the highest grade, but Zakharov, who was the jury chair, said, laconically, 'Where's the beauty?' Clearly, Braun design was far removed from Zakharov's Stalinist aesthetics, so my grade was lowered by one point.

In 1969, I started working as a designer and a research associate at the VNIITE (Institute for Industrial Design) in Moscow. One day, our director Yuri Soloviev came down to the design studio where my friend Evgeny Bogdanov and I were working on experimental furniture. He informed everybody that the Italian lighting company Artemide had announced an international design competition for 'Furniture of the Future'. 'It's time for our institute', said Soloviev, 'to enter the international arena.'

Figure 1.6 Grigory Zakharov's column 'Abundance' in the underground hall at Kurskaia metro station, 1949. Source: Vladimir Paperny.

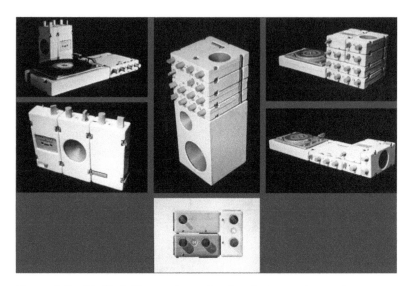

Figure 1.7 Vladimir Paperny's graduation design project at the Stroganov Art Academy, 1964. Source: Vladimir Paperny.

Evgeny and I eagerly accepted the challenge and came up with a proposal. We called it 'Isolo-Sphere': it was a set of rocking-chairs that could be assembled into a sphere, providing total isolation. We were convinced that everybody in the world wanted to escape from their surroundings and would be happy to crawl into our Isolo-Sphere. Now I realise that behind this proposal was *our own* subconscious desire to escape from the oppressive Soviet Union.

Did our entry have a chance of winning, or at least of being published? I think so. Coming from the USSR in 1972, such an entry would probably attract some attention. But it was not to be. Soloviev said he did not understand the idea and, in any case, sending our package to a 'capitalist country' would require quite a few approvals and permissions, for which we simply did not have enough time. Another failed attempt to get in touch with the outside world.

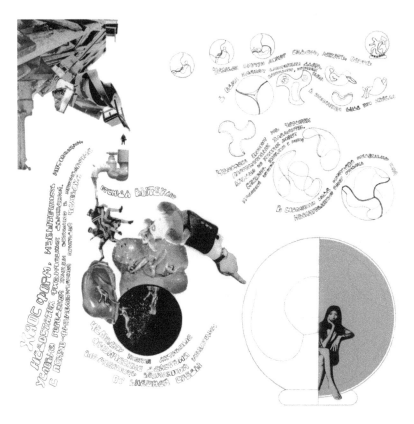

Figure 1.8   Vladimir Paperny and Evgeny Bogdanov's 'Isolo-Sphere', Artemide competition entry, never submitted. Source: Vladimir Paperny.

IV

In 1975, I entered graduate school at the Institute of the Theory and History of Architecture and started working on my PhD thesis. The subject, 'The 1935 general plan for the reconstruction of Moscow', was suggested by my professor Vyacheslav Glazychev. Working in libraries and archives, I soon realised that in order to understand the tectonic shift that occurred in Soviet architecture in the 1920s and 1930s (one manifestation of which was the general plan itself) I needed to dig deeper and to look at what was happening in the Soviet culture as a whole.

One point of departure was Erwin Panofsky's *Gothic Architecture and Scholasticism*. Panofsky succeeded in answering Heinrich Wölfflin's rhetorical question 'Where exactly is the path leading from the scholastic's cell to the architect's studio?' This path, as Panofsky found, went through a *monopoly on education*, that is, through the special form of social organisation by which a style of thought was translated from philosophy into architecture. Philosophy and architecture, according to Panofsky, were 'primary and secondary spiritual forms'. This, as Panofsky noted, was valid only in a specific time and a specific place: between 1130 and 1270 and in a 100-mile zone around Paris. Even though Panofsky's scheme was not directly applicable to Soviet culture, it reassured me that a connection between architecture and seemingly unrelated fields is possible.

The second point of departure was my family history. In 1923, my great-grandfather and two of his children were free to move from the USSR to Palestine. How did it happen that an unauthorised crossing of the Soviet border became punishable by death? Why couldn't Bogdanov and I send our design to Italy without approvals and permissions? Why wasn't I ever allowed to travel to Greece to study the Parthenon? Or to San Carlo alle Quattro Fontane in Rome, which was so passionately described by our art history professor at Stroganov?

The third point of departure was the Tartu–Moscow Semiotic School and the works of Juri Lotman, Vyacheslav Ivanov, Alexander Piatigorsky and others. Additionally, Aaron Gurevich's book *Categories of Medieval Culture* helped me realise that a culture can be studied as a whole, and that to understand a culture you need to discover its basic categories. The works of Lévi-Strauss showed me the descriptive power of binary oppositions.

Looking at the paradigm shift that occurred between the 1920s and the 1930s, I came to the conclusion that there had been a clash between two different cultural modes; I called them Culture One and Culture Two, using numbers to avoid any appearance of value judgement.

The binary oppositions that I used to contrast the two cultural modes included *beginning–end*, *movement–immobility*, *horizontal–vertical*, *uniform–hierarchical* and others. Here I will concentrate on *horizontal–vertical*. 'Workers of the world unite!' This Marxist slogan, appearing in Culture One on the covers of nearly all architectural publications (and totally absent from them in Culture Two), indicates that the idea of the international unity of a single class in Culture One clearly dominated over the concepts of either national or state unity. This is the reason why writers of the Proletkult (Proletarian Culture) group so carefully looked after 'the purity of the membership in studios. Only those who, by the nature of their activities, are genuine members of the proletariat, those with a proletarian background, can join studios'.

Lenin never supported Proletkult, but his own thinking revealed no lesser degree of horizontality. One of the decrees he signed suggested 'establishing relations with foreign Marxists to commission them to write a number of textbooks'. The word 'foreign' in Culture One almost always had positive overtones; what happened beyond the border was often a paradigm to follow. Thus, for example, the decree introducing the international time zone system in Russia justified it as 'unification with all the *civilised world* in the accounting of time'. The decree 'On the Improvement of the Life of Scientists' suggested freedom to go abroad and to receive literature from abroad. 'Overseas', wrote an architectural journal, 'in the North American United States, the radio-telephone and radio-telegraph are available to almost all citizens.' That meant 'our citizens' must have this too.

By the late 1920s, however, this horizontal intention underwent a metamorphosis. In 1926, 'for Soviet citizens who have completed a foreign higher education and have returned to work in the RSFSR', special tests in social science were arranged. A 1927 decree made for 'a sharp reduction in foreign business trips'.[5] In 1931, all citizens were forbidden to keep the products of trade with foreigners in the territory of the USSR without prior special permission. In 1935, TORGSIN (the Department for Trade with Foreigners) was liquidated. The final replacement of the horizontal strivings of the culture by verticality was manifested in a resolution of the Presidium of TsIK in 1929: 'The refusal of a citizen of the Soviet Union working in the capacity of a functionary in a state institution or establishment of the USSR acting abroad to return to the USSR upon the suggestion of an organ of state authority will be considered desertion to the camp of enemies of the working class and will qualify as a treason.' In a resolution of 1934, this is stated still more definitively: 'Fleeing or flying abroad will be punished by the highest measures of criminal

punishment – execution by shooting with confiscation of all possessions.'
The centre of the world had moved permanently to Moscow, while the
world itself shrank to the borders of the USSR.

Sacralisation of borders was apparent in architecture in the omni-
presence of statues of a border guard with a rifle and a German shep-
herd dog. The importance of borders could also be seen in the treatment
of entrances as points of crossing the boundary between exterior and
interior or between above-the-ground and the dangerous underground
space.

Figure 1.9 Pavel Balandin's border-guard sculpture at the All-Union
Agricultural Exhibition, Moscow, 1953. Courtesy of the Shchusev State
Museum of Architecture, coll. 11, 11790.

Figure 1.10 Matvei Manizer's border-guard sculpture at Ploshchad'
Revoliutsii metro station, 1938. Source: Vladimir Paperny.

An important source of information about the unique character of
Culture Two architecture was my random wandering through the streets
of Moscow. In the 1970s, I did not know much about Guy Debord and
French Situationism (precisely because of the sacrosanct status of physical and ideological borders, one of the few features of Culture Two that
survived the 'thaw' and the relatively relaxed Brezhnev's epoch). Still, to
some degree, my random exploration of the city was similar to Debord's
Psychogeography with its goal of taking pedestrians 'off their predictable
paths and jolting them into a new awareness of the urban landscape'.

The feature that struck me while walking the streets of Moscow was
the two scales that existed in architecture. A balcony that could actually

Figure 1.11   Architect Leonid Poliakov, sculptor Georgy Motovilov. Interior of the entrance pavilion to Kaluzhskaia metro station, 1949. Source: Vladimir Paperny.

be used by residents was often incorporated into a much bigger balcony, which functioned almost as Plato's 'ideal form' of a balcony. Similarly, an ornate gold-plated gate at an underground station could lead to a 'No Trespassing' sign behind it. A pavilion at the Agricultural Exhibition, standing about 100 metres behind a statue of Lenin, would have the door so tall that it could have allowed Lenin to walk in.

When my manuscript was finished, I gave it to my professor. The next day he returned it and said gloomily, 'Brilliant, please hide it and never show it to anybody.' Obviously, I had touched some untouchable subjects. Two years later I emigrated to the US without a PhD.

Twenty years after finishing my thesis, having published it as a book in Russian and English (and later in Czech and Italian), I was talking to the head of the RGGU (Russian State University for the Humanities), Yuri Afanasyev,[6] who said that RGGU would be happy to award me the missing degree. I went through all the bureaucratic formalities (which had not changed since the 1970s) and received a very impressive document bound in red imitation leather with a double-headed eagle embossed in gold on the cover. Inside, there was a piece of paper saying that I had become a 'Doctor of Culturology'.

Figure 1.12 Two scales: a balcony inside a balcony on the façade of Arkady Mordvinov's building 'B' on Gorky Street, 1938. Source: Vladimir Paperny.

Figure 1.13 'No Trespassing' sign on the door behind the ornate gates at the entrance to the Arbatskaia metro station. Source: Vladimir Paperny.

Figure 1.14 Georgy Shchuko and others. The main pavilion at the All-Union Agricultural Exhibition, Moscow, 1954. Source: Vladimir Paperny.

Figure 1.15 Georgy Shchuko and others. The main pavilion at the All-Union Agricultural Exhibition, Moscow, 1954. The size of the door corresponds to the size of the Lenin statue in front of the building. Source: Vladimir Paperny.

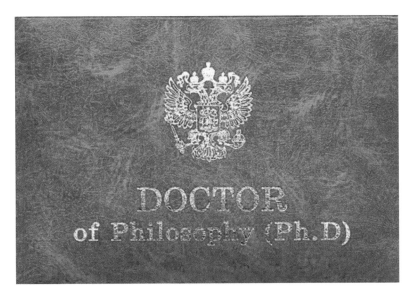

Figure 1.16 The cover of Paperny's PhD certificate, 2000. Source: Vladimir Paperny.

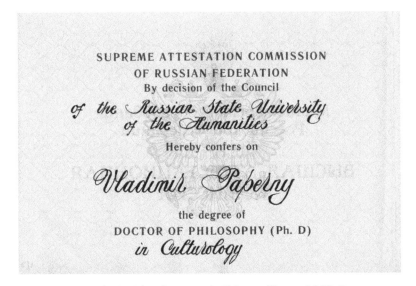

Figure 1.17 The inside of Paperny's PhD certificate, 2000. Source: Vladimir Paperny.

My first reaction was disappointment: this was the most progressive Russian cultural institution, and they didn't know how to translate *Культурология* (Cultural Studies) into English! But then I thought that maybe my disappointment was misplaced. We have psychology and philology; why not culturology. So, I started writing emails to my friends announcing my new title, and my computer immediately replaced the word Culturology with Cult Urology. This dubious degree allowed me to become an American professor and to get back to my academic studies. Here I am, still on the West coast, on the edge of the hemisphere, half a globe away from my birthplace. The personal journey continues.

Notes

1. «Дажди ему килу» instead of «Дажди ему силу».
2. Also spelled Kostanay, now in Kazakhstan.
3. NKVD (People's Commissariat for Internal Affairs) was a precursor of the KGB.
4. Stroganov is also famous for inventing the beef stroganoff dish.
5. RSFSR is the Russian Soviet Federative Socialist Republic.
6. Yuri Afanasyev (1934–2015), Russian historian, active in the era of Gorbachev's reforms.

2

Fortress City: the hegemony of the Moscow Kremlin and the consequences and challenges of developing a modern city around a medieval walled fortress

Clementine Cecil

The Kremlin is the universally recognised symbol of Russia; some would say, it *is* Russia, at least in terms of its political life. There is even a name for those who study Russian politics and its secrets: Kremlinologists. The entire country, but particularly Moscow, is in a symbiotic relationship with the Kremlin: it dictates both the form of the city which flows towards and away from it in ever-increasing concentric circles, and the radial roads that cross these. The form of the metro follows the same plan, and the railway stations are also placed at regular intervals, loosely following the Garden Ring Road. All these rings reinforce the basic form and dynamic of the city. The Kremlin is synonymous with the Russian state and its central idea at any one time: it is a theatre, heavy on pomp, circumstance and secrecy. Its very presence in the city centre hampers Moscow's growth and development and leads to some startling town planning and architectural decisions, often caused by fear generated by being so close to the seat of power. Just as the form of the Kremlin reflects the national idea at any one time, its very presence at the centre of the city makes any kind of sustainable growth impossible, thus negating the very thing it sets out to achieve – a sense of stability and continuity. The contemporary needs of the city are subjugated to the quirks of the medieval town plan, and its historic buildings are sacrificed and mutilated to serve changing needs.

At the first press conference of the campaign group the Moscow Architecture Preservation Society, in May 2004, which took place about 100 metres from the Kremlin in the Shchusev State Architecture Museum, architect Mikhail Khazanov said that as long as the Kremlin held such a position of dominance in the city, the pressure on the historic centre would not let up.[1] He saw the problem as primarily one of town planning; the city has its medieval ground plan at its heart and emerges centripetally from the Kremlin. This dynamic creates enormous pressure on the historic centre of the city, or Kamer-Kollezhsky Val, which roughly follows the line of the Garden Ring. This dynamic is, of course, also an ideological one: everyone wants to be close to the Kremlin and therefore, inevitably, there is huge pressure on the historic city to transform and mutate and to fulfil newly emerging needs such as those for modern office space, apartments and underground parking.

The word *kremlin* means 'fortress'. Many Russian towns and cities have *kremlins*, but the Moscow one tops them all. The history of Russia is reflected in its buildings and walls; it is the site of the birth of the city, originally a wooden fortress on a hill. Today, the Kremlin makes up the sum of Russia's history – political, spiritual and cultural. Only a fraction of it is open to the public; the rest of it used for affairs of state, reflecting Russia's relationship to its citizens – restricted and secretive. It is as if the Prime Minister of the UK had their centre of operations in the Tower of London. We would be allowed in to see the beefeaters and the Crown jewels, but the rest of it would be out of bounds, a place of mystery and power akin to the sacred area behind the 'golden gates', or altar, in a Russian Orthodox church.

The religious metaphor is appropriate. Even while the imperial court and associated administrative functions went north to St Petersburg between 1703 and 1918, coronations always took place in the Kremlin; it holds sway in terms of religious significance for the country. After the revolution it became a Red Fortress where Lenin and Stalin had apartments. Returning the capital to Moscow was part of the revolutionary idea, and physically moving into the Kremlin was a manifestation of dramatic change. The Kremlin alters with every ruler, and each regime tries to deploy it to project stability, strength and permanence. The only continuity is, in fact, where it is sited.

During his first term as president in the early 2000s, Vladimir Putin tried to reassign certain administrative duties to St Petersburg, but largely failed; only the courts have moved there. During his third term (2012–18), however, Putin brought many of the state rooms in the Kremlin back into use as the *mise-en-scène* for television broadcasts, most notably his victory speech following the annexation of the Crimean Peninsula. The white-and-gold Georgievsky Hall of the Great Kremlin Palace projected the scale, might and wealth of the state.

The Kremlin plays an important psychological role: it reflects the current ruling idea back to the citizens of the country. As historian Catherine Merridale described it in her book about the Kremlin, 'It is … a theatre and a text, a gallery that displays and embodies the current governing idea.'[2] Putin also wishes to make his mark in Moscow: his contribution has been the new 25-metre-high sculpture of St Vladimir on Borovitksaya Square, right next to the Kremlin.

The spate of demolitions that led to the rebirth of the preservation movement in Moscow in 2004 with the founding of Moskva, Kotoroy Net ('Moscow, Which Is No More'), the Moscow Architecture Preservation Society and later Arkhnadzor ('Arch-Watch', or 'architecture watch') began with the destruction of three buildings within spitting distance of the Kremlin. They were replaced, to varying extents, with 'sham replicas', distorted copies vaguely resembling their former selves:[3] the Moskva Hotel was replaced with a simplified replica, the Manezh Exhibition Hall was given an underground level and a new roof structure, and Voyentorg, the former Central Military Department Store, was replaced by a bloated sham replica with little resemblance to the original. This troika of destruction represented a crisis in the approach to historic buildings in Moscow, which was as much to do with the ground plan of Moscow and these buildings' proximity to the Kremlin as with a disregard for planning controls, including policies on historic buildings.

These three Kremlin-adjacent destructions were soon followed by the knocking down of the Middle Trading Rows just behind Red Square, and the enormous 1960s modernist Rossiya Hotel, abutting Red Square and overlooking the River Moskva. The demolition site of the Rossiya Hotel, meanwhile, has been transformed into an enormous park – a sign, for some, of shifting priorities and the emergence of a more nuanced set of aesthetic priorities within the Moscow administration.[4]

Borovitskaya Square is a formerly empty plot between Borovitsky Gates and the Pashkov House, a stunning piece of eighteenth-century classicism that sits on a hill beside the Kremlin. Its nod to civic values and its balance with the Kremlin in Moscow's cityscape makes for a very Muscovite pairing. This enormous statue of Vladimir, the Kievan prince and founder of Russian Orthodoxy, is reflective of several tendencies within the Russian state today. They include:

- the rising power of the church – its active promulgation and domination of space with churches, images and sculptures; and

- the centrality of nationhood and nation building in the state's ideology, particularly in its connection to the seizure of Crimea and the ongoing war in eastern Ukraine.

It also appears to represent the absence of an idea at the heart of the contemporary Russian state. Merridale writes:

> The Kremlin's story, like that of Russia as a whole, is fragmented, and much has been lost. In the midst of the fires, revolutions and palace coups, however, the single genuinely continuous thread is the determination of successive Russian rulers to rewrite the past so that the present, whatever it turns out to be, will seem … deeply rooted and organic.
>
> Merridale, 2016: 13

This is certainly the case with this statue, which evokes a feeling either of nationalism or of despair, depending on the viewer's political and aesthetic sensibilities.

The site of Borovitskaya Square was cleared for equally ideological reasons: to tidy up the city ahead of the 1980 Olympic games, and specifically for the historic visit of US President Nixon. The square was a vacuum for over thirty-five years, until Prince Vladimir made his appearance. The prince was searching for a new home after his monumental sculpture's proposed site on Sparrow Hills, one of the highest points in the city on the axis leading from the centre of the capital to Moscow State University, was rejected, thanks to an intervention by planners and conservationists.

Another contested site in close proximity to the Kremlin today is the empty space left after the demolition of the Hotel Rossiya. The late-Soviet-era hotel was demolished in the second half of the 2000s. Initial plans were for a hotel and a business quarter with a finely grained medieval street plan, somewhat resembling the historical layout of this ancient city region before its demolition during the 1930s to 1950s. However, it is said that Putin was fond of this void at the heart of the city and declared that it should be a park. The winning competition entry for the new park – which gathered 'landscape typologies' from throughout Russia, including portions of steppe, forest, marsh and tundra – is the work of New York architectural practice Diller, Scofidio + Renfro, authors of Manhattan's famous High Line park.[5]

So, what is the actual effect of these constant reconfigurations of Moscow's core on the city's inhabitants? The most immediate and obvious effect of this pressure is evident in the city's traffic jams, a paradigmatic phenomenon of twenty-first-century Moscow. This is partly because of the build-up that inevitably happens when you have a circular city plan, but also because of the low number of roads compared to cities of higher density, such as London and New York.

It is challenging to find a solution for this in Moscow. The formation of the street plan reflects the historical Russian traditions of kin-habitation as much as the Kremlin reflects hyper-centralised Russian power structures. Historically, in Moscow people built their homes around courtyards, one room at a time. Merchants would build a room, and when they had more money, or they married, or their mother-in-law came to live with them, they would build another. The entrance to the street was nothing in particular; the glory was inside – an inviting courtyard leading to a splendid and cosy interior.[6] The city has developed in a similar way, with a similar generous disregard for the limitations of space: buildings are constructed around pleasant, leafy courtyards. This means that a dense road grid is not possible. It is also interesting how the Kremlin's own inward-looking morphology (a walled edifice) is reflected in Moscow's early domestic dwellings and continues to this day in the formation of domestic courtyards (*dvori*).[7] The pressure on the area immediately around the Kremlin will not abate and it will continue to mutate, grow and change. There are calls at present to remove Lenin's embalmed corpse from the Mausoleum on Red Square; this could lead to the removal (total demolition is unlikely) of the ziggurat-like 1920s Mausoleum that has been a fixture of the square since his death in 1924.

The pressure of the centre is also moving out, centrifugally, to other parts of the city, but in a manner which nevertheless observes the centripetal city plan: the undertaking by Mayor Sergey Sobyanin to demolish some 8,000 apartment blocks, known as *Khrushchevki* (most of them five-storey buildings raised during the building boom of the Khrushchev-era 1950s and 1960s), entails their replacement with a ring of commercial high-rises that will be visible from the city centre. This follows a trend, already underway, for building enormous-scale residential blocks around the outer ring road, the Moscow Automobile Ring Road (MKhAD). At the time of writing, plans are also afoot for the construction of yet another ring road, again reinforcing the centrality of the Kremlin, ideologically as well as geographically.

Attempts have been made to alleviate this pressure. Some preservationists have called for presidential functions to be moved out of the

Kremlin and for the old fortress to be opened to the public, arguing that if the Kremlin stopped being the seat of power the 'pressure' on Moscow's historic centre would lift and historic buildings in the centre would be easier to preserve. During Dmitry Medvedev's presidency of Russia (2008–12), there was even a plan to move the Russian parliament to the Kommunarka district of the Moscow Region, to the south-west of the city, about 30 km from the Kremlin. Eventually, however, this initiative – whether it can truly be considered de-centralising or is, in fact, a re-centralising one – was dropped on account of Kommunarka's excessive distance from the Kremlin.[8]

There is a widespread sense among Muscovites that the present ground plan is creating a paralysis in the city centre; things are too close to the Kremlin to be replaced with anything radically different, and sites are often left empty for a long time through inertia caused by fear. Everyone is second-guessing what the chief-in-command wants – whether that is the mayor of Moscow or the president of Russia. The site of the Hotel Moskva, following demolition, lay empty for a long time. The city enjoyed the new vistas that opened up. The city's chief architect of the time promulgated a rumour that President Putin was fond of the new space that had been created. We began to wonder, would the void be replaced at all? The same thing happened following the demolition of the Hotel Rossiya.

One reflection of the inherent instability that this perceived stasis is desperately trying to cover up is the fact that plans for demolished sites are not approved until after demolition. Often, these sites are enormous, and they are rebuilt several times (as with the Zaryade district, the site of the former Hotel Rossiya). The closer the site is to the Kremlin, the more say the mayor or the president will have in the decision. This is a continuation of a political-architectural practice widespread during Soviet times, and indeed, during the Tsarist era; the state – or its private subsidiary corporations – is client, commissioner and implementer all at once. This has happened with major building projects in Moscow throughout its history: the Cathedral of Christ our Saviour when first built during the later decades of the nineteenth century, the gargantuan Stalin-era Palace of the Soviets for which the Cathedral was demolished but which was itself never built, the Central House of the Artist, and more recently, Zaryadye. The patron is the Kremlin (as a political entity), and the Kremlin is characterised by the same traits of hegemony and apparent stability hiding instability as is Moscow's concentric city structure.

Notes

1. I founded the Moscow Architecture Preservation Society (MAPS) while living in Moscow in 2004. For more background on MAPS, and on historical destruction and reconstruction in Moscow during the 2000s, see Cecil, 2011. Also see Cecil and Harris, 2007.
2. Merridale, 2013: 3.
3. See Harris, 2009: 227.
4. This is a view represented, to some extent, by Daria Paromonova's contribution to this volume.
5. For some background on the park project, see Ulam, 2017.
6. Robert Edelman, 'Каждый имеет право на жилище'. In *Жилище в России: век XX*, edited by William Craft Brumfield and Blair A. Ruble. Moscow: Three Squares, 2002 (= Edelman 1993).
7. A critical-theoretical, provocative take on the relationship between centralised spatialities and Russian cultural 'traditions' is provided in Medvedev, 1997.
8. More background on plans to build a 'new Moscow' to the south-west of the old city is provided in Chubukova, 2016.

Bibliography

Cecil, Clementine. '"We shall soon have the newest ancient heritage in the world": the rise of the sham replica under Moscow Mayor Yuri Luzhkov and its implications for Russia's architectural heritage', *The Historic Environment: Policy and Practice* 2, no. 1 (2011): 68–102.

Cecil, Clementine and Edmund Harris, eds. Московское архитектуоное наследие: точка невозврата/*Moscow Heritage at Crisis Point, 2004–2007*. Moscow/London: MAPS/Save Europe's Heritage, 2007.

Cecil, Clementine, Anna Bronovitskaya and Edmund Harris, eds. *Moscow Heritage at Crisis Point*. 2nd edn. Moscow/London: MAPS/Save Europe's Heritage, 2009.

Chubukova, Margarita, ed. *Kak Postroit' Novuyu Moskvu?* [How to build a new Moscow.] Moscow: KB Strelka, 2016.

Edelman, Robert. 'Everybody's got to be someplace: organizing space in the Russian peasant house, 1880 to 1930'. In *Russian Housing in the Modern Age: Design and Social History*, edited by William Craft Brumfield and Blair A. Ruble, 7–24. Washington, DC: Woodrow Wilson Center Press/Cambridge and New York: Cambridge University Press, 1993.

Harris, Edmund. Муляжи/'Façading and sham replicas'. In *Moscow Heritage at Crisis Point*, edited by Clementine Cecil, Anna Bronovitskaya and Edmund Harris, 2nd edn., 226–36. Moscow: Save Europe's Heritage, 2009.

Medvedev, Sergei. 'A general theory of Russian space: a gay science and a rigorous science', *Alternatives: Global, Local, Political* 22, no. 4 (1997): 523–53.

Merridale, Catherine. *Red Fortress: The Secret Heart of Russia's History*. London: Penguin, 2013.

Ulam, Alex. 'In Putin's Moscow, an urban wilderness emerges', *CityLab*, 17 May 2017. Accessed 23 May 2017. https://www.citylab.com/design/2017/05/in-putins-moscow-an-urban-wilderness-emerges/526872/.

3
Appropriating Stalinist heritage: state rhetoric and urban transformation in the repurposing of VDNKh

Andreas Schönle

A sprawling park and exhibition site in the north of Moscow, known by its Russian acronym VDNKh, has been a bellwether of Russia's history since its opening in 1939. Conceived initially as a display of Soviet agriculture, it became the Exhibition of the Achievements of National Economy under Nikita Khrushchev, at once a technology and trade show and an amusement park. It went through a rough patch after the collapse of the Soviet Union, when it was partially privatised and many of its grand pavilions were taken over by shady trade overseen by mafia groups. In 2014, the Government of Moscow obtained custody of it, promptly embarking on an energetic regeneration programme, which will be the subject of this chapter.

Extending over 235 hectares – almost equivalent to the entire City of London – VDNKh contains forty-nine listed objects and has become one of the focal points of the battle over architectural preservation. If initially it displayed grand Stalinist architecture, in the 1960s and 1970s it underwent a partial modernist makeover, including the construction of new metal-and-glass pavilions and the retrofitting of modernist elements onto existing structures.[1] In addition to its iconic architecture, it comprises an amusement park, vast trade exhibition spaces, a farm, riding stables, a panoramic cinema, a green theatre, restaurants, a model soviet village and a system of fountains and ponds. It is surrounded by two landscape parks – the Moscow Botanical Garden of the Academy of Sciences and the country estate of Ostankino – which can now be accessed seamlessly from it, further extending the area to 540 hectares.

Figure 3.1 Central Pavilion, VDNKh. Source: Andreas Schönle.

Many of its pavilions are currently closed, and some are in disrepair. But after some initial cosmetic refreshing of the façades, more fundamental and ambitious restoration is underway, and the park is beginning to live up to its potential as a prime exhibition space.[2] So far, it has gained perhaps its greatest notoriety from the enormous skating rink it houses in the winter, allegedly the largest in the world. A project to build a new observation wheel, the highest in Europe, was announced in the summer of 2016, although, in 2018, construction had not yet started. In any case, VDNKh doesn't *do* small. The exhibition park already claims the third-largest footfall in Russia after the Moscow Kremlin and the St Petersburg Hermitage, though this includes repeat local visitors. Numbers of visitors are one of the park management's main preoccupations and the VDNKh website obsessively records the footfall for its many activities. The current management aspires to turn VDNKh into one of the most iconic tourist destinations of the world, no less, banking on its ability to encapsulate Russian history.

Ilya Oskolkov-Tsentsiper is one of Moscow's movers and shakers in urban issues, and his company was retained to develop a new master plan for the exhibition. In an interview he gave me, he showed great pride in having convinced city officials that everything at VDNKh had to be grand, if not grandiose – new buildings needed to become bold statements. All elements of the customer experience, 'from the entrance ticket, to the sausages, not to speak of the architecture, should contribute to this feeling of something marvellous, something incredible', as he put it to me, implying that every detail of the exhibition had to go through an aesthetically coherent design process. Most stakeholders agree that VDNKh's *raison d'être* is to inspire awe in its visitors, but if in the past this sublimity aimed to sustain Stalinist ideology and enhance economic production, we will have to work out its purpose in the current context.

The challenges are daunting. One complex issue is the role of the state in institutional terms, but also in the visual and emblematic vocabulary of the exhibition. The park is saturated with statist rhetoric, expressed in the pompous Stalinist idiom of much of its architecture and sculpture, as well as through numerous emblems, banners, reliefs and wall paintings – all this omnipresent, often gloriously executed claptrap of socialist propaganda.

In its Soviet incarnation, the exhibition was meant as a celebration of the achievements of the state, and this ideology continues to weigh heavily on it. In an interview, Anna Kovalevskaya, the then Director of the Department of Territorial Development, told me that the management

Figure 3.2   Ukrainian Pavilion, VDNKh. Source: Andreas Schönle.

team envisioned the park as a 'demonstration of the individual and collective achievements of human beings', rather than as a display of state might. In their view, its many pavilions represent a magnificent shell, into which one can inject 'new content'. Hence, they aspire to house an eclectic range of exhibits aimed at different segments of the public and curated in collaboration with various institutions, the main criterion being that through their resonance these exhibits contribute to revamping the VDNKh brand.

The ideology behind the repurposing of VDNKh finds its roots in the Government of Moscow's efforts to reshape Moscow and to make the city more attractive and liveable for its inhabitants. The reconstruction of VDNKh follows in the footsteps of other urban projects such as the revamping of Gorky Park, the redesign of city streets, the development of bicycle paths and the creation of the new Zariad'e Park adjacent to the Kremlin.[3] Sergei Kuznetsov, the Chief Architect of Moscow, writes about it in very ambitious terms. The reconstruction of VDNKh is a 'reprogramming' or a 'reincarnation'.[4] It utilises the powers of architecture in order to 'manage life'.[5] What is at stake is 'the fight for the minds and hearts' of its visitors.[6] The park 'competes for people's attention – for their intellect'; in other words it aims to supply city residents and visitors with attractive and enjoyable opportunities for intellectual and cultural development. It is engaged in a struggle against the destructive logic of consumerism. By offering educational entertainment, the exhibition attracts new visitors, but also raises the cultural and intellectual standards of its existing patrons. As he puts it pithily, 'the [VDNKh] phenomenon is a matter of the right offer giving rise to the right demand'.[7]

One may be forgiven for asking who decides what the 'right' offer is, and there are clear paternalistic undertones to this rhetoric. Kuznetsov takes the *shashlyk* barbecue stands that proliferated at VDNKh in the 1990s as an example of the cultural degradation to which society succumbs when left to its own devices: 'In such cases development instantly sinks to the level of the most primitive and affordable pleasures.'[8] Thus, the reconstruction of the exhibition is a top-down initiative whose ultimate aim is social engineering – the fashioning of a new kind of public and by extension the transformation of society. Elena Pronicheva, the General Director of VDNKh until September 2018, adds that 'in a situation where the key resource for economic growth is innovation, the development of intellectual and creative potential is taking on new significance'.[9]

The repurposing of VDNKh thus responds to a utilitarian demand from the state, fostering creativity. This requires the instillation of a specific kind of everyday ethics, which Pronicheva calls 'a responsible attitude to free time' – the practice of useful, formative leisure – which the exhibition seeks to foster.[10] Of course, the model for this kind of utilitarian functionality is close at hand; it is in the Soviet Union, after all, that the concept of a 'park of culture and recreation' was developed, parks assuming explicitly educational, and ideological, functions. Pronicheva unabashedly draws on this genealogy. Writing about Soviet parks, she states that 'this model of an environment which constantly pushes people to study something new strikes us as incredibly relevant in today's world'.[11] The emphasis here is both on addressing as broad a section of the public as possible and on foisting new learning experiences upon it.

The Russian pavilion at the Venice Architecture Biennale in 2016 was devoted to the reconstruction of VDNKh, and the statements above come from the lavishly produced catalogue of this exhibition. In fairness, the military rhetoric of fighting for the hearts and minds of people in these quotations may have been inspired by the Biennale's theme of 'Reporting from the Front'. Nevertheless, it is symptomatic that for Russian officials the 'front' is not about sustainable development, housing, migration or dealing with natural and human-made catastrophes. Instead, the 'front' means shaping the citizenry in a way that makes it useful to society and to the government; in other words, it is about reinventing the compact between citizens and the state. Indeed, one of the problems the Government of Moscow has sought to address in recent years is citizen apathy, in particular the residents' disaffection with the urban environment, a leftover from Soviet collectivisation. Under the stewardship of Sergei Kapkov, the director of the city's Department of Culture until 2015, the absence of a habit of civic involvement in public matters was seen as an obstacle to creating a more user-friendly urban space, and ultimately a more integrated society.[12] Thus, for the revamping of Gorky Park, city authorities applied methods of 'agile' development, creating prototypes which were presented to the public for consultation and reworked correspondingly. Only younger generations, Moscow's so-called 'hipster' set, contributed to the design, which resulted in the creation of a park deliberately equipped for a young, active, mobile, loud and well-to-do demographic. In reaction to this state of affairs, the management team at VDNKh are keen to underscore their intention to appeal to all segments of Russian society. Accordingly, they aim to provide an eclectic range of activities and exhibitions, as well as to accommodate plural uses of the premises, while fostering the integrative virtues of encounters across generations and professions.[13] Some of the city government's user-responsive thinking endures: the management invites feedback from the public on its website, conducts informal public consultations on certain questions, and regularly monitors the feelings of its visitors through sociological surveys. And yet, the redevelopment of the park remains largely a paternalistic top-down affair: in Pronicheva's words, the exhibition is to 'impart meaning and dignity to the leisure enjoyed by various social groups'.[14] What makes this rhetoric particularly salient is the fact that the park management knows from its surveys that its main consumer base is a working-class public, in contradistinction to the young professionals who congregate in Gorky Park.

Architectural preservation is one of the main bones of contention in the reconstruction of VDNKh. Although the park management pays lip service to the need to preserve the exhibition's historical architecture, preservationist groups have accused it of a lax, if not illegal, handling of its heritage. The preservationists' contention is that the park should be seen as an architectural ensemble, which by law would require the preservation of everything in it and prohibit any new construction. Anatolyi Zhukov, the chief architect who developed the exhibition in the early 1950s, had clearly conceived it as an integrated, carefully designed whole and incorporated principles of eighteenth-century landscape design in it: it featured a grand principal alley flanked with stately pavilions and punctuated with fountains, while the outlying areas were conceived as places of lower height and density, which allowed the gaze to catch sight of the main pavilions from almost everywhere in the park.

Zhukov wrote of the park's architectural design as an 'integral whole', in which all the elements related to one another in meaningful ways, both thematically and in terms of form and size.[15] Even small service buildings, such as the park's 200 food kiosks, were carefully integrated into the design of alleys.[16] Although it features unremarkable architecture, the model Soviet farm, for example, has spaced-out buildings that create an atmosphere of laid-back country life, contrasting with the dramatic architecture of the main alley.

In 2015, in the context of a revision of heritage preservation legislation, the preservation status of the park was in fact downgraded to that of a 'notable zone'.[17] Even if individual listed pavilions are still protected, this new designation allows construction in some areas. The preservationists' fear is that, in line with the management's ambitious aims for the park, this new construction will significantly change the height and density parameters of some areas in the exhibition and therefore destroy the subtle balance between its various zones. For example, the area of the model Soviet farm is slated for the creation of a 'Park of Knowledge', which will offer professional development courses for adults and residential educational camps for children from all of Russia. The erection of

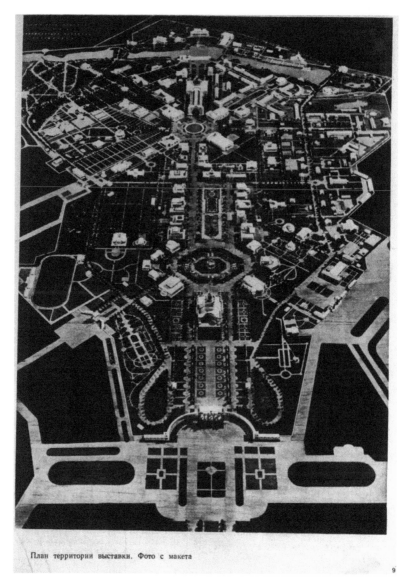

План территории выставки. Фото с макета

Figure 3.3 A. F. Zhukov's plan for VSKhV. A. F. Zhukov, *Arkhitektura vsesoiuznoi sel'skokhoziastvennoi vystavki*. Moscow: Gos. izd. literatury po stroitel'stvu i arkhitektury, 1955. Public domain.

the required facilities, including classrooms and dormitories for 3,000 schoolchildren, will inevitably dwarf the buildings that survive the necessary cull.

The preservationists' distrust of VDNKh management is fanned by several recent events. In the winter of 2013, construction began on a huge oceanarium in close and visible proximity to the main alley in a zone previously devoted to crop research. The construction involved the destruction of historic greenhouses, and took place at the time when VDNKh's status as a 'protection zone' legally prohibited any new construction. Subsequent to enquiries initiated by Arkhnadzor, the architectural preservation society, it transpired that the construction rose without any of the required official authorisation, indeed without any paperwork at all. This was a blatant case of *samostroi*, illegal construction. By the spring of 2015, when the building was completed, VDNKh had been lumbered with an enormous 30-metre-high structure that profoundly defaced the surrounding areas.

The construction began before the city took over the park, but it unfolded on its watch, and the current park management could easily have constrained its height. The construction was legalised retroactively in a flurry of documents in the summer of 2015. Planning permission, signed by Kuznetsov, was given on 26 June 2015, the beginning

Figure 3.4   Oceanarium. VDNKh. Source: Andreas Schönle.

of construction was signed off on 9 July, and the permission to start exploitation of the building was given on 17 July. In other words, according to official documents, construction had lasted just over a week![18] Not without some galling chutzpah, the document authorising the construction of the oceanarium also stipulated that in case of reconstruction, 'in order to lower its negative visual impact on objects of cultural heritage', its height should be lowered to 9–12 metres.[19]

Secrecy also affected the development of VDNKh's new master plan. Developed by the Tsentsiper agency and the company Strategy Partners Group without public consultation and kept under tight control, the master plan was presented to Vladimir Putin in August 2015, who gave it his approval, as was reported in the media.[20] Thereafter, one would have expected an official unveiling, but nothing happened. The master plan was eventually leaked to the internet, although it remained difficult to find.[21] When I asked Kovalevkaya what had prompted this secrecy, she stated that, since the plan had been leaked, it required no further release. Clearly, the park management aimed to evade a critical discussion of its intentions, despite its professed openness to user input. It was only in April 2017 that Moscow mayor Sergei Sobianin finally unveiled the plans officially.

In 2014, shortly after the city gained control over the exhibition, the panels of the neo-modernist façades of two listed buildings were hastily dismantled, in defiance of the law. This cladding had been added to the Stalinist buildings in the 1960s. Whatever one thinks of their aesthetic merit, these panels had historic value, showing the transformations of a monument over its life, something which according to the Venice Charter for the Conservation and Restoration of Monuments and Sites ought to be preserved.[22] Following an outcry by the public, the park management left the underlying metal skeletons standing and invited interested parties to phone in their views.[23]

The signs announcing this three-week-long consultation in August 2014 were still standing in April 2016, while its results had not been announced and plans had ground to a halt. By the summer of 2018, only one of the two pavilions was under refurbishment. Yet again, the park management had taken a rash decision in defiance of preservation laws and without public consultation. In fact, this modus operandi has become the rule. When Pavilion 57 was dismantled and reconstructed in 2015, the public was similarly kept in the dark.

On the aesthetic plane, recent transformations raise the question of what general orientation the park management wishes to pursue. The

Figure 3.5 Computer Engineering Pavilion between 1967 and 2014. VDNKh. Public domain.

Figure 3.6 Computer Engineering Pavilion in 2016. VDNKh. Source: Andreas Schönle.

fate meted out to modernist buildings, including the projected levelling of two (admittedly rather unsightly) pavilions of the 1970s, suggests the intent to return to the stylistics of the 1950s. This, too, goes back to Soviet practice, namely the principle in Soviet architectural preservation of choosing an 'optimal date' and stripping buildings back to it.[24] In the spring of 2016, tall, mature fir trees on the main alley were felled and replaced with young linden trees, which can be trimmed into geometric shapes more in keeping with Stalinist neoclassicism. In the summer of 2017, the layout of the flowerbeds was redesigned in keeping with their look in the 1950s. And although these interventions are partially rooted in archival research (albeit not strictly: the trees on the main alley were initially apple trees), they give short shrift to the fact that gardens are always evolving in time and never reach an 'authentic' fixed condition. In the same spirit, a new restaurant serves the typical cuisine of the former Soviet republics in an appropriately Stalinist retro-chic setting, with toilets adorned with reproductions of Moscow metro mosaics.[25]

Is the park management gripped by nostalgia for Stalinist stylistics? And if so, how does the exhibition handle the baggage of totalitarian politics that comes with this idiom? When interviewed by Gazeta.ru, Eduard Boiakov stated that 'VDNKh is a vertical, it is the image of heaven on earth'. Boiakov is a prominent theatre director and producer who was hired to curate the newly renamed Kultprosvet (formerly Culture and before that Uzbekistan) pavilion on behalf of Russia's Ministry of Culture. According to him, this pavilion is so remarkable that 'as soon as you enter, you feel like a barbarian'. Previous users of the pavilion had closed it off into separate boxes, which, he states 'comes from Postmodernism, from the liberal idea of fighting against any vertical'. Instead, all that is required 'is to study this space, to relate to it with respect and love … and not to fear being called "Stalinist"'. In this heady stew of culture, religion and politics, which echoes Putin's long-standing rhetoric on the 'vertical of power' and positions itself explicitly against 'liberal ideas', architectural preservation is enlisted in the service of some loyalist multi-disciplinary grand happening, succeeding where the Centre Pompidou in Paris is alleged to have failed, so as 'to fill the monument with live energy'.[26]

In my interview with her, Kovalevskaya breezily dismissed any link between culture and politics. The commissar of the Russian pavilion at the Biennale, Semen Mikhailovskii, set the 'decontamination of sites contaminated with ideology' as one of the goals of the Venice installation. He too emphasises that VDNKh is not about 'restoring the Empire', but about 'preserving imperial monuments and filling them with new content'.[27] To bring about this decontamination, the pavilion presented

Figure 3.7 'The Crypt' in the Russian Pavilion. 15th Venice
Architecture Biennale, 2016. Source: Andreas Schönle.

decontextualised reduced-scale copies of VDNKh's architectural detail in
the 'Crypt', displayed as antique artefacts.

Upstairs, a map of the exhibition was modelled as a computer
'motherboard', suggesting that its architecture is no more than underlying circuitry and thus compatible with any sort of operating system (or
ideology, that is).

And finally, gloriously shot views of a largely depopulated
VDNKh across the seasons emphasised its connections with nature.
Astonishingly, the pavilion succeeded in presenting VDNKh from various angles without revealing actual plans for development. In the catalogue, Mikhailovskii draws analogies with the historical practice of
religious conversion of monuments, for example, the transformation of
the pagan temple of the Pantheon in Rome into a Christian church. What
makes this analogy problematic is the foreshortening of the time scale.
There are still many people alive who bear the scars of Stalinist purges
and it will take time until VDNKh can be approached like the Egyptian
pyramids, through an antiquising gaze that effaces the memory of des-
potic cruelty. Furthermore, the examples of religious conversion that
Mikhailovskii mentions were precisely motivated not by a concern

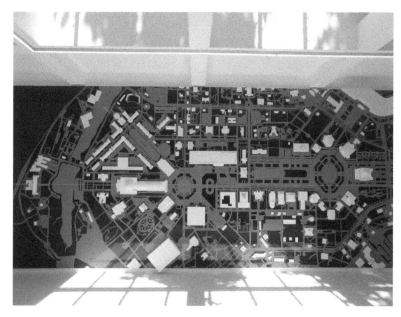

Figure 3.8 'The Motherboard' in the Russian Pavilion. 15th Venice Architecture Biennale, 2016. Source: Andreas Schönle.

forpreservation, but by a desire to adapt a structure for new political and religious uses. Thus, unwittingly, he concedes the point that preservation, which requires some form of distancing, is not the prime drive of VDNKh's repurposing.

The *genius loci* of the exhibition continues to haunt the premises. Initially, one of the main themes of the exhibition was the friendship of nations, embodied not only in the pavilions allocated to each Soviet republic, but also in the glorious fountain called precisely 'Friendship of Nations'.

The cornerstone of this marriage of nations was the 'everlasting fraternal union' between Russia and Ukraine, expressed visually through the prominence given to Ukraine in the layout of the park. The decoration of the Ukrainian pavilion directly celebrates this union between the two Slavic countries, notably with its central stained window of the Pereiaslav Council in 1654, when the Cossack Hetmanate pledged allegiance to the Russian Tsar, an event that Soviet historians treated as the (re)unification of Ukraine with Russia.[28] Thus, much of VDNKh's rhetoric ironically highlights the collapse of the communist dream of creating a world beyond nationalism.

Figure 3.9   The Friendship of Nations Fountain. VDNKh. Source: Andreas Schönle.

In an attempt to revitalise these bonds, the current administration invited friendly countries of the Commonwealth of Independent States to lease their former pavilion on nominal terms, provided they assumed the cost of restoration and used their premises for meaningful exhibitions. A few accepted these terms, but so far only Belarus has fully stepped up to the plate, although it remains embroiled with the park administration in a lawsuit over unpaid rent. Armenia, Kazakhstan and Kyrgyzstan have also expressed interest, but restorations are proceeding at snail's pace. Ukraine initially accepted the deal but reneged after the Russian military interventions began in 2014. Clearly it won't be easy to re-energise the exhibition's cosmopolitan import. Meanwhile the façades of the Ukrainian pavilion, renamed Agriculture, have been refurbished in 2018 with plans to house an exhibition devoted to 'Slavonic writing'.

The early signs of VDNKh's ideological repositioning are not encouraging. Pavilion 57 was rebuilt at great speed to accommodate a historical theme park, commissioned by the Patriarchate of the Orthodox Church.[29] It consists of colourful multimedia displays that tell the story of the Russian state through its rulers. Despite a few ethnographic displays, its mainstay is not artefacts or even facts, but a collection of quotations about Russian history from prominent Russian historians, philosophers, politicians and religious figures – all of them men! – and enhanced, for good form, by quotations from Russia's 'national' poet, Alexander Pushkin. These citations (including a few fake ones) are displayed on sham banners against the walls. Their general tenor is to celebrate the consolidation and unification of the Russian state under the savvy rule of its princes and tsars and under the spiritual, and political, guidance of the Orthodox Church. President Putin features prominently, highlighting the defining role of the Church in secular matters and its overwhelming contribution to Russian identity.

In an interview, Varvara Gogulia, the then Deputy Director of the Museum and Exhibition Department, strenuously denied that this exhibition exemplifies the curatorial aims of the current management team. 'Just as in a retail park', she told me, 'it would be incorrect to consider Leroy Merlin or Auchan as a leaseholder that defines the orientation of the entire park. The exhibition in Pavilion 57 is just one among many.' It is true that there are plenty of less ideologically minded exhibitors displaying their wares on the premises, from the Moscow Zoo to the Polytechnic Museum and the Museum of Oriental Art, but it is also obvious that VDNKh is subject to pressure from the highest echelons of power. In the summer of 2016, VDNKh retained the services of Michel Péna, a prominent French landscape designer, who claims to 'militate for lovers' and aimed to arrange intimate places in the landscape park he designed.[30] Perhaps there is thus hope that the official, ideologically suffused idiom of the exhibition will become less dominant.

The repurposing of VDNKh exemplifies the post-post-socialist condition.[31] Instead of a rejection of the past, we face a selective reappropriation of it. While there is nothing pernicious about this in principle, the challenge is on the one hand to avoid reifying the past into some sort of fixed, homogeneous entity inspired by sentimental nostalgia, and on the other hand to eschew a cavalier, postmodernist nonchalance towards it. VDNKh exhibits in concentrated forms the layerings of history and represents a unique opportunity to rethink historical continuity through multiplicity and diversity, rather than in a discriminatory fashion. It could also foster public debate about the dark moments of Russian history, allowing democratic reckoning. Yet the current administration of the park reveals not only a propensity to play down the multi-layeredness of its history, but also to redefine in narrow, aesthetic terms what it means. In my interview with him, Tsentsiper argued that it would be immoral to aestheticise Stalinist architecture, but his proposals have fallen on

Figure 3.10 Banner with quotation from historian S. M. Solov'ev, 'Centralisation is beneficial and indispensable, for without it everything would fall apart and drift away'. Exhibition 'Russia – my history'. Pavilion 57. VDNKh. Source: Andreas Schönle.

deaf ears. VDNKh is seen as a repository of visually effective tropes of greatness, as a sublimity that has become intransitive; its greatness is abstract, seemingly without reference to any underlying historical (and often even political) reality. In this decontextualised way, the exhibition is made available for the glorification of the contemporary state, where the concentration of cultural capital in one place is meant to function as a metaphor for its resurgent power and radiance while visitors become the target of social engineering instigated from above. In this profoundly patriarchal paradigm, VDNKh, rather than catalysing grassroots creativity, ultimately demonstrates what the state does, in its munificence, for its grateful, bedazzled and supine citizens.

Will the new VDNKh exert a transformational impact on Moscow? Initially built on the periphery of Moscow, it has long been overtaken by the expansion of the city, although the park nevertheless remains outside the centre. Authorities hope that through it, a second gravitational pole will emerge for Moscow, in line with their aim to de-centre economic and cultural activity. The economy has clearly picked up around the exhibition, yet surveys show that residents of the centre do not take much heed of what happens there. One can surmise that VDNKh's heavy-handed, paternalistic statist rhetoric may deter liberal professionals. At best, one can expect the emergence of a bipolar system of socially stratified cultural activity. In any case, the talk of creating a second *centre*, rather than spreading economic and cultural activity across the city, is itself symptomatic of the continuing centripetal propensities of urban development in Russia.

The VDNKh project is thus full of contradictions. Obsessed with its own branding, its stated aim is to resist the mindless consumerism of its patrons, while it operates with categories derived from marketing and packages culture as a consumer product. It deploys user-responsive practices yet arrogates to itself the right to top-down management of creativity. While being allegedly in the business of ideological decontamination and expending substantial rhetorical resources to rebrand Stalinist architecture, it simultaneously gives pride of place to heavy-handed nationalist propaganda. It claims to inject new content into Stalinist shells, but also capitalises on Stalinist nostalgia. And even though it studiously speaks the language of architectural preservation, it energetically transforms buildings as it repurposes them, certainly in their interior spaces, but also, often, in retro-refurbishing their façades.

VDNKh unashamedly embraces these sorts of contradictions. It takes the divorce of form and function as a point of departure and approaches history as an aesthetic repository.[32] But nor does it aim to orchestrate disjunctions, collisions or distortions in the manner of Bernard Tschumi's deconstructivist Parc de la Villette.[33] VDNKh's co-joining of incompatible ideas, forms, styles and times is that of a mild-mannered grand eclecticism which aims to please various focus groups. The master trope of the exhibition is neither coherence nor contradiction, but co-optation. In appropriating and repurposing a complex history, it first and foremost affirms the modernising power of the state, which posits itself as the ultimate redeemer of a troubled past. The yield from its considerable financial investment lies not in commercial profit, nor, fundamentally, in public amenity, but in the symbolic assertion of a historical resurgence that manifests itself in breezy pride at its achievement, measured first and foremost by visitor footfall.

Notes

1. For an overview of VDNKh's architectural history see Zinov'ev, 2014. On the various historical incarnations of the exhibition, see Mariia Silina, 'VDNKh vozvrashchaetsia', http://www.colta.ru/articles/specials/4084?part=8 (accessed 5 October 2018). VDNKh's official website provides a somewhat sugar-coated overview in English of the exhibition's history and reconstruction, http://vdnh.ru/en/about/history/ (accessed 28 October 2018).
2. On the new phase of restoration starting in 2016, see http://vdnh.ru/news/mer-moskvy-sergey-sobyanin-otkryl-posle-restavratsii-gorelef-evgeniya-vucheticha-na-vdnkh/ (accessed 5 October 2018). See also Nefedov, 2016.
3. Walker, 2015.
4. *V.D.N.H. Urban Phenomenon*: 105, 121.
5. *V.D.N.H. Urban Phenomenon*: 105.
6. *V.D.N.H. Urban Phenomenon*: 121.
7. *V.D.N.H. Urban Phenomenon*: 109.
8. *V.D.N.H. Urban Phenomenon*: 115.
9. *V.D.N.H. Urban Phenomenon*: 64.
10. *V.D.N.H. Urban Phenomenon*: 64.
11. *V.D.N.H. Urban Phenomenon*: 113.
12. These issues are discussed at length in *Urban Agenda*, the publication of the *Moscow Urban Forum*, which organises regular meetings of Moscow's urban stakeholders. See in particular *Urban Agenda*, no. 2 (spring 2013).
13. *V.D.N.H. Urban Phenomenon*: 109.
14. *V.D.N.H. Urban Phenomenon*, 65.
15. Zhukov, 1955.
16. Zhukov, 1955: 11.
17. For an analysis of this law and its practical implementation, see Konstantin Mikhailov, 'VDNKh – dostoprimechatel'noe mesto', 4 August 2015, http://hraniteli-nasledia.com/articles/proekty/vdnkh-dostoprimechatelnoe-vmesto-/ (accessed 5 October 2018). See also 'VDNKh – dostoprimechatel'naia i neokhraniaemaia territoriia', http://www.archnadzor.ru/2015/05/13/vdnh-dostoprimechatelnaya-i-neohranyaemaya-territoriya/ (accessed 5 October 2018).
18. See Irina Trubetskaia, 'Okeanarium na VDNKh: uzakonennyj samostroi', http://hraniteli-nasledia.com/articles/proekty/vdnkh-dostoprimechatelnoe-vmesto-/ (accessed 5 October 2018).
19. Mikhailov, 'VDNKh – dostopimechatel'noe mesto'.
20. Sobianin predstavil Putinu dolgosrochnyi plan razvitia VDNKh, https://ria.ru/moscow/20150804/1162240719.html (accessed 5 October 2018).
21. See https://politota.dirty.ru/vdnkh-vskore-unichtozhat-809878/ (accessed 5 October 2018). An extensive critical discussion of the master plan had been removed from the yodnews.ru site by the time this article was being prepared for publication (October 2018).

22. Irina Trubetskaia, 'VSKhV protiv VDNKh' (accessed 5 October 2018). For a history of these pavilions, see Anna Bronovitskaia, 'Ot VSKhV k VDNKh: transformatsiia vystavochnogo ansamblia v Ostankino 1950-kh – 1960-kh gg'. *Archnadzor*, 13 March 2015, http://archi. ru/russia/54559/ot-vshv-k-vdnh-transformaciya-vystavochnogo-ansamblya-v-ostankino-v-konce-1950-kh-1960-kh-gg (accessed 5 October 2018).

23. Fedot Pukhlov, 'Obespokoennyi gorozhanin o tom, kak proiskhodit rekonstruktsiia VDNKh', *The Village*, 21 March 2014, http://www.the-village.ru/village/city/direct-speech/144211-mestnyy-zhitel-o-rekonstruktsii-vdnh (accessed 5 October 2018).

24. See Kelly, 2015.

25. For the press release about the opening of this restaurant, see http://vdnh.ru/news/na-vdnkh-otkroetsya-pervyy-semeynyy-restoran-moskovskoe-nebo-/ (accessed 05/10/2018).

26. 'Ne nado boiat'sia, chto tebia nazovut "stalinistom"', http://www.gazeta.ru/culture/ 2015/12/14/a_7967057.shtml (accessed 5 October 2018).

27. *V.D.N.H. Urban Phenomenon*, 52.

28. Needless to say, in the eyes of Ukrainian nationalists, this interpretation remains highly controversial.

29. In April 2016, when I visited, only the exhibition on the Riurikids was open.

30. See a brief interview with him at http://vdnh.ru/news/mishel-pena-dlya-menya-chest-byt-avtorom-kontseptsii-landshaftnogo-parka-vdnkh/, 10 August 2016 (accessed 5 October 2018).

31. For a brief discussion of the post-post-socialist condition, see Schönle, 2015.

32. On the political import of architectural forms and the uses of monumentality, see Murawski, 2019.

33. Blundell Jones, 2012.

Bibliography

Blundell Jones, Peter. 'Parc de La Villette in Paris, France by Bernard Tschumi', *Architectural Review*, 7 June 2012. Accessed 5 October 2018. https://www.architectural-review.com/buildings/ parc-de-la-villette-in-paris-france-by-bernard-tschumi/8630513.article.

Kelly, Catriona. '"Scientific reconstruction" or "new oldbuild"? The dilemmas of restoration in post-Soviet St. Petersburg', *Revue des études slaves* 86, no. 1/2 (2015): 17–39.

Murawski, Michał. 'Radical centres: the political morphology of monumentality in Warsaw and Johannesburg', *Third Text* 33, no. 1 (2019): 26–42. DOI: 10.1080/09528822.2016.1275188.

Nefedov, Pavel. 'Vosem' zhiznei odnoi vystavki' [Eight lives of one exhibition]. In *V.D.N.H. Urban Phenomenon: The Exhibition at the Russian Pavilion at the 15th International Architecture Exhibition – La Biennale di Venezia*, 150–87. Moscow: Ministry of Culture of the Russian Federation, 2016.

Schönle, Andreas. 'Introduction: Les défis de la condition post-postsocialiste: architecture et histoire en Europe centrale et orientale', *Revue des études slaves* 86, no. 1/2 (2015): 9–14.

V.D.N.H. Urban Phenomenon: The Exhibition at the Russian Pavilion at the 15th International Architecture Exhibition – La Biennale di Venezia. Moscow: Ministry of Culture of the Russian Federation, 2016.

Walker, Shaun. 'Is the "Moscow experiment" over?', *Guardian*, 8 June 2015. Accessed 5 October 2018. https://www.theguardian.com/cities/2015/jun/08/is-the-moscow-experiment-over-gorky-park-sergei-kapkov-alexei-navalny.

Zhukov, A.F. *Arkhitektura vsesoiuznoi sel'skokhoziastvennoi vystavki*. Moscow: Gos. izd. literatury po stroitel'stvu i arkhitektury, 1955.

Zinov'ev, Aleksandr. *Ansambl' VSKhV. Arkhitektura i stroitel'stvo*. Moscow: no publisher, 2014.

4

The city without a centre: disurbanism and communism revisited

Owen Hatherley

The centre of Moscow has almost disappeared. The Boulevard Ring, the Garden Ring, the theatres, department stores, tenements and winding streets are gone, replaced with linear strips of road and parkland, lined by industry and small modernist houses, with their own allotment gardens, which stretch out endlessly, with the main feature of the city – if you can call it that – being the workers' clubs and Palaces of Culture, in the shape of steel pyramids, or globules of glass suspended from gantries, with wide sports fields around. Everyone gets around in a small car, and family life seems to have disappeared, as individuals move from one small, prefabricated house to another according to their job, their interests, whomever they've met. Travel further and further out from the city and you find more of the same, an endless low-rise constructivist suburb, which has mixed almost imperceptibly with the kibbutz-like structures of the collective farms. But travel into the dead centre, and you find something quite surprising. Here, at the heart, still, is the Kremlin. It's not the centre of power any more – that has long since been devolved into the hands of the local Soviets – but instead it's a sort of architectural park, lovingly restored by architectural historians. But nobody lives or works here; it is a museum of itself, surrounded not by asphalt but by luscious, somewhat overgrown parkland, overflowing onto the river. The architecture of power as anything other than a historical curio, however, has totally disappeared.

This, only slightly travestied, is the vision of the Communist city of the future presented by the constructivist architects of the USSR, circa

Figure 4.1 Disurbanist development between Moscow and Yekaterinburg, 2017. Source: Owen Hatherley.

1930, at the start of the first Five-Year Plan, when architects who at the start of the 1920s dreamed of modernist megacities suddenly saw the Plan as an opportunity to make concrete the 'dissolution of the divide between city and country' demanded in *The Communist Manifesto*.[1] The movement that coalesced around this was known as 'disurbanism', and the name most associated with this idea, the sociologist Mikhail Okhitovich, is Soviet architecture's most famous martyr. In the 1990s, as the archives were opened, Hugh D. Hudson's study *Blueprints and Blood* revealed that Okhitovich was a former oppositionist who was readmitted into, then re-expelled from, the Party, before disappearing into the Gulag in the late 1930s.

What is less often considered is how this sudden shift into an architecture that abhorred any kind of power, and a city that had no room for it, occurred. For much of the 1920s, the key reference for constructivist architects and urban planners was Chicago, an industrial, skyscraping megacity that had come out of nowhere; rapidly industrialising Soviet cities such as Yekaterinberg (then Sverdlovsk) and Kharkiv were routinely described as 'Chicagos'; Novosibirsk's description as the 'Siberian Chicago' became semi-official.[2] You can see this moment in the emblematic buildings of that decade, new socialist city centres such as that built around the Derzhprom building in Kharkiv, which were huge, dramatic, megalopolitan and, most of all, centres of state power. Suddenly, all this is rejected, in favour of cities without centres, without power, without even obvious spatial differentiation of any kind. How and why does this sudden shift at the turn of the 1930s happen, and why is it equally suddenly reversed?

In all the theoretical debates on urban planning during the 1928–32 period, it was practically unanimously agreed that a principal part of the Plan should be an attempt to erase, or at the very least considerably lessen, the divide between city and country. The historian and biographer of Konstantin Melnikov, S. Frederick Starr, considered the attempt to, as Moisei Ginzburg put it, let workers 'listen to the songs of skylarks' by 'destationing' society somewhat macabre.[3] Certainly this seems to be the case if we examine the career of Nikolai Miliutin, old Bolshevik, commissar, occasional architect, author of the famous study *Sotsgorod* (a portmanteau of 'socialist' and 'city'), and occupant of the Narkomfin building's penthouse.[4] For an insight into just how far from 'utopianism' his world actually was, there is the single anecdote on Miliutin in Victor Serge's *Memoirs of a Revolutionary*, in a section dealing with the trials and executions of entirely innocent (and often, as in the Shakhty 'wreckers' trial, foreign) alleged 'saboteurs' during the first Five-Year Plan. Serge sketches the reason for the apprehension of one of the victims, the Menshevik Groman, who had been working in the Planning Commission, attempting to make this Stalinist instrument follow reality rather than diktat. Serge writes: 'many were punished for having actually foreseen the disastrous consequences of certain government decisions. The old socialist Groman was arrested after having had a sharp quarrel at the Planning Commission with Miliutin. Groman, at the end of his tether, shouted that the country was being led to the abyss.'[5] He would soon be a defendant in one of the USSR's earliest show trials, and Miliutin could continue imagining ultra-modern socialist cities without reality intruding. Hence, it's unsurprising that Starr calls the disurbanists' Arcadian proposals in the midst of an unprecedented crisis 'cynical' or 'grotesque'.[6]

However much constructivist theorists and architects like Okhitovich or Ginzburg appear to be complicit with this, there is a counter-argument that theirs was the more realistic, not to mention more humane response to the massive rupture that industrialisation and agricultural collectivisation created between city and country, as opposed to the hyper-urbanism of primitive accumulation, with all its overcrowding and groaning infrastructure that actually resulted. The historian Moshe

Figure 4.2 Disurbanist development between Moscow and Yekaterinburg, 2017. Source: Owen Hatherley.

Lewin claims that an ad hoc dissolution of the fixed divide between city and country was the inadvertent consequence of the 'socialist offensive', creating a space somewhere between the two. '[A]t one pole, collectivization "de-ruralized" the countryside; at the other, urbanization did the same; and industrialization, another potent demiurge, operated at both poles.'[7]

In this sense, it is possible to argue that the 'dreams' of the disurbanists were not especially utopian, that in fact they were a description of contemporary reality, a suggestion for how processes already set in motion could be continued without coercion, as a positive factor rather than a messy, indistinct space, in flux between city and country and waiting to ascend to the former. Okhitovich imagined a 'city' where 'no function would be pinned to any one place … individual functions and individual human beings would for the first time be free to move anywhere'. On one level, disurbanism emerges from the assembly line; Okhitovich writes that 'the planning of an industrial enterprise can now reflect the possibilities of conveyor belt production on the scale of the whole national economy, and eventually of the whole world economy', which, when combined with 'the automobilization of the territory', offers a new urbanism based on 'the principle of maximum freedom, ease and speed of communications possibilities'. The resultant entity, he implies, is something that could only emerge after world revolution, 'the red city of the planet of communism', which doesn't stop him from advocating it as an immediate solution.[8]

Disurbanism can be seen as a form of Soviet cargo cultism; whereas earlier, architects had dreamed of the socialist Chicago, now they dreamed of the communist Los Angeles; but if it is looked at in the context of the chaos of the Five-Year Plan, it appears in fact to be one of the few attempts during Stalin's 'Great Change' to retain a libertarian, democratic conception of communism. It is a conscious transformation of the reality described by Lewin in which 'on the one hand, millions of peasants tried out living in the towns, or in the case of richer peasants, sought refuge from persecution there; on the other hand, masses of people abandoned – even fled – urban areas. This was a veritable human maelstrom'.[9] It was also fully anticipated by Okhitovich's apparently unworldly, utopian studies, hence the advocacy of a means to manage, or improve and make liveable, this flux, without the internal passports, arrests and deportations that were actually used.

However, the constructivists were also remarkably astute in noticing the trends of twentieth-century capitalist urban development, although perhaps overestimating its usefulness for socialist purposes. Without the infrastructural components advocated by avant-garde planners – the electrical and transportation networks that made 'destationing' possible in the first place – the result could have been more comparable to Latin American disurbanism. S. Frederick Starr notes that B. Strogova, one of the rival group of 'urbanists', had 'complained bitterly about the shantytowns springing up on the periphery of Moscow like Latin American *barriadas*'.[10]

That is, people were erecting and demounting their own self-made houses in the spaces between country and city, which is certainly a major component of Okhitovich's theory. Starr also notes in passing that the Disurbanist Socialist settlement was based to a large degree on North American archetypes, or rather that Okhitovich 'defended his proposals in terms of his reading of American and Australian experience', with the suburbanisation of the Midwest considered more appropriate than Manhattanism: 'Minneapolis was hailed as holder of the world record for downtown green space and cited as justification for tearing down parts of Moscow.'[11]

It is the very suburbanism of Okhitovich and his colleagues around *Sovremmennaia Arkhitektura (SA)* that makes it, for Hugh D. Hudson, in his archival study of the 'Stalinisation' of Soviet architecture, *Blueprints and Blood*, an exemplar of an attempt to fulfil the real dreams and desires of the working class, a retreat, dictated by events rather than ideology, from the behaviourist implications of their previous advocacy of the ultra-urban 'social condenser'. Hudson argued that this was an example of the constructivists' responsiveness to direct working-class desire; they were learning, via questionnaires given out to workers, 'from worker assessments of housing and urban design. This communication formed the basis for bridging, at least in housing, the cultural gap between revolutionary elites and common people'.[12] In Hudson's analysis, what Okhitovich's opponents alternately called 'automobile socialism' or, in exemplary Stalinist manner, 'social-fascism', was driven by what he frequently refers to as the workers' 'desires' and 'dreams'.[13] In essence, Hudson's argument is a familiar one from the last half-century of architectural and town-planning discourse: what the workers really want is *suburbia*.

Lenin's widow and educational minister Nadezhda Krupskaya, like Okhitovich briefly an oppositionist, publicly criticised his ideas in *Komsomolskaya Pravda* at the end of 1929: 'any talk about "disurbanisation", reproducing attitudes of the bourgeois mind, which is afraid of the concentration of the proletariat, the Leo Tolstoy detestation of the big cities, is to be rejected'.[14] This was not limited to aesthetic traditionalists such as Krupskaya; a similar argument was made by the modernist architect Nikolai Dokuchaev, who saw disurbanism as little more than a series of 'self-built dacha colonies', an unserious proposal, a utopian distraction from the serious task of urbanisation and industrialisation.[15] This was also the position taken by Lazar Kaganovich when he ended the town-planning debate by fiat in 1932, and proposed instead another mega version of the bourgeois city: a tightly planned neo-Haussmannism, which – like the original Haussmann – hid peri-urban chaos behind grandiose façades, a situation not seriously tackled until well into the Khrushchev era.[16]

This all assumes that disurbanism was serious, but in reality there is an element of *Alice's Adventures in Wonderland* about many of the urban proposals of the time. The controversy over the socialist city truly broke out in 1930 over the 'Green City' competition for a sort of spa town outside of Moscow, and a proposal which was taken less seriously by the administrators of the Plan was submitted by Konstantin Melnikov.[17] His Green City was a city of sleep for a country descending into coercion and surveillance and with ever-increasing working hours. Apparently innocently, Melnikov wrote of how the inhabitants' sleep would be subliminally affected by smells, sounds and spatiality, so that even in dreaming they were reachable by the authorities. Melnikov writes, apparently poker-faced, as the Soviet workers' living standards plummeted, famine started to seep into the countryside, the first show trials began and fascism began its rise in Germany, 'the whole world has fallen asleep'. Maybe in the ultra-urban city of Stalinism, with its ruthless urban hierarchies, grand boulevards and shanty towns, skyscrapers and overcrowded *kommunalki*, a few people did dream of the disurbanist city.

Figure 4.3   Disurbanist development between Moscow and Yekaterinburg, 2017. Source: Owen Hatherley.

Naturally, nothing like it was built in the hyper-centralist Stalinist city, with its grand boulevards, axes and high-density housing; although it resembles disurbanism a little more closely, the 'mikrorayon' planning of the Khrushchev era and beyond, though undeniably often 'green' and geographically dispersed, presented a decidedly urban image of a city of mass-produced towers, dominating and teeming rather than low-rise, bucolic and self-produced. It is very probable that nothing resembling Okhitovich's city was possible in the way he had imagined it in 1930, among other reasons because of the inability of the Soviet car industry to even begin to keep up with the assumed car-per-person that would make the system work. A more planned, gradual shift between city and country, that created a commonality between the two, could have had some positive effects, but the chaos of the Five-Year Plan made this sort of sophistication unlikely. There is evidence that some novel urban forms were created in that period. 'Linear cities' and some semblance of a '*Sotsgorod*' did get created in new 'socialist settlements' in industrial cities such as Gorky, Sverdlovsk, Kharkiv and Zaporizhia, where abundant (albeit deliberately unproductive) green space was interspersed with low-rise, non-hierarchical housing. Most of all, the dacha colonies that gave the USSR one of the highest levels of second-home ownership in the world are certainly self-built and linear, and are strung informally along transport networks. These places, encouraged from the mid-1950s onwards by Soviet governments, were the nearest disurbanism ever came to becoming reality, and in the 1990s they had a major role in stopping Russians, Ukrainians and others from starving during the social devastation that followed the USSR's collapse. No utopia, but a crucial emergency refuge.

Disurbanism was a heroic challenge to the fetish for power and hierarchy that beset Russian politics and Russian cities in the 1930s, and that clearly continues to do so to a lesser degree, in the neo-Stalinist re-planning of Moscow under Mayor Sobyanin. Even so, the idea is at striking variance with how urbanism has been envisaged in the last few decades by socialist thinkers such as Mike Davis, Doreen Massey, David Harvey and Michael Sorkin, who have imagined a dense city connected by public rather than private transport, that is easily walkable – something that precludes the endless panoramas of single-family houses looping along infrastructure networks that the disurbanists imagined. There are very good reasons for this. Such a city would be completely petrol-based, horrendously wasteful of energy and space, and extremely polluting, as the American exurbs that inspired Okhitovich make very clear. In fact, the Stalinist city, however vicious and unjust it was at the time, may actually appear more 'modern' by today's standards, with its superb public transport and the concentration of housing in mid-rise blocks of flats around public spaces. If there is a political force that would want to build (and that, in a sense, is building) the disurbanist city today, it is capitalist and libertarian. The 'dream' of the dissolved city that Okhitovich imagined was revolutionary is now more often dreamt by those for whom the city means migrants, minorities and socialists.

Notes

1. The key text on this moment is still Kopp, 1970; on the long history of neither-city-nor-country hybrids and social planning, see Darley, 1978.
2. On the 'Americanist' movement in the Soviet 1920s, see the first part of Ball, 2003, or Hatherley, 2016.
3. Starr, 1984, p. 223.
4. *Sotsgorod* was published in English translation by MIT Press in 1974, with extensive appendices on the period.
5. Serge, 1975, p. 249.
6. My preferred study on the urban–rural crisis that came with the first Five-Year Plan is Lewin, 1994.
7. Lewin, 2005, p. 62.
8. Okhitovich, 1929.
9. Lewin, 2005, p. 63.
10. Starr, 1984, p. 236.
11. Starr, 1984, p. 230.
12. Hudson, 1992, p. 448; see also Hudson, 1994, pp. 51–63.
13. Hudson, 1992, p. 457.
14. Quoted from Nevzgodin, 2006.
15. Dokuchaev, 1930.
16. Stites, 1989, pp. 237–8.
17. Melnikov, 2002, pp. 62–9.

Bibliography

Ball, Alan M. *Imagining America: Influence and Images in Twentieth-Century Russia*. Lanham, MD: Rowman and Littlefield, 2003.

Darley, Gillian. *Villages of Vision*. London: Paladin, 1978.

Dokuchaev, Nikolai. 'The competition for the planning of Magnitogorsk', translated by Ross Wolfe, *Stroitel'stvo Moskvy* ('The construction of Moscow'), 4 (1930): 28.

Hatherley, Owen. *The Chaplin Machine: Slapstick, Fordism and the Communist Avant-Garde*. London: Pluto Press, 2016.

Hudson, Hugh D. 'Terror in Soviet architecture: the murder of Mikhail Okhitovich', *Slavic Review* 51, no. 3 (1992): 448–67.

Hudson, Hugh D. *Blueprints and Blood: The Stalinization of Soviet Architecture, 1917–1937*. Princeton, NJ: Princeton University Press, 1994.

Kopp, Anatole. *Town and Revolution: Soviet Architecture and City Planning, 1917–1935*, translated by Thomas E. Burton. New York: Braziller, 1970.

Lewin, Moshe. *The Making of the Soviet System: Essays in the Social History of Interwar Russia*. New York: New Press, 1994.

Lewin, Moshe. 'Social flux and "Systemic Paranoia"'. In *The Soviet Century*, edited by Gregory Elliott, 52–65. London: Verso, 2005.

Melnikov, Konstantin. 'The Green City'. In *Architecture of Konstantin Melnikov, 1920s–30s*, edited by Rishat Mullagildin, 62–9. Tokyo: Toto, 2002.

Miliutin, N.A. *Sotsgorod: The Problem of Building Socialist Cities*, translated by Arthur Sprague. Cambridge, MA: MIT Press, 1974.

Nevzgodin, Ivan. 'The socialist city behind the scenes: the crucial theoretical debates in Moscow in 1929–31 and daily practice in Soviet urbanism'. In *The Socialist City: Concepts and Realities between Pragmatism and Utopianism*. Stockholm: European Association for Urban History, 2006.

Okhitovich, Mikhail. 'Zum Problem der Stadt', *Sovremennaia Arkhitektura* 4 (1929): 130–4.

Serge, Victor. *Memoirs of a Revolutionary, 1901–1941*, edited and translated by Peter Sedgwick. London: Oxford University Press, 1975.

Starr, S. Frederick. 'Visionary town planning during the Cultural Revolution'. In *Cultural Revolution in Russia, 1928–1931*, edited by Sheila Fitzpatrick, 207–40. Bloomington: Indiana University Press, 1984.

Stites, Richard. *Revolutionary Dreams: Utopian Vision and Experimental Life in the Russian Revolution*. New York: Oxford University Press, 1989.

5

Mutant centralities: Moscow architecture in the post-Soviet era

Daria Paramonova

It is common to hear criticism of post-perestroika architecture in Russia, and in particular Moscow – whether from architects, critics or the general public. The architecture, they say, is weak, compromised, dubious. But the architecture of this period was incredibly significant in giving form to the age, and it produced a great many buildings of note.

Today Moscow is facing another stage of development. One that is centred not so much on buildings, but on space. The city is in the middle of an ambitious programme of urban renewal. It is renovating streets and public spaces, transforming the city into a high-quality urban environment. There is a new emphasis on pedestrians, safety, ecology, technology. We may with some certainty state that one epoch has finished and another has begun.

The Rubicon seems to have been at or around 2010, when the then Moscow mayor Yuri Luzhkov was removed in favour of Sergey Sobyanin. Before his sacking, Luzhkov was well known for his personal involvement in urban development. However, it is important to trace the full sweep of architecture over the almost three decades since the collapse of the USSR in order to understand what is really new in ongoing development, and what is just a new form of old practices.

After the disappearance of the Soviet Union, socialist values were swept aside and replaced by ideological emptiness. 'Labour, justice and equality' – the values of the Soviet past – became 'profit, property and democracy'. Meanwhile, the material world, seemingly scorned by Soviet ideology, had to be built from scratch. What we can see now is that between the late 1980s and 2010 we went through a period of transition – a move from one social paradigm to another. This period is extremely difficult to describe. Dynamics and transformation are at its core, but there is no single element. There is not one defining character-istic or trait.[1]

But over this period, Russian architecture, and in particular Moscow architecture, went through an extremely intensive period of develop-ment. One of the first manifestations of change taking place in society was the elevation of personal over public priorities. In architecture, we saw similar developments – an appearance of architectural pluralism. The foundation of this phenomenon was undoubtedly provided by the political pluralism of the time. The ability to be yourself – both outstand-ing and unique – became a new paradigm for architects previously used to centralised design institutes, and prefabricated and standardised structures.

These new structures were built mainly in the centre of the city. 'Creative egoism' was an explosion of styles and visions, of aping and perfecting, of statements and ambitions. In the main, such structures ignored the existing context of the city, or, at the least, used it as a source for developing a new context. The establishment of the individual's right to a personal opinion defined the political axis of the first decade of Luzhkov's rule. An anti-Soviet notion of individualism was synonymous with that time's understanding of modernity and progressiveness.[2]

Alongside that explosion of personal visions, another important development introduced a new aesthetic of a dominant but artificially developed vernacular style. It was artificial because it was mostly a pro-jection of the personal preferences and imagination of city officials and, in particular, the often hyperactive Mayor Luzhkov. The 'Luzhkov style' became possible because of his merging of two styles of leader – domi-nating Soviet-style director and efficient city manager. The city came to be perceived as the property of one person, and his personal taste started to translate into physical space. The personal aesthetic preferences of one person emanated, centripetally, throughout the architectural fabric and urban shape of the entirety of Moscow.

Not only did this period introduce a whole array of forms and styles, it also in many cases saw a return to the past. Social housing is perhaps the clearest example of this. Soviet industrial-scale construction of prefabricated buildings enjoyed a renaissance in post-Soviet times. It became integrated into the system of private property. Sophisticated prefabrication systems were the source of fast-to-build – and, equally important, fast-to-sell – housing developments. At the same time such developments generally ignored the social functions of Soviet *micro-rayon*, 'micro-districts'. The constructions were diverse and beautified, but none of that social infrastructure was built. It was a mutant – a Soviet skeleton dressed in the latest fashions.[3]

Another important architectural phenomenon all about reinterpreting the past – but in a more radical format – was a search for the new sacred. The first dialogue between church and state began in the final years of the Soviet Union. And the first result of these new links was programmes to rebuild churches – the redemption of the past. Yet it was a modernised process, and so the churches were radically transformed in appearance and function. They played an important role in influencing secular architecture too. Demolition became a popular tool as a new type of creation of an improved past, when the meaning of authenticity was completely reconsidered.[4]

In the first years of perestroika, at the end of the 1980s, public spaces were already beginning to take on new functions. This was a result of the emergence of new types of entrepreneurial and commercial activity, which allowed them to adapt the city to their own purposes. This gave rise to new forms of commercial architecture, from advertising billboards to vast markets and shopping centres, that subjugated swathes of the city to the laws of profit and investment. One phenomenon that radically transformed the post-Soviet city could be defined as 'commercial functionalism', or the possibility of using any property or plot of land for profit, an opportunity previously restricted in Russia.[5]

The possibility of acquiring and appropriating space with the help of new types of structures provided opportunities to adjust the parameters of the city's scale. But these haphazard constructions, which have sprouted up all over Moscow during the past decades, have fallen victim to systematic attempts by city officials to take back control of the fabric of the city. Commercial functionalism has gone through several stages of torment, but the last was the most spectacular and radical, perhaps the most obvious example of a break with the Luzhkov era. It actually happened in one night, called 'the night of the long diggers' by the mass media. More than 100 structures of commercial architecture, considered illegally built, were demolished in the early hours of 9 February 2016. This dramatic event was widely discussed by society. What was surprising was that the kiosks and shopping malls – previously scorned, especially by architects and critics – began to be appreciated by the same people. Many came to their defence. Interestingly, the main topic of discussion was the status as private property, rather than the 'ugly' visual nature, of these buildings.

Today, the time of uncontrolled appropriation of space, typical of any new democratic society with unclear rules on private property, has passed. The renovation of streets has been the main focus of the current mayor and his team since the 2010s. Today, we are again undergoing a process of defining a proper style and language for new development – the fight between a never-existing past and a frightening future is happening in the design of lamps, benches and other forms of infrastructure. There is already a so-called 'Sobyanin style', highlighting the extent to which officials such as the mayor continue to play an important role in city development.

Today we are facing a new march for identity, together with the development of spaces that have been forgotten for twenty years. It is obvious that this is a necessary turn of evolution, but at the same time as creating public space we have begun to fight the achievements of the recent past. They were proud achievements: the freedom of each individual to participate in the city economy, to provide services and goods on the scale of small businesses (totally eliminated in Soviet times), to influence, transform and fix the environment that we live in, and the right to be imperfect in the end. If all these parameters can be incorporated in a new programme of city development, that will represent an even prouder achievement.

For now, however, whether it will be is anyone's guess.

Notes

1. Gutnov and Glazichev, 1990.
2. Goldhoorn and Meuser, 2006. See also the architectural guide book on Moscow and the Moscow region from 1987 to 2007: Korobyna, 2007.
3. Paramonova, 2012.
4. Cecil and Harris, 2007.
5. Paramonova, 2012.

Bibliography

Cecil, Clementine and Edmund Harris, eds. *Moscow Heritage at Crisis Point, 2004–2007*. Moscow: Save Europe's Heritage, 2007.

Goldhoorn, Bart and Philipp Meuser. *Capitalist Realism: New Architecture in Russia*. Berlin: DOM Publishers, 2006.

Gutnov, A. and V. Glazichev. *Mir Arhitekturi*. Moscow: Molodaya Gvardia, 1990.

Korobyna, Irina. *Novaya Moskva 4*. Moscow: Center of Contemporary Architecture/CCA, 2007.

Paramonova, Daria. *Mushrooms, Mutants and Other Oddities: Architecture of the Luzhkov Era*. Moscow: Strelka Press, 2012.

Part II
Off-centre: palatial peripheries

6

Berlin's empty centre: a double take

Jonathan Bach

In the centre of Berlin, halfway between the Brandenburg Gate and the commercial heart of Alexanderplatz, lies a peculiar palimpsest: the reconstructed Berlin City Castle that now occupies the site of the former East German Palace of the Republic. The former socialist parliament and cultural centre was itself built on the site of the original City Castle. In dialectical fashion, today's reconstructed Castle erased the Palace, which in turn erased the Castle. These two buildings – the City Castle and the Palace of the Republic – have come to both structure and suture the socialist and post-socialist eras and the accompanying division of the city into East and West. They form competing images and discourses of the centre of the city, the symbolic point from which it radiates and converges. Yet, as with all binaries, the Palace/Castle dialectic hides as much as it highlights.[1]

While the next chapter in this book examines the present-day plans for the site, this intervention seeks to direct attention to what is potentially overlooked in the focus on the buildings themselves: key periods when no building stood on the site. Most visitors today, if they are aware at all of the existence of the GDR-era Palace of the Republic, most likely do not realise that the Palace existed only for the last fourteen years of the GDR. For considerably longer – twenty-three years, not counting the construction phase – the site was unbuilt, windswept and desolate, a place caught between becoming and being. Between 1950, when the Castle was destroyed by the Communist government, and 1973, when construction on the Palace of the Republic began (it opened in 1976), Berlin's centre was not merely metaphorically empty. This situation was echoed briefly again between 2008, when the Palace was fully demolished, and 2012, when work on the new Castle began (finished in 2019).

I argue here that this period of absence is important not only for understanding how the centre of Berlin came to acquire its contemporary contours, but also as a useful case study for theorising centrality. Roland Barthes, in his famous essay on Tokyo in *Empire of Signs*, posited a 'synesthetic sentiment of the City, which requires that any urban space have a center to go to, to return from, a complete site to dream of and in relation to which to advance or retreat; in a word, to invent oneself'. For Barthes, the 'emptiness' of Tokyo's central imperial palace was a 'precious paradox' because it enabled this sentiment despite being 'empty'.[2] Yet in Berlin the post-war central emptiness was not intended in the same sense, but rather created by the destruction of the Castle in order precisely to reinvent the national self.

It was not, like the Tokyo palace, a strictly forbidden space, but it was in its emptiness at times a forbidding one, and it exerted a phantom

Figure 6.1 The Absent Castle, East Berlin, 1950. Courtesy of Bundesarchiv Berlin.

pull not unlike the eye of a storm, with extravagant plans and a rebuilt city rising around it (Figure 6.1).

Thus the void at Berlin's centre signified a restless emptiness, always seeking to be filled, always awkwardly aware of its emptiness as a lack. The attempt to deal with this central problem, which is also the problem of the centre, encompasses what I call here the logic of the double take. The double take is both dialectical and performative. It is dialectical because history is never completed in one take. It is performative because the double take is a form of non-verbal communication in which something that seems obvious is made to seem shocking or astonishing. A double take is itself double: in acting, the actor does the double take, and the audience, in watching the double take, also takes a second look. In this sense the logic of the double take is the logic of getting people to look twice, to see differently the second time, or perhaps to see for the first time by looking twice. In this spirit I wish to cast a second glance at the space now occupied by the restored Castle.

Take 1: Centre

Berlin is famous for its sprawling cityscape. Especially after the expansion of the city limits in 1920, Greater Berlin consisted of many disparate districts with distinct geographical identities. Yet the city's pivot remained the islands of the River Spree and especially the site of the fifteenth-century Berlin City Castle, sitting astride the medieval city site to its east and the modern grid of Friedrichstadt to its west. The Castle lost its royal function after the abdication of the emperor in 1918, yet it remained a potent symbol of Prussia and the German empire, and survived the bombings of the Second World War with serious, but not fatal, damage.

In the early post-war period, as Berlin's decimated architecture and urban space was being elevated to ideological proxies in the new struggle for control of the not yet divided city, the Castle came to play a key role for East German leader Walter Ulbricht. In those preliminary days of the Cold War, a decade before the construction of the Berlin Wall, East Germany initially hoped to unify the country on *its* terms. As part of these plans, Ulbricht placed importance on a radical visual remaking of Berlin, and the Castle was the central point. Almost immediately after the founding of the GDR in 1949 he solicited two proposals for the site. The first, by Richard Paulick, would have preserved the Castle and integrated it into a 'Forum of Democracy'. The other, by Helmut Hennig, would have demolished the Castle and created a great flat 'Central Building'. Ulbricht preferred Hennig's proposal, and in short order the Castle was demolished in the second half of 1950 in a massive series of explosions that served to underscore the determination of the new regime to create a new Germany.

The rest of the plans, however, were not so fast in coming, and herein lies the rub. Future plans would turn around the question of the phantom 'Central Building' (*Zentrales Gebäude*). The term itself is empty, bureaucratic, generic and vague. It marks the centre in a declarative way. Hennig's flat building idea quickly gave way to various ambitious plans to build a skyscraper along the Soviet model (Figures 6.2 to 6.4). As a symbol of a socialist future for all of Germany, it was to be the tallest building in Germany. The skyscraper version of the Central Building became part of what Peter Müller called 'an all-embracing work of art' that radiated out for 100 kilometres from the skyscraper, with buildings, factories and nature all rippling out from the centre of the German socialist world.[3]

The Central Building was to replace the Castle in spirit, yet Ulbricht never actually intended to build directly on the site of the former Prussian Residence. This was not out of any deference to the Prussian past. On the contrary, he wanted to replace the Castle, once representing the national body in the form of king and emperor, with a massive parade ground

Figure 6.2   Richard Paulick, model of the Central Building, 1951. Courtesy of Bundesarchiv Berlin.

Figure 6.3   Gerhard Kosel's Central Building design in Stalinist 'wedding cake' style, 1951. Courtesy of Bundesarchiv Berlin.

Figure 6.4   Gerhard Kosel's design for the Central Building, 1959. Courtesy of Bundesarchiv Berlin.

larger than Moscow's Red Square: where once German imperialism was literally enthroned, now the literal bodies of the people, in columns by the thousands, would trample the Castle with their boots. The massive size of the square was achieved by combining the former Castle grounds with the adjoining *Lustgarten* (pleasure garden) that the Nazis had paved over in 1934 for their staging of mass rallies (Figure 6.5).

Thus it was across the river that Ulbricht sought to replace the symbolic imperial edifice with the Central Building, which he described as a 'nerve centre' of the new government, for which the parade grounds would be the hinge in its new urban axis of power extending from the Brandenburg Gate to the stretch of neoclassical monoliths along Stalin Boulevard (later Karl Marx and Frankfurter Boulevard).[4]

The first take, then, was a series of double takes that sought to draw the eye towards the centre. Look again, the plans said, and see one double: a rebuilt Berlin that, as the mayor of East Berlin put it, 'must not become a city of ruins like Rome'.[5] Look once more, and see another double: the mimetic might of Moscow, in the plans echoing Stalinist skyscrapers in their odd mixture of baroque and Gothic forms and, uncannily, the plans for the never-built Palace of the Soviets. Look yet again, as the plans change, and see yet another double: something that looks perhaps like Western skyscrapers, but built, as the 1955 slogan for the

Figure 6.5 From castle to parade ground, 1951. Courtesy of Bundesarchiv Berlin.

first GDR construction convention (*Baukonferenz*) put it, 'better, faster, cheaper' than the capitalist West.[6]

These takes were destined to remain first takes, for the government could not settle on a design for the Central Building, stuck between support for plans for Stalinist wedding-cake-style skyscrapers that expressed a 'national tradition' and more modernist forms that contrasted high-rise office towers with low-rise government buildings. Hermann Henselmann's modernist ensemble seemed to have won the day, but was precipitously cancelled in 1961 for reasons of disagreement about both its modernism and money, just two years after the plan had been approved, and two years before construction was to begin. It was cancelled, ironically, on 3 October, the date that would be the day of unification in 1990. Thus ended the first take.

Take 2: De-centre

If the first take was to create a centre for a united socialist Germany, then once the division of East and West had congealed into what seemed like a permanent state of affairs the second take was to 'de-centre' West Germany. From claiming the mantle of united Germany, the GDR now focused all its energies on establishing its sovereignty as an independent state. The Central Building gave way to the Television Tower (Fernsehturm, built 1964), with its practical ability to counter West German broadcasts and its lower cost.

The Television Tower, too, was a double take: Look again, and see Sputnik; look again and see a Western commercial idea – television – in the service of socialism; look again and see the material instantiation in this originally named 'Signal Tower' of the German chorus of the Internationale: 'People, hear the signal!' (*Völker, hört die Signale!*). The Television Tower, in turn, existed as part of the larger Marx-Engels Forum, emerging triumphant from an earlier 1959 plan, again by Hermann Henselmann, that, in its modernism, once seemed an affront to party elders.

During the period 1963 to 1973, from the abandonment of the Central Building to the Palace of the Republic, the former Castle-turned-Red Square became an even more vacant space. The massive parades had shifted to Karl Marx Boulevard, in part to accommodate large vehicles, and in part because the exhaust tended to overwhelm the reviewing tribunal. More often than not, it was mostly a giant car park serving the new buildings that rose around its perimeter, in 1962 the State Council building and in 1964 the Foreign Ministry, both buildings that would have been part of the ensemble with the missing Central Building, but now stood guard around a perimeter that overlooked rows of parked pastel-coloured East German cars.

Take 3: Re-centre

When Ulbricht's successor, Honecker, decided to build the Palace of the Republic, it was therefore both a version of the Central Building and a break with its structuring absence. Most prosaically, perhaps, the Palace of the Republic allowed Honecker to claim he could build what Ulbricht could not. But what he built was also not quite what Ulbricht had had in mind.

Rather than providing a backdrop for parades and rallies, it more pragmatically eliminated the embarrassing emptiness of the parade ground-turned-car park. Built in a different location from the one that had been planned for the earlier Central Building, it did not connect easily with the expansive green space of the Marx-Engels Forum stretching to the Television Tower and Alexanderplatz. The story goes that where Ulbricht had dreamt of a skyscraper, Honecker wanted to maintain the landscaping of the opposite river bank because he became emotionally attached to it during the planning of the 1973 World Festival of Youth, for which he had been responsible.

Modern to a fault, it was a relatively modest white box that bore no architectural resemblance to the perceived excesses of past socialist state projects. It resembled more the convention centres of Hamburg and Helsinki than the architecture of power. This, of course, was on purpose, since earlier projects, such as Stalin Boulevard, had famously strained resources to the point of mass revolt.

The Palace also reflected the government's desire to provide leisure outlets, and its everyday accessibility, for everything from birthday parties to first dates, drew explicitly on the nineteenth-century *Volkshaus* ('People's House') tradition that, in 1960s GDR, had come to signify a yearning for a place outside direct state control that was open to all. The chief architect of the Palace himself, Heinz Graffunder, openly wrote, perhaps in reference to the expressionist architect Bruno Taut, that it was a 'light-filled People's House'.[7] This was in stark contrast to Walter

Ulbricht, who died the year construction began, and whose distaste for dancing was part of a hard line against the growing demand for leisure in a country experiencing a shift to the post-war generation.[8]

Looking back, the Palace anticipated the changes to come. Its focus on interior life mirrored the withdrawal of the GDR into small pleasures as its 1970s-chic restaurants, discos, theatres and bowling alleys fashioned a dreamland GDR bordering on the absurd. Its attraction was the lure of consumption, and the aspirations to middle-class enjoyment that exploded with the consumer frenzy of the unification period.

A final take?

The new castle formally contains the Humboldt Forum, and showcases a museum of non-European ethnographic collections that dates from the imperial era. Yet the absence that once structured the plans for the Palace and the reconstructed castle is not wholly gone; rather, it persists in modified form, to the east of the new castle, where the Central Building was once supposed to have been built, and where since the mid-1960s a green expanse known by its GDR-era name, 'Marx-Engels Forum', stretches from the Spree to the Television Tower and Alexanderplatz.

What one notices is how both the Palace of the Republic and today's Humboldt Forum are, in a way, the product of planning failures to coherently relate the former castle space to the 'empty' stretch of park extending eastward towards Alexanderplatz. This space, once the core of medieval Berlin, has now inherited from the original castle site the role of a structuring absence. This once dense urban space was, like the Castle, damaged by bombs during the war and then razed by the GDR government to create space for the never-built Central Building and, in its place, the Marx-Engels Forum park. Today the very space where Ulbricht wanted to build his skyscraper is the focus of discussion, driven by conservatives, about whether to rebuild the old city by giving back the plots to private owners, an idea complicated by the site's formal status as parkland.[9]

The emptiness of Berlin's post-war centre thus forms its own kind of detour round an empty subject. This subject, though, is not the 'opaque' power of Tokyo's centre as described by Barthes. Both of the post-war central buildings – the Palace and the reconstructed Castle – emerged from lengthy periods of 'emptiness' in which attempts to replace each other resulted in a performance of the centre as a space of absence and projection, of transformation and transgression. What will we see when, once again, we take a second look?

Notes

1. See my fuller treatment of the post-unification trajectory of the Palace of the Republic and plans to rebuild the city castle in Bach, 2017, chapter 3, which this essay draws on in part. For a definitive work on the Palace of the Republic itself, see Kuhrmann, 2006.
2. Barthes, 1982, pp. 30–2.
3. Müller, 2005, p. 103.
4. On this specific history see Flierl, 2009; Gomez Gutierrez, 1999; Beyme, 2000.
5. Mayor Friedrich Ebert, cited in Ladd, 1998, p. 56.
6. This slogan extended Khrushchev's use of this phrase at the All-Unions Building Conference in Moscow the year before. See Rubin, 2016, p. 23.
7. Cited in Hain, 2001; Meyer, 2005, p. 79.
8. On the history and origin of the German *Volkshaus* and its trajectory in the GDR, see Groschopp, 1994, and Hain, 2001. On the shift in the Soviet Union to a rigid ideological approach to cultural palaces, see Siegelbaum, 1999, pp. 78–92. On the question of leisure in the Palace of the Republic, see Kuhrmann, 2006.
9. On the development of the area between the Humboldt Forum and Alexanderplatz, or more precisely between the Television Tower (Fernsehturm) and the River Spree, see Flierl, 2010 and, more generally, Goebel, 2018.

Bibliography

Bach, Jonathan. *What Remains: Everyday Encounters with the Socialist Past in Germany*. New York: Columbia University Press, 2017.

Barthes, Roland. *Empire of Signs*, translated by Richard Howard. New York: Hill and Wang, 1982.

Beyme, Klaus von. 'Ideas for a capital city in East and West'. In *City of Architecture, Architecture of the City: Berlin 1900–2000*, edited by Thorsten Scheer, Josef Paul Kleihues and Paul Kahlfeldt, 239–49. Berlin: Nicolai, 2000.

Flierl, Bruno. 'Zur historischen und stadträumlichen Bedeutung des Areals Mitte Spreeinsel in Berlin' ('On the significance, historically and within the city surroundings, of the Mitte Spreeinsel area in Berlin'). In *Humboldt Forum Berlin: Das Projekt*, edited by Thomas Flierl and Hermann Parzinger, 108–15. Berlin: Theater der Zeit, 2009.

Flierl, Bruno. *Berlin – Die neue Mitte: Architektur und Städtebau seit 1990*. Berlin: Gegenstand und Raum, 2010.

Goebel, Benedikt. *Mitte! Modernisierung und Zerstörung des Berliner Stadtkerns von 1850 bis zur Gegenwart*. Berlin: Lukas Verlag, 2018.

Gomez Gutierrez, Juan Jose. 'Building homes, building politics: Berlin's post-war urban development and ideology', *Central Europe Review* 1, no. 21 (1999). Accessed 23 July 2019. https://www.pecina.cz/files/www.ce-review.org/99/21/gomez21.html.

Groschopp, Horst. 'Kulturhäuser in der DDR: Vorläufer, Konzepte, Gebrauch: Versuch einer historischen Rekonstruktion'. In *Kulturhäuser in Brandenburg: Eine Bestandsaufnahme*, edited by Thomas Ruben and Bernd Wagner (Brandenburger Texte zu Kunst und Kultur), 97–176. Potsdam: Verlag für Berlin-Brandenburg, 1994.

Hain, Simone. '*Das* Volkshaus der DDR: zur Entwurfsgeschichte und Funktionsbestimmung'. In *Ein Palast und seine Republik: Ort – Architektur – Programm*, edited by Thomas Beutelschmidt and Julia Novak, 76–89. Berlin: Bauwesen, 2001.

Kuhrmann, Anke. *Der Palast der Republik: Geschichte und Bedeutung des Ost-Berliner Parlaments- und Kulturhauses*. Petersberg: Michael Imhof, 2006.

Ladd, Brian. *The Ghosts of Berlin: Confronting German History in the Urban Landscape*. Chicago: University of Chicago Press, 1998.

Meyer, Christine. *Kulturpaläste und Stadthallen der DDR: Anspruch und Realität einer Bauaufgabe*. Hamburg: Dr. Kovač, 2005.

Müller, Peter. 'Counter-architecture and building race: Cold war politics and the two Berlins', *German Historical Institute Bulletin* Supplement 2 (2005): 101–14.

Rubin, Eli. *Amnesiopolis: Modernity, Space, and Memory in East Germany*. Oxford: Oxford University Press, 2016.

Siegelbaum, Lewis H. 'The shaping of Soviet workers' leisure: Workers' clubs and palaces of culture in the 1930s', *International Labor and Working-Class History* 56 (1999): 78–92.

7
Phantom palaces: Prussian centralities and Humboldtian spectres

Jonas Tinius and Khadija von Zinnenburg Carroll

Introduction

This chapter analyses monumentality along two axes: centrality as a spatial horizontality and as a vertical temporality. We take the rebuilding of the Berlin Stadtschloss, or City Palace, and its overarching conceptual framing as the Humboldt Forum, as a case study.

Built on the cleared-up remains of the previous City Palace and the German Democratic Republic's parliamentary building, the Palast der Republik, the Palace has become a projection screen for reconstructed and appropriated universalisms and centralities of Germany's and indeed the Global East's past, thus echoing the topographical and psychoanalytic heuristics for describing Berlin's role in European imagination and socialist history more broadly.[1] The Forum functions as a conceptual frame, espoused for the multiple institutions contained within the rebuilt Palace. It claims to contain a link to universalism by rewriting Prussian imperialism as a Humboldtian cosmopolitanism that allows it to encompass, in supposedly progressive and horizontal gestures, all the cultures of the world. Housing selected sections of the vast collections of the Museum of Asian Art and the Ethnological Museum, among other institutions and collections, it presents itself as a forum for seeing *into*, and encountering, the world, from Berlin. At the same time as it thus proposes a horizontal expansionist cosmopolitanism, it is also built on a vertical temporality, a deep historical recurrence of centrality illustrated by the fact that the Forum emerges on the remains of several previous centres of power, including the previous Prussian Stadtschloss and the socialist Palast der Republik. These two axes, along which we discuss aspects of the ongoing reimagining of heritage for Germany's cosmopolitan futures, serve as potential lenses to take a closer look at the notion of centrality in twentieth-century urban space and the future of past heritage.

(Re)framing the centre I: Verticality

On the north-eastern tip of Berlin's Museum Island, on the artery of the avenue Unter den Linden in what was the heart of East Berlin, the Berlin City Palace has been reconstructed. This palace, encompassing over 41,000 square metres of space, is custom-built to house a number of museum, exhibition and research spaces, which together are known under the umbrella concept of the Humboldt Forum. The Forum, which is thus at once contained within, and a larger conceptual framework for, the reconstructed architectural shell, is full of contradictions and challenges, not least about centrality, authenticity and colonial memory culture. The Forum constitutes, in effect, an attempt to revisit Berlin's past by erasing 'difficult heritage', while at the same time (and in the same place) displaying artefacts associated with Germany's colonial past (in spite of growing concern over its collections and their provenance), and seeking to reach otherwise ostracised audiences in a diverse capital city.[2] It does all of the above in an eclectic classicist architectural frame that cost over half a billion euros to construct. However, it is also therefore a complex and explosive prism through which Berlin refracts and puts on display its vexed relationship with its social, cultural and political heritage. And yet, it has as much to tell us about how Berlin – and Germany for that matter – would like to project itself into a cosmopolitan and horizontal future, as it does about how it locates itself, historically or vertically, in the city's and the country's post-colonial and post-socialist past.

Since the first idea for the reconstruction of the Schloss began as early as the fall of the Berlin Wall, one can hardly speak of a time-sensitive planning process. Yet because the conceptual frame for the content and design of the constituent parts of the Humboldt Forum was publicly announced as late as 2016, and revealed to the public in late 2019, its planning and design was until fairly late in the process open to critical debate with the professionals working on and studying such undertakings, and so was the possibility for integrating reflexive anthropological thought. The role of anthropological and artistic reflections on its planning process and local historical context can thus exceed that of the detached commentators, and try to inform and scrutinise the complexities condensed in such monumental architectural nodes in the broader urban ecology of the city.[3]

Completed in 1451, the Stadtschloss was the principal residence of the Hohenzollern kings of Prussia during the eighteenth and early nineteenth centuries, by which point it was already composed of an eclectic assemblage of architectural props and additions (see Figure 7.1). It was heavily damaged during the Second World War, and subsequently demolished and replaced by the Palast der Republik in 1976. Following reunification, the German government ordered yet another destruction, completed in December 2008, of this socialist monument, erasing a historical testament to Germany's Cold War division. About a decade before this act of architectural iconoclasm, an influential lobby of private investors had gathered plans for the reconstruction of the original Stadtschloss, convincing both government and private sponsors to agree on a vast £500 million project that, by 2020, aims to re-create an architectural frame for Berlin's self-presentation. The new Schloss is presented as a monument to German history, only selectively remembered. Berlin-based activist groups such as No Humboldt 21! have been protesting against the reconstruction and the display of ethnological collections in a city still marked by European imaginations of class and race.[4] Such critiques do not go unnoticed, and indeed, as Thomas Thiemeyer suggests, this space creates the possibility of a 'genealogical memory culture' (*genealogische Erinnerungskultur*) based on a national narrative of diversity, wherein constituent parts of the new Forum are addressing these challenges by incorporating experimental and institutional critiques.[5]

The GDR's Palast der Republik accommodated both chambers of the East German parliament, and provided public space for over 5,000 people in its auditoria, restaurants, galleries and discothèque. Located in the central district of Mitte just south of Marx-Engels Forum and Berlin Alexanderplatz, and accommodating in its space five iconic museums, including the Pergamon, as well as Berlin Cathedral, the burial cathedral of the Hohenzollern family, built in the 1890s, the area is arguably one of the city's most prominent and representative public cultural spaces. Appropriately enough for a site dominated by museums, this is a space layered by different temporalities in which phantom palaces, imperial and socialist, are built on top of each other, erased and recurring. Yet despite sitting among buildings dedicated to preserving artefacts of the past, and notwithstanding a strong focus on memory culture in post-Second World War and post-Cold War Germany, no evident adaptation or integration of this intact albeit contaminated socialist glass palace was foreseen by the unified government and subsequent planning authorities.[6] Its inclusion in the new stratum of architectural future was denied.

Figure 7.1   Berliner Schloss, 1685. Public domain.

(Re)framing the centre II: Horizontality

The public discourse that addressed and ridiculed post-colonial German *Vergangenheitsbewältigung* and cast the GDR's *Palast* as mere *Ostalgie* became the departure point of several artistic research projects, which not only commented on the invisible historical verticality of the palatial zombies, but also critically viewed its pseudo-cosmopolitan horizontalities. *The Museum in a Book/Pour ouvrir ce musée* documents a series of participatory, photographic and poetic interventions into the idea of conflating the ethnographic museum with the Prussian castle in the Forum (see Figures 7.2 and 7.3).[7] The form of *The Museum in a Book* is inspired by André Malraux's *Le Musée imaginaire* ([1947] 1996), in which the pages of contemporary art books were the new walls on which to hang art, replacing, as Malraux thought, the need to build new museums. The second reference for the format of this exhibition in a book is Seth Siegelaub's *January 5–31, 1969*, which featured works by many of the then emerging minimalists.[8] Rejection of ornament of the kind loaded onto

Figure 7.2 Khadija von Zinnenburg Carroll, *The Museum in a Book*, 2009. Source: Khadija von Zinnenburg Carroll.

the Forum's palatial architecture took the form of a minimal and anti-monumental artist's book, in which the campaign for funding the palace's ornaments was mocked. The discourse revolving around and anticipating the post-palatial, post-socialist palace as far back as 2009 appeared as a colossal decoy to the refugee crisis and the problematics of funding a new ethnographic museum in a palatial European envelope. *The Museum in a Book*'s pages extend the performance 'Humboldt's Meal', also by Khadija von Zinnenburg Carroll, in which indigenous Australian spices were ground up and sent through the international post in transparent envelopes.[9] These parcels to and from Berlin incited notices of quarantine, impoundment and destruction. Interpreting these quarantine laws as an index of anxieties about cultural contamination, 'Humboldt's Meal' was an experiment with the fear and confusion that government instils on the crossing of borders.

Lars Ramberg's large installation *Palast des Zweifels* operated on fears and anxieties by scaling its artistic critique of the palatial recurrences on Berlin's museum island down to the conflicts around the destruction and rebuilding of the palaces on the site, and then up again to national self-perception. Ramberg placed the word *ZWEIFEL* ('doubt') in large capital letters on top of the Palast der Republik, transforming the defunct architecture into a monument to Germany's uncertainty over its new identity (*Palace of Doubt*, 2005).[10] It might have been an appropriate gesture to place the installation back on the

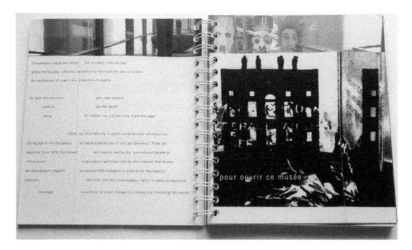

Figure 7.3 Khadija von Zinnenburg Carroll, *The Museum in a Book*, 2009. Source: Khadija von Zinnenburg Carroll.

Forum of today, as some indeed suggested during a faint debate on the erection of a Christian cross on the new palace's cupola.[11] Between 2006 and 2008, the Palast's last days were presented as a ruin to the public (and documented by the artist Reynold Reynolds as such in his film *The Last Days*). The temporality of the demolition was theatrically stretched and thereby politically leveraged for all to see, a visible iconoclasm. The Palast's own 'dismantling', a euphemism for 'demolition', restaged the Allied levelling of Berlin for a reunified yet often unresolved German nation today. A viewing platform that reached the length of a city block allowed this slow tearing-down of the spectacular ruin of the former communist regime to be witnessed. The Berlin Senate Department for Urban Development streamed the process of demolition via webcam.

In a promotional video made for an early stage of the Humboldt Forum, accompanied by ambient techno music, the palace gets whisked back and forth in time and through space across the site on the island.[12] Glorious palatial moments from 1910, 1925 and 1930 appear as stills. These Potemkin structures complete the as yet skeletal centre being rebuilt behind. Some horrified witnesses of the centre's ruins in 1945 flick by and 1950 is hurried in. Unter den Linden was a bustling centre of East Berlin and was crowned by the Palast der Republik, yet in this promo the years 1978–2009 are skipped in a beat of techno, leading up, in an imagined and inevitable trajectory, to the year 2009, leaving only the new tabula rasa for the city centre. Suddenly, the viewer is given a stilted hallucination of world travel. Traversing the world as an all-seeing god-like observer, picking up bits of artefacts on strings or cables to pull them out of their own chaotic cultural realities onto museum plinths – all of this leads to an all-unifying mosaic of world cultures shown and gathered in Berlin. The conceptual frame – a reflection on colonial object histories, the involvement of indigenous artists and source communities – envisions the Humboldt Forum as 'a palace in Berlin for the whole world', as one official publication has it.[13] And, one might be led to imagine, the whole world in a palace in Berlin.

Architect Franco Stella's winning design for the new Stadtschloss, however, stands in contrast to such an open-ended vision. Instead, it articulates a desire to reconstruct and complete a larger urban section of Prussian heritage in Berlin, the museum island. Furthermore, for those associated with a key player in the reconstruction process, a private foundation called Förderverein Berliner Schloss E.V., the castle represented Berlin itself.[14] The dome and façades, complete with hand-crafted replicas of Prussian heraldry, are carefully rendered within a larger model of how the whole reconstructed centre of Berlin will look.

Promotional videos, like other public statements and press releases, change over time as the programming and reasoning for the curated objects and constituent institutions in the Humboldt Forum change. What we are pointing out here, however, is a second logic, or axis, along which the Humboldt Forum and the Stadtschloss are constructed, and which we describe as an expansionist horizontal cosmopolitanism. For Hermann Parzinger, the chairman of the Prussian Heritage Foundation, for instance, the Humboldt Forum represents a focal point of extensive nodes to other stakeholders and communities of implication in the collections of the Forum. He has adopted the rhetoric that provenance research and the accessibility of contentious heritage collections from colonised countries form a way to 'decolonise and democratise museums'.[15] Yet, as the subtitle of one of his essays reads, to speak of 'administering the cultural goods of mankind', of letting 'nations that we once colonised' 'participate' in such shared investigations, or to ask whether such contentious 'objects should not be allowed to travel more frequently', reinterprets their accommodation and the patronage of legally acquired objects from other parts of the world in a cosmopolitan framework of horizontal sharing. Through the notion of shared heritage, the Humboldt Forum is imagined by Parzinger as 'an epicentre of such new forms of relations with the world'.[16] Yet as Bénédicte Savoy and Felwine Sarr have outlined in their report for the French government on repatriation, talk of temporary loan and global circulation controlled from Berlin is not nearly sufficient. Savoy is a former member of the Forum's board, and her criticism of the Forum is rearticulated in the way forward for restitution that France will lead in sub-Saharan Africa. Titled *The Restitution of African Cultural Heritage: Toward a New Relational Ethics,* their report breaks down the different forms of appropriation and enjoyment of an item and the morally reprehensible acts of 'rape, pillaging, spoliation, ruse, forced consent, etc.' under which they were acquired.[17] While Parzinger and the Forum have absorbed the rhetoric of new horizontal relations with the world, and the German parliament discussed decolonisation in 2018, the French government is negotiating a 'new relational ethics', addressing the real complexity of how to engage in colonial repair through restitution.[18]

In contrast to Sarr's *Afrotopia* (2016), a neatly neutralised statement from the Federal Government Commissioner for Culture and the Media, Monika Grütters, speaks of the new Forum as allowing visitors to experience 'the tradition of the Enlightenment; the idea of self-assured, open-minded encounters between the world's peoples; peaceful dialogue as an ideal'.[19] But the tradition of Enlightenment certainly did not create 'open-minded encounters' in colonial settings themselves, and it is remarkable to frame a twenty-first-century ethnological museum as motivated, in Grütters's words, by 'a virtually insatiable thirst for knowledge about the world … [a] thirst for knowledge about the Other'.[20] The Forum's International Team of Experts, which supports the steering committee and founding directors, appears to diversify the decision-making, the 'orientation and the interaction of the collections and ideas' of the Forum, but it only does so on a temporary, limited basis.[21] Therefore, some of the Forum's encompassing rhetoric of guardianship still causes disgruntlement among those who actually engage with or come from that 'wider world' but do not see representatives in the highest positions of power in the institutions represented by the Forum, which are defining the futures of how Prussian heritage and Germany will be remembered and witnessed as guardians of shared global heritage.[22] As Berlin anthropologist Beate Binder puts it, 'Centred around the notions of encounter, openness and cultural experience, the Humboldt Forum is designed as a space for reflection in which the national is stabilised in a globalised world, and it speaks at the same time of the tolerance and openness of the German nation'. (Our translation.)[23]

Conclusion

Our argument in this contribution is that Germany engages in the projection of a quasi-cosmopolitanism, through notions of shared heritage, with a building that links to Prussian imperialism, and constructs a contemporary, national centrality. Centrality in this case is asserted through a horizontal global expansion which, in turn, is reconstituted in Berlin's city centre, embodied thus by a vertical structure and temporality. This recurring palatial zombie moves up and across at the same time, and it has a façade of horizontality (diversity, multiculturalism) that belies a pretence of non-hierarchy, actually asserting a dominant structural regime, based in a capital city intent on controlling the self-representation of horizontality.

The Forum thus frames its colonial collections in terms that purport to transcend the notion of a purely national collection, while resting on the difficult heritage of its past monumentality and imperial centrality.[24] One of the ways in which it can address the complexity of the challenges posed by its reawakened palatial recurrence in the new centrality of Berlin, we submit, is by truly articulating its horizontal vision. This can be done in a number of ways, such as by conceiving of the Palast and its Humboldtian framing as a starting point for satellite engagement in the peripheral sprawl of Berlin, inviting curators, artists and activists to engage in the difficult legacies of colonialism and socialism that have marked the city's centre by moving outwards rather than inwards, relationally rather than monumentally, in neighbourhoods rather than avenues.[25] A second possible trajectory of inclusive engagement is to realise the horizontal ecology of the Forum's collection and heritage through an expansive and sustainable project of transdisciplinary provenance research that not only looks at the past, but is open to imagining what a future of international and collaborative heritage research and permanent restitution would set in motion.[26] A shift of memorial culture due to changing perspectives on the Shoah also enabled de-colonial discussions to arise where for a long time they had not been a topic in Germany. Holocaust studies since the 1980s have shifted from a single focus on the question of German guilt to comparative genocide studies, allowing for different and new interrogations of organised violence and ways of exhibiting and collecting in post-Holocaust, post-colonial European museums.[27]

A rethought anthropological museum of the future could then become no longer simply a guardian, but a decolonising forum for an ethics of listening, with a sense of responsibility and reciprocation, with the co-owners of objects turned from collected artefacts into mediating agents of difficult heritage.[28] The vast accumulations of material from around the world held in the museum stores of European capitals can provide a sense of what was lost in the process of their acquisition. The sheer volume of accumulated objects and relations embedded within them, for the most part stored out of sight, can be subjected to the critical awe and also the anger of de-colonial witnessing, rather than being presented with the finality and 'Vitrine-logic' of the fixed museum display.[29] Museums can thus be interrogated in their spatialisation of privilege and 'whiteness as property', as symbolised in the global hegemony of the permanent white cube display of cultural hierarchy.[30]

The rebuilt Stadtschloss and Humboldt Forum thus combine two complicated aspects, which we interrogated along two axes of horizontality and verticality. Leaning and building on a difficult imperial past, articulated architecturally, embedded within curatorial modes of operating, and complex collection histories that face questions of shared investigation, the project at the centre of Berlin relates to a 'vertical' sense of temporal inheritance. Providing a view to the complex layering and selecting of strands that are allowed to break through into the present, this axis directed our analytical attention to what we described as the palatial recurrence of problematic imperial dispositions. The decision to frame the project by appealing to a Humboldtian cosmopolitanism created a second, horizontal, entry point into the complex palatial assemblage. By internalising a set of arguably global relations through

Figure 7.4   Humboldt Forum, 2019. Public domain.

the proposition of shared collections with non-European ancestry, international advisory teams, and a broadly configured set of constituent institutions, the horizontal axis herein sketches the multiplicity of colonial legacies in twenty-first-century Berlin. These two axes are not invisible, but are being addressed by the many agents – critical, complicit and otherwise mediating – involved in creating the Humboldt Forum and the Palace. Both purport to contain and relate to a shared world, but this guardianship is maintained on problematic and unstable grounds, on the sandy strata of Berlin's central island, among the imperial remains and the cleared socialist rubble of undead palaces, hastily discarded, perhaps to reappear one day, like Lenin's four-ton head, unearthed a few years ago in a Berlin forest, to be exhibited on the Spandau fringes of Berlin in a peripheral medieval citadel.[31] The razed palaces hidden beneath those of today and tomorrow offer much to a contemporary archaeology and anthropology of palatial recurrences, of phantom palaces.

Jonas Tinius's research for this publication was funded by the Alexander von Humboldt Foundation as part of the research award for Sharon Macdonald's Alexander von Humboldt Professorship'. Khadija von Zinnenburg Carroll's research was supported by her fellowships from the Alexander von Humboldt Stiftung and the Sackler-Caird.

Notes

1. See Bach, 2017, Borneman, 1992, and Webber, 2008.
2. MacDonald, 2009.
3. See Binder, 2009, Mostafavi and Doherty, 2010, Murawski, 2017, and Bose, 2016.
4. Ha, 2014
5. See Thiemeyer, 2016, and Bose, 2013.
6. See Carroll La, 2010, Macdonald, 2013, and Schug, 2007).
7. See http://www.inflexions.org/tangents/berlin/humboldtsmeal.html (accessed 10 August 2016) for the video and photographic documentation and larger Society of Molecules project of which it was also part. Carroll, 2009.
8. The artists' pages were commissioned by the curator Jean-Charles Agboton-Jumeau for the exhibition *January 5–31, 2009* at the Musée des beaux-arts Cherbourg-Octeville, which was a forty-year anniversary homage to Sieglaub's *January 5–31, 1969*.
9. Carroll, 2009.
10. See http://www.larsramberg.de/1/viewentry/3890 (accessed 10 August 2016).
11. Justifying their decision, the founding directors Horst Bredekamp, Neil MacGregor and Hermann Parzinger argued for the 'capacity' of the castle to bear its own history. See https://humboldtforum.com/de/storys/im-zweifel-fuer-das-kreuz (accessed 21 February 2019).
12. See https://vimeo.com/170197165/ee4c56e8a8 (accessed 6 May 2017).
13. See SPK, 2015.
14. See Stephan, 2016.
15. Parzinger (2016) notes that considering contentious collections as a form of shared heritage, which is made accessible to their 'cultures of origin' (*Herkunftskulturen*), entails 'eine Art Dekolonialisierung und Demokratisierung der Museen'.

16. 'Das Humboldt Forum könnte das Epizentrum einer solch neuartigen Beziehung mit der Welt sein' (Parzinger 2016).
17. See Sarr and Savoy, 2018.
18. This is the topic of a forthcoming book on repatriation by Khadija von Zinnenburg Carroll, Chicago University Press, based on Carroll, 2017. Also, see Sarr, *Afrotopia*, 2016.
19. See Sarr, 2016.
20. See SPK, 2015.
21. See https://humboldtforum.com/en/pages/international-experts/ (accessed 6 May 2017).
22. See Bloch, 2016, and Modest, Oswald and Ndikung, 2017.
23. 'Zentriert um die Begriffe Begegnung, Offenheit und kulturelle Erfahrung wird das Humboldt-Forum als Reflexionsraum entworfen, in dem das Nationale innerhalb einer sich globalisierenden Welt verstetigt werden kann und zugleich von der Toleranz und Offenheit der deutschen Nation spricht' (Binder, 2013, p. 114).
24. See Meskell, 2009.
25. See Tinius, 2018.
26. See Förster, 2016, and Sarr and Savoy, 2018.
27. See Bajohr and Löw, 2015, Taberner and Berger, 2009, and Moses, 2007.
28. See Deliss, 2013, and Oswald, 2018.
29. Carroll, 2013.
30. Harris, 1993, and Moreton-Robinson, 2015. See also Filipovic, 2005, and Simpson, 1996.
31. See Reich, Perdoni and Plaga, 2015.

Bibliography

Bach, Jonathan. *What Remains: Everyday Encounters with the Socialist Past in Germany*. New York: Columbia University Press, 2017.
Bajohr, Frank and Andrea Löw, eds. *Der Holocaust: Ergebnisse und neue Fragen der Forschung*. Frankfurt am Main: Fischer Taschenbuch, 2015.
Binder, Beate. *Streitfall Stadtmitte: Der Berliner Schlossplatz*. Cologne: Böhlau, 2009.
Binder, Beate. 'Vom Preußischen Stadtschloss zum Humboldt-Forum: der Berliner Schlossplatz als neuer nationaler Identifikationsort'. In *Rekonstruktion des Nationalmythos? Frankreich, Deutschland und die Ukraine im Vergleich*, edited by Yves Bizeul, 99–120. Göttingen: V&R unipress, 2013.
Bloch, Werner. '"So etwas wie Unterwerfung": Was soll das Humboldt-Forum? Ein Gespräch mit dem Wissenschaftler und Documenta-Kurator Bonaventure Ndikung', *ZEIT Online*, 7 January 2016. Accessed 6 May 2017. http://www.zeit.de/2016/02/humboldt-forum-documenta-kurator-bonaventure-ndikung.
Borneman, John. *Belonging in the Two Berlins: Kin, State, Nation*. Cambridge: Cambridge University Press, 1992.
Bose, Friedrich von. 'The making of Berlin's Humboldt-Forum: Negotiating history and the cultural politics of place', *darkmatter* 11, 18 November 2013. Accessed 7 April 2017. http://www.darkmatter101.org/site/2013/11/18/the-making-of-berlin's-humboldt-forum-negotiating-history-and-the-cultural-politics-of-place/.
Bose, Friedrich von. *Das Humboldt-Forum: Eine Ethnografie seiner Planung*. Berlin: Kadmos, 2016.
Carroll, Khadija von Zinnenburg. 'Humboldts Meal', *Inflexions: A Journal for Research Creation* 3 (*Micropolitics: Exploring Ethico-Aesthetics*) (2009). Accessed 6 August 2019. https://www.inflexions.org/tangents/berlin/humboldtsmeal.html.
Carroll, Khadija von Zinnenburg. 'Le Musée comme la silhouette / The museum in a book'. In *Exposition 5–31 Janvier 2009 / January 5–31, 2009*, edited by Jean-Charles Agboton-Jumeau, 22–9. Cherbourg-Octeville: Ecole des beaux-arts de Cherbourg-Octeville, 2009.
Carroll, Khadija von Zinnenburg. 'Vitrinendenken: vectors between subject and object'. In *The Challenge of the Object*, edited by G. Ulrich Großmann and Petra Krutisch, 316–18. Nuremberg: Germanisches Nationalmuseum, 2013.
Carroll, Khadija von Zinnenburg. 'The inbetweenness of the vitrine: Three parerga of a feather headdress'. In *The Inbetweenness of Things: Materializing Mediation and Movement between Worlds*, edited by Paul Basu, 23–36. London: Bloomsbury Academic, 2017.

Carroll, Khadija von Zinnenburg. *The Disputed Crown: An Aztec Enigma in the Heart of Europe*. Chicago: Chicago University Press, forthcoming.

Carroll La, Khadija. 'The very mark of repression: The demolition theatre of the Palast der Republik and the new Schloss Berlin', *Architectural Design* 80, no. 5 (2010): 116–23.

Deliss, Clémentine. 'Trading perceptions in a post-ethnographic museum', *Theatrum Mundi*, 17 June 2013. Accessed 28 July 2019. http://theatrum-mundi.org/library/trading-perceptions-in-a-post-ethnographic-museum/.

Filipovic, Elena. 'The global white cube'. In *The Manifesta Decade: Debates on Contemporary Art Exhibitions and Biennials in Post-Wall Europe*, edited by Barbara Vanderlinden and Elena Filipovic, 63–84. Cambridge, MA: MIT Press, 2005.

Förster, Larissa. 'Plea for a more systematic, comparative, international and long-term approach to restitution, provenance research and the historiography of collections', *Museumskunde* 81, no. 1 (2016): 49–54.

Ha, Noa. 'Perspektiven urbaner Dekolonisierung: Die europäische Stadt als "Contact Zone"', *Sub\ urban: Zeitschrift für kritische Stadtforschung* 2, no. 1 (2014): 27–47.

Harris, Cheryl I. 'Whiteness as property', *Harvard Law Review* 106, no. 8 (1993): 1707–91.

Macdonald, Sharon. *Difficult Heritage: Negotiating the Nazi Past in Nuremberg and Beyond*. London: Routledge, 2009.

Macdonald, Sharon. *Memorylands: Heritage and Identity in Europe Today*. London: Routledge, 2013.

Malraux, André. *Le Musée imaginaire*. Paris: Gallimard, [1947] 1996.

Meskell, Lynn, ed. *Cosmopolitan Archaeologies*. Durham, NC: Duke University Press, 2009.

Modest, Wayne, Margareta von Oswald and Bonaventure Soh Bejeng Ndikung. 'Objects/subjects in exile', *L'Internationale Online*, 9 March 2017. Accessed 6 May 2017. http://www.internationaleonline.org/research/decolonising_practices/89_objects_subjects_in_exile_a_conversation_between_wayne_modest_bonaventure_soh_bejeng_ndikung_and_margareta_von_oswald.

Moreton-Robinson, Aileen. *The White Possessive: Property, Power, and Indigenous Sovereignty*. Minneapolis: University of Minnesota Press, 2015.

Moses, A. Dirk. 'Conceptual blockages and definitional dilemmas in the "racial century": Genocides of indigenous peoples and the Holocaust'. In *Colonialism and Genocide*, edited by A. Dirk Moses and Dan Stone, 148–80. London: Routledge, 2007.

Mostafavi, Mohsen and Gareth Doherty, eds. *Ecological Urbanism*. Baden: Lars Müller Publishers, 2010.

Murawski, Michał. 'The Palace Complex: A Stalinist social condenser in Warsaw', *Journal of Architecture* 22, no. 3 (2017): 458–77.

Oswald, Margareta von. 'Post-ethnological: An essay based on a panel with Clémentine Deliss and Dan Hicks'. In *Otherwise: Rethinking Museums and Heritage*, edited by Sharon Macdonald and Jonas Tinius, 55–67. Berlin: Centre for Anthropological Research on Museums and Heritage, 2018.

Parzinger, Hermann. 'Gemeinsam geerbt: Das Humboldt Forum als Epizentrum des shared heritage', *Dossier Humboldt Forum – Stiftung Preußischer Kulturbesitz*, 17 October 2016. Accessed 7 April 2017. https://www.preussischer-kulturbesitz.de/?id=2056.

Reich, Anja, Silvia Perdoni and Corinne Plaga. 'Kopf hoch, Lenin! Abgerissen, begraben, auferstanden: Die unglaubliche Geschichte des Berliner Lenin-Denkmals', *Berliner Zeitung*, 12 May 2015. Accessed 10 August 2016. https://berlinerverlag.atavist.com/lenin.

Sarr, Felwine. *Afrotopia*. Paris: Philippe Rey, 2016.

Sarr, Felwine and Bénédicte Savoy. *The Restitution of African Cultural Heritage: Toward a New Relational Ethics*, translated by Drew S. Burk. Paris: Ministère de la Culture, 2018. Accessed 30 December 2018. http://restitutionreport2018.com/sarr_savoy_en.pdf.

Schug, Alexander, ed. *Palast der Republik: Politischer Diskurs und private Erinnerung*. Berlin: Berliner Wissenschafts-Verlag, 2007.

Simpson, Moira G. *Making Representations: Museums in the Post-Colonial Era*. London: Routledge, 1996.

SPK (Stiftung Preußischer Kulturbesitz). *Humboldt Forum: Ein Berliner Schloss für die Welt*. Berlin: Tempus Corporate, 2015.

Stephan, Peter. 'Das Schloss lag nicht in Berlin – Berlin war das Schloss', *Förderverein Berliner Schloss e.V.*, 13 September 2016. Accessed 7 April 2017. http://berliner-schloss.de/blog/das-schloss-lag-nicht-in-berlin-berlin-war-das-schloss/.

Taberner, Stuart and Karina Berger, eds. *Germans as Victims in the Literary Fiction of the Berlin Republic*. Rochester, NY: Camden House, 2009.

Thiemeyer, Thomas. 'Deutschland postkolonial: Ethnologische und genealogische Erinnerungs-kultur', *Merkur* 70, no. 806 (2016): 33–45.

Tinius, Jonas. 'Awkward art and difficult heritage: Nazi collectors and postcolonial archives'. In *An Anthropology of Contemporary Art: Practices, Markets, and Collectors*, edited by Thomas Fillitz and Paul van der Grijp, 130–45. London: Bloomsbury Academic, 2018.

Tinius, Jonas and Khadija von Zinnenburg Carroll. 'Palace coups: Reconstructing history in the heart of Berlin', *Calvert Journal*, 9 June 2016. Accessed 7 April 2017. http://calvertjournal.com/features/show/6141/power-and-architecture-humboldt-forum.

Webber, Andrew J. *Berlin in the Twentieth Century: A Cultural Topography*. Cambridge: Cambridge University Press, 2008.

Further reading

Cuno, James, ed. *Whose Culture? The Promise of Museums and the Debate over Antiquities*. Princeton, NJ: Princeton University Press, 2012.

Tinius, Jonas and Khadija von Zinnenburg Carroll. 'Palace coups: Reconstructing history in the heart of Berlin', *Calvert Journal*, 9 June 2016. Accessed 7 April 2017. http://calvertjournal.com/features/show/6141/power-and-architecture-humboldt-forum.

8

Palatial socialism, or (still-)socialist centrality in Warsaw[1]

Michał Murawski

> There can be no city or urban reality without a centre … there can
> be no sites for leisure, festivals, knowledge, oral or scriptural trans-
> mission, invention or creation without centrality.[2]

These words, written in 1970 by the French Marxist spatial theorist Henri
Lefebvre, echo – with quite uncanny precision – a pronouncement made
fourteen years earlier by Edmund Goldzamt, a leading architectural ideologue in Warsaw during the Stalinist 1950s, 'There can be no such thing
as a city without a centre. The very idea of the city incorporates within
itself the fact of the existence of the primary catalyst of the urban organism: the central ensemble or arrangement.'[3]

It may seem far-fetched to claim an affinity between Lefebvre's
and Goldzamt's ideas about centrality. Lefebvre's own political
anti-Stalinism is well known, as are his hostility to the aesthetics of
Stalin-era Socialist Realism and his broader lack of enthusiasm for
state socialist planning and architecture's capacity to produce a 'differential' space.[4] In Lefebvre's assessment, under actually existing socialism, 'no architectural innovation has occurred, … no specific space has
been created'.[5]

I would like to suggest, however, that there is common ground
between Lefebvre's and Goldzamt's ideas about architecture, the city,
centrality and socialism. Further, I would like to challenge Lefebvre's
judgement concerning the failure of state socialist space, by suggesting
that Warsaw's Palace of Culture – as designed, as implemented and as
still functioning today – in fact constitutes an instance of a remarkably

Figure 8.1   Edmund Goldzamt with his wife, the architect Elena Guryanova, outside the Palace of Culture, late 1950s. Courtesy of Anna Guryanova.

successful, actually existing instance of Goldzamtian-Lefebvrean centrality in action.

Goldzamt's thoughts on centrality were formulated with explicit reference to the Palace of Culture, Warsaw's then brand-new Stalinist skyscraper, a 'gift' from the Soviet Union to the newly formed Polish People's Republic. Now, the Palace of Culture was consciously intended to endow Warsaw with an entirely new political morphology, focused on itself – and the surrounding 25-hectare Parade Square – as a pivot and *dominanta*.[6] According to the totalising morpho-logic of the day – as verbalised by Goldzamt and other Stalinist architectural ideologues – the Palace was to function as the 'vital and territorial centre of gravity'[7] of Warsaw, the new 'urban epicentre', to which the remainder of the city would be 'harmoniously subordinated'.[8]

The Palace was suffused with transformative social, political and economic intent. On both vertical and horizontal planes, it rode rough-shod over (what survived of) Warsaw's pre-existing urban structure and aesthetic. The radical multiplicity of functions encompassed by the build-ing – three major theatres, three cinemas, a vast 'Palace of Youth' com-plete with resplendent marbled swimming pool, a 3,000-seat Congress Hall, municipal offices, two museums, numerous libraries, research and educational institutions, and much else – *condensed* enormous numbers of people within its walls and environs, inculcating Varsovians with a profuse concentration of socialist culture. The Palace was to serve, in the words of Warsaw architect Szymon Syrkus (a lifelong communist, but a leading International Style modernist until the onset of the Stalinist period in 1949), an 'immovable guiding star on our journey to transform old Warsaw, princely Warsaw, royal, magnates', burghers', capitalist Warsaw, into socialist Warsaw'.[9]

Stalinist architectural thinking, therefore, saw no unresolvable con-tradiction between revolutionary social content, and morphological cen-tripetality or monumentality. Echoing German expressionist architect and theorist Bruno Taut's influential notion of the *Stadtkrone*,[10] or crown of the city, Goldzamt writes that the 'particular destiny and ideological role' of the central ensemble 'determine[s] the deployment in its con-struction of only the most monumental types of public construction and architectural form, *which crown the aesthetic unity of the city*' (emphasis original). Furthermore, adds Goldzamt, 'the dominating role of the cen-tral ensemble is the effect of the concentration therein of *architectural power*' (emphasis original).[11]

But how does Goldzamt square the egalitarian imperative behind socialist urbanism with the Stalinist elevation of the all-dominant cen-tre? He distinguishes between, on the one hand, the levelling effect of socialist town planning and the distribution of wealth and access to dig-nified living conditions and, on the other, the *architectural* differentiation between centre and periphery, which the realisation of an egalitarian urban environment necessarily entails:[12]

> Socialist urbanism eradicates class differences within the city, creating across all districts identical conditions for living, in terms of dwelling, work, communal services and aesthetic experiences … But

the eradication of the social contradiction between the city centre and the suburbs does not entail the elimination of all differences in architectural solutions; nor does it entail the eradication of central ensembles, with their particular form and spatial role. To the contrary, the democratism of socialist societies … necessitates the enormous significance of the centres of socialist cities.

In Goldzamt's account – quite jarring, I think, to the parameters of today's democratic-peripheralist political morphology – the distinction between socialist and capitalist centrality lies precisely in the fact that, on all counts, the former exceeds the latter: in scale, in intensity, and in agentic capacity. In contrast to capitalist urban cores, which are merely 'material carriers of the dominant worldview', socialist centres function as 'actual tools of ideological impact'.[13] 'What is more,' Goldzamt continues,

> their prominence in the life of socialist cities must become incomparably higher than that of the ceremonial or financial-commercial centres of feudal and capitalist cities. The foundation of the strengthening of the role of the centre in the practice of Soviet, Polish and other People's Democracies is the *transformation of the infrastructure of social ties carried out by central ensembles*.[14] (Emphasis added.)

The centre of the urban organism, when possessed of the right characteristics, is able to, and should, become a powerful agent in the transformation of society, simultaneously actualising and illustrating the 'coming unity of interests in socialist society, the unity of the interests and ideals of the entire population of the socialist city'.[15] The socialist centre is thus never at loggerheads with the remainder of the city.

Like Goldzamt, Lefebvre also emphasises that there is more than just one kind of centrality, and that the nature of centrality's social functioning depends on more than merely its shape, size and appearance. Having declared that 'there can be no city or urban reality without a centre', Lefebvre makes an important clarification: 'But as long as certain relationships of production and ownership remain unchanged, centrality will be subjected to those who use these relationships and benefit from them.'[16] The question of the urban, then, is not one of periphery versus centre. The victory of a more collective, more egalitarian, more just or otherwise better urbanism does not depend on the vanquishing of the middle by the margins. It is, instead, a question of progressive and regressive centralities: those owned by and open to the collective, or those held and guarded by the few, and those whose design – its aesthetic, scalar and morphological characteristics – is founded on *planned* use value, or those determined by *calculated* exchange value.

Socialist verticality

Just as there is a socialist centrality, there is also a long tradition of socialist verticality. In the Soviet incarnation, this dates back to unrealised constructivist experiments with *anti*-skyscrapers or *horizontal* skyscrapers, such as Vladimir Tatlin's Monument to the Third International, Nikolai Ladovsky's Communal House and El Lissitzky's *Wolken-bügel* ('cloud-irons'), and to the early Stalinist dream of the Palace of the Soviets, which was to stand on the site of demolished (and now rebuilt) Christ the Saviour Cathedral on the banks of the River Moskva. But its most vivid realisation came in the shape of the spate of 'tall building' construction in Moscow between 1947 and 1953. Seven towers, their heights ranging from 130 to 250 metres, were built at commanding sites ringing the central core of the Soviet capital (Lev Vladimirovich Rudnev, head of the Warsaw Palace's design team, came to prominence as the architect of Moscow State University, the tallest of the Moscow towers). The perceived correlation between capitalism and architectural verticality was an issue that the designers of the Soviet high-rises and the ideologues of Stalinist Socialist Realism were very eager to address, all the more so given the extent to which Stalinist skyscraper architecture made use of stylistic and engineering solutions borrowed from inter-war boom-era American skyscrapers. An illustrative 1953 article in the Warsaw weekly *Stolica*, about high-rise construction, cites Maxim Gorky's condemnations of American skyscrapers as 'square, lacking any desire to be beautiful … bulky ponderous buildings towering gloomily and drearily', and diagnoses 'the American skyscraper' as 'a product of highly developed capitalism, at the kernel of which lies ground rent'.[17] According to the author of the *Stolica* text, the Soviet tall building constitutes the 'absolute opposite of this image … in its entire figure one can see the will to a beauty, whose form is appropriate to its humanistic content'.[18]

A citation from a key tract of the time by Goldzamt, meanwhile, makes it clear that the difference between the American 'skyscraper' and the Soviet 'tall building' has to do not merely with architectural form, but also – and especially – with the morphology of the city as a whole.

> American skyscrapers reflect the chaos and internal contradictions of the capitalist economy. They pile up alongside one another in random, clumsy heaps. They grow thoughtlessly, without any consideration for function or composition. They grow without concern for the city, whose streets they transform into ravines. The tall buildings raised among the expansive squares and boulevards of the new Moscow, by contrast, form a system appropriate to the needs and structure of the city, attesting to the emotional unity of its figure and image.[19]

In the words of the architectural historian Alessandro De Magistris, the Soviet 'tall building' was the 'culminating element and the expression of the new urban morphology of Communism'.[20] It was to be the negation (by appropriation, as De Magistris points out) of its capitalist corollary. These towers were set in sprawling expanses of empty space, rather than piled onto one another; they fulfilled public or residential functions, rather than revenue-accumulating ones; their appearance was dictated not by a will-to-profit, but by a will-to-beauty; and they were to be distributed around the city not at random, but according to a higher-ordained, total plan – whose function it would be to reduce the complexity of the ravenous, random and fragmented city of capital.

Centrality after socialism

More than a quarter-century has passed since the collapse of Poland's state socialist regime in 1989, and yet the Palace of Culture continues to work much as Goldzamt and the other planners and ideologues of Stalinist urbanism intended it to. The vast majority of Warsaw's residents – 80 per cent, according to a large-scale survey I carried out in Warsaw – consider it (and the surrounding Parade Square) to constitute Warsaw's singular central or core site (*centrum*). What is more, none of the many post-1989 plans for filling the space around it with a triumphant coterie of money-making skyscrapers – whether in the form of a circular 'crown' or an asymmetrical 'forest' – have been carried out. Neither the Palace's centrality, nor its verticality, has yet been superseded in the urban morphology of the capitalist city.

Public and private discussions between architects, decision-makers and audiences dedicated to the future of Parade Square continually circulate around the issue of whether a particular architectural solution will successfully *undermine* the Palace's dominance over its surroundings, or whether it will, conversely, *underline* this dominance, surrendering (intentionally or not) to the Palace's scale, and to the symmetry and axiality emanating from it. These are precisely the issues that occupied the attention of experts grouped together in the mayor's architectural advisory councils, during meetings held in the three years leading up to the ratification of the currently binding (but, of course, unrealised) Parade Square master plan.

During the latter stages of the final round of discussions that preceded the 2010 ratification, the council chair implored the municipally employed planner-bureaucrats who had produced the Parade Square master plan to put more effort into 'designing asymmetry' and undermining the Palace's 'axiality'. The chair emphasised that all Parade Square planning work should aim to 'depart from the symbolism of crowning the Palace'. Their new master plan – which was supposed to drown out the Palace's grandeur in an asymmetrical forest of low- and high-rise buildings of varying heights, shapes and styles – was, in their view, actually still too symmetrical, too deferential to the Palace's spatial logic.

As the council chair moved towards their closing statement, the tone of their pronouncements subtly shifted. Instead of berating the authors of the municipal master plan for having been 'defeated' by the Palace's triumphant morphology, they began to concede that such a defeat may have been inevitable, whatever spatial strategies are used. It is all well and good trying, they said, and the 'elimination of symmetry in the Palace's surroundings' would, in theory, be a desirable achievement. Ultimately, however, 'in all the variants' presented so far for the council's evaluation, 'the Palace is underlined, and it has not been possible to avoid this'.

Still-socialist centrality

Against Lefebvre's dismissal of state socialism's capacity to produce differential space, I would argue that the Palace is an example of one extraordinary state socialist building, which – on Lefebvre's own terms – *did* produce a new space, *did* exert an enormous creative effect on daily life, language and space. And furthermore, I argue that this differential space not only endures today, but remains 'still-socialist' – functioning as a non-capitalist enclave and a potential force field of revolutionary influence – despite the collapse of the political-economic system that created it.

I do not interpret the twentieth-century Palace, then, as an *ex-communist* building, which has been 'tamed' by capitalism. It is not a formerly tyrannical and oppressive thing, which has now been turned into nothing other than a cute and pliable mechanism for the accumulation of profit. It cannot be reduced to a commercialised object of *Ostalgie*. The Palace of Culture is a uniquely effective piece of communist architecture, spatial planning and social engineering. It is a building that functions as well as it does because the land on which it stands was expropriated from its pre-war owners and has not yet been 're-privatised'. It is a building that resists the 'wild capitalist' chaos – of property restitution, twenty-storey billboards, inner-city poverty and rampant gentrification – that surrounds it. The Palace, in other words, is not so much a 'post-socialist' building as a 'still-socialist' one – a building which – in large part thanks to the radical centrality built into it by its designers – is able to endure as an enclave of a 'non-capitalist' aesthetic, spatial and social world at the very core of a late capitalist city.

I want to put the Palace forward, then, as a powerful architectural embodiment of what anthropologist Kristen Ghodsee has referred to as 'the left side of history',[21] but also – since its magnificent solidity makes it likely to be around well into whatever future comes along – of what Jodi Dean calls the 'communist horizon'.[22] The Palace is a building which exists at once as an anachronism, an undead survivor of a dead (or dormant) property regime, ideology and aesthetic, and as an edifice alive with subversive public spirit, whose 'architectural power' embodies a powerful challenge to the privatising political economy and exclusionary spatiality of the post-socialist city.

There is nothing clear or inevitable, however, about the communist horizon, which the Palace's enduring socialist verticality allows us to glimpse. The Palace-as-non-capitalist-enclave of socialist centrality may not hold out for ever. Since the early 2000s, Warsaw has been in the grip of a violent and unregulated wave of property restitution, and many public spaces and facilities (schools, universities, kindergartens, public gardens, sports facilities), communal and social housing developments in the city – as well as human lives – have fallen victim to it.[23] Parade Square itself is slowly being chopped up and parcelled out to the descendants of pre-war owners, or – more often – to plunderous property developers, who have spent most of the last twenty years buying up land claims, more often than not for extremely low ('non-market', in the capitalist parlance) prices. In order to remain socialist, then, the Palace has to remain public. The difference between progressive and reactionary centrality is, in the last instance, a question of political economy.

Notes

1. This chapter reproduces edited versions of a fragment of the following article: Michał Murawski, 'Radical centres: the political morphology of monumentality in Warsaw and Johannesburg', *Third Text* 33, no. 1 (2019) and short fragments from the Introduction and chapters 5 and 6 of my book, *The Palace Complex: A Stalinist Skyscraper, Capitalist Warsaw, and a City Transfixed* (Bloomington: Indiana University Press, 2019).
2. Lefebvre, 2003 (first published in 1979), p. 79.
3. Goldzamt, 1956, p. 11. All translations are the author's own except where indicated otherwise.
4. Léger, 2012, p. 145.
5. Lefebvre, 1991, p. 55. I expand on my critique of Lefebvre in Murawski, 2018.
6. The connection between the Maussian theory of the gift and the idea of the 'total social fact' is explored in connection with skyscraper urbanism, from a contrasting point of view, in Vyjayanthi Rao's contribution to this volume. For a more detailed treatment of this topic, see chapter 2 in Murawski, 2019.
7. Goldzamt, 1956, p. 22.
8. Sigalin, 1986, vol. 3, p. 10.
9. Sigalin, 1986, vol. 2, p. 460.
10. Taut, 1919.
11. Goldzamt, 1956, p. 52.
12. Goldzamt, 1956, p. 18.
13. Goldzamt, 1956, p. 16.
14. Goldzamt, 1956, p. 18.
15. Goldzamt, 1956, p. 20.
16. Lefebvre, 2003, p. 97.
17. Kawa, 1953, p. 7.
18. Kawa, 1953, p. 7.
19. Goldzamt, 1956, pp. 329–30.
20. De Magistris and Korob'ina, 2009, p. 8.
21. Ghodsee, 2015.
22. Jodi Dean, 2012.
23. I elaborate on this non-process of property restitution and the 'infrastructural violence' which drives it in Murawski, 2018.

Bibliography

Dean, Jodi. *The Communist Horizon*. London: Verso, 2012.
De Magistris, Alessandro and Irina Korob'ina, eds. *Ivan Leonidov, 1902–1959*. Milan: Electa architettura, 2009.
Ghodsee, Kristen. *The Left Side of History: World War II and the Unfulfilled Promise of Communism in Eastern Europe*. Durham, NC: Duke University Press, 2015.
Goldzamt, Edmund. *Architektura zespołów śródmiejskich i problemy dziedzictwa*. Warsaw: Państwowe Wydawnictwo Naukowe, 1956.
Kawa, Franciszek. 'Łamigłówka techniczna budowy wysokościowej', *Stolica*, 24 May 1953.
Lefebvre, Henri. *The Production of Space*, translated by Donald Nicholson-Smith. Oxford: Blackwell, 1991.
Lefebvre, Henri. *The Urban Revolution*, translated by Robert Bononno. Minneapolis: University of Minnesota Press, 2003.

Léger, Marc James. *Brave New Avant Garde: Essays on Contemporary Art and Politics*. Winchester: Zero Books, 2012.

Murawski, Michał. 'Actually-existing success: economics, aesthetics and the specificity of (still-) socialist urbanism', *Comparative Studies in Society and History* 60, no. 4 (2018): 907–37.

Murawski, Michał. 'Marxist morphologies: a critique of flat infrastructures, fuzzy property and complexified cities', *Focaal: European Journal of Anthropology* 82 (2018): 16–34.

Murawski, Michał. *The Palace Complex: A Stalinist Skyscraper, Capitalist Warsaw, and a City Transfixed*. Bloomington: Indiana University Press, 2019.

Sigalin, Józef. *Warszawa 1944–1980: Z archiwum architekta*. Warsaw: Państwowy Instytut Wydawniczy, 1986.

Taut, Bruno. *Die Stadtkrone*. Jena: Eugen Diederichs, 1919.

Part III
Looking inward: re-centring the sacred

9

The Architecture of the Seventh Day: building the sacred in socialist Poland

Kuba Snopek with Izabela Cichońska and Karolina Popera

Between 1945 and 1989, despite the communist state's hostility towards religion, over 3,000 churches were built in Poland: the Architecture of the Seventh Day. Built by their parishioners, these churches represent a truly communal architecture that contrasts with the rigid modernism of the centralised state.

Parallel architectures

Socialist housing estates form a remarkably consistent type of urban landscape. Housing projects developed by Eastern European architects between the 1960s and the fall of the USSR do represent a certain level of diversity. Their scale, as well as their square footage of apartments, increased with every decade. Their architectural form differs: Eastern European governments developed many alternative production systems, as well as repetitive projects, the so-called 'housing series'. Notwithstanding these nuances, the overwhelming visual impression produced by the socialist city is one of sameness and repetitiveness. Designed for dozens of hectares at once, the socialist housing estates were populated with rows of similar boxy houses, prefab schools and kindergartens.

   In Poland, too, this monotonous architecture, fully prefabricated and industrialised, became one of the predominant kinds of urban landscape. But there is an inherent component of the Polish estates that breaks this paradigm: the parish church. The towers of Catholic churches break through the orthogonal skyline of every district built in

Figure 9.1 The Church of Our Lady Queen of Poland in Krakow's Nowa Huta neighbourhood (1967–1977) by Wojciech Pietrzyk, a rupture in the rigid urbanism of the centralised state. Source: Igor Snopek.

communist Poland. The brick façades, parabolic concrete shells and triangular forms of these churches strongly contrast with the prefabricated background. The infinite diversity of over 3,000 churches stands in clear opposition to the generic architecture produced by the socialist state.

Counter-intuitively, many of these churches were designed and built by the same architects who raised the housing estates that surround them. The huge visual difference between those two parallel architectures was created by the forces that produced them. Housing estates were generated by the power of a centralised state, designed in hierarchical and well-organised institutions, produced in factories, and erected on site by machines. The churches were designed by lone architects, and built from scavenged materials by highly motivated volunteers. Poland's architecture of the six working days – factories, schools, kindergartens or housing units – bears strong analogies to the modernist architecture developed in other countries. The Architecture of the Seventh Day, however, built ad hoc and in the grey zone, is Poland's most distinctive contribution to global architecture in the twentieth century.

Between Moscow and the Vatican

The duality of Polish post-war architecture reflects precisely the political situation in the country after 1945. After the devastation of the
Second World War, Poland found itself behind the Iron Curtain and in
the political orbit of the USSR. But the country didn't strictly follow
the Soviet economic and political model. Despite the attempts made
in the 1940s and 1950s, two important communist projects failed: the
collectivisation of agriculture and the subordination of the institutional
church. In 1956, when the Stalinist system broke down, Poland stepped
into the next epoch with private property in the countryside, along
with a well-organised ideological alternative to the Communist Party,
maintained by the Catholic Church. Both breaches in the consistency
of the Soviet system would soon be reflected in architecture. The short
period of liberalisation brought about by the 1956 de-Stalinising 'thaw'
resulted in a wave of church construction. Dozens of new churches
were erected spontaneously, predominantly in the rural areas of eastern Poland, and in newly built socialist cities.[1]

Nowa Huta (literally 'new steelworks') was one of the most ambitious projects of the Polish communist government. The construction
of the new city started in the late 1940s. Nowa Huta was designed
for 100,000 workers and squeezed between Kraków and a huge
steel-production plant. Both its architecture and its master plan were
defined by the rules of Stalinist Socialist Realism: strict hierarchy, order
and symmetry. Housing blocks were supplemented by schools, kindergartens and other services usual for a communist city. Missing from this
template was a parish church, a component strongly desired by the newly
proletarianised peasantry, many of whom had very recently moved to
the city from the villages.[2] Just a few months after the October thaw,
the authorities of Nowa Huta granted a permit for a parish church. The
parishioners marked the construction site with a wooden cross and the
state-run Association of Polish Architects organised a nationwide competition. Similar competitions were arranged in a few other cities, including
Tychy, another perfect socialist settlement, built from scratch in the coal-
rich region of Silesia.

The thaw didn't last longer than a few years. As early as 1960, the
government had tightened its policy towards the Church. The building permits given a few years earlier were all cancelled and dozens
of competition designs remained on paper. This led to unforeseen
consequences. The removal of the wooden cross that marked the

Figure 9.2a and b   The Church of St John the Baptist in Tychy (1957–1958) by Zbigniew Weber and Tadeusz Szczęsny. The temple appeared before the surrounding structures, preceding the growth of the city. Source: Igor Snopek.

construction site in Nowa Huta was seen by the traditional local community as an act of outrageous blasphemy, which resulted in several days of brutal street riots. For the next few decades, the construction of the church was an issue that united and mobilised the citizens against the authorities.

In Tychy, the thaw had initiated not one, but several, church constructions. One of them, the Church of St John, was finished before the window of opportunity closed. Unlike other churches from the 1950s, the construction of St John's didn't follow the formal procedures. Instead of a lengthy competition, there was a direct order from a local priest for an architectural design. Materials and labour were organised entirely within the local parish. The church was also built in a very specific location, in a rural area directly adjacent to the city. This location granted more independence from the state; the plot was donated to the parish by the local farmers. A few years later, when the city grew and took over these lands, the church was already there.

Although the thaw ended very quickly, it had a fundamental importance for the Architecture of the Seventh Day. The scale of the riots in Nowa Huta changed the general attitude of the government towards church construction. From this moment on, the building of Catholic churches in Poland moved into the grey zone. Although it was not desired by the government, it was not directly prohibited. The authorities would abstain from issuing building permits, selling building materials or renting construction machinery, but until 1989 church construction sites would not be directly assaulted or closed down. The Church of St John in Tychy, in turn, showed what path a parish community should choose in order to build a church. To be successful, parishes should depend only on their own resources: labour, materials, plots and architectural designs.[3] These lessons remained in the collective memory of churchgoing Poles and were redeployed two decades later.

The unrecognised architecture of 'solidarity'

The two decades following the thaw (an epoch sometimes called the 'small stabilisation') were a time of rapid urbanisation. In cities all over Poland, new neighbourhoods grew following the construction of heavy industry. Directly after the Second World War, two out of three Polish citizens lived in rural areas. In the next few decades this proportion was inverted; by 1980, two-thirds of the Polish population lived in cities.[4] Thousands of families fled to the cities to become first-generation proletarians. In their new homes, they would not find a parish church, the traditional centre of rural life. The tension between the architectural reality of new housing estates and the expectations of their tradition-bound communities was growing with every year. The two decades of 'small stabilisation' comprised an epoch in which almost no Catholic churches were built; occasional constructions were exceptions to this general rule. Permits were granted exclusively in those areas where the social pressure to build them was extreme. Some limited church construction was permitted directly after the social unrest of 1970 and 1976, in order to calm a restless society. Unintentionally, the authorities designed a mechanism in which determined resistance to the state was 'rewarded' with the gift of a church – a time bomb that was about to explode.

In 1978, Karol Wojtyła, a Pole, became Pope John Paul II. With his election, Polish church builders gained a powerful ally. In his previous position as the archbishop of Kraków, Wojtyła was known for his strong support for erecting new churches. Wojtyła can be found in dozens of photographs with architectural models of new churches, discussing the details directly with their architects. He would also visit construction sites in person to cheer on parishes under construction. With John Paul II in the Vatican, the matters of Polish sacral architecture ceased to be only local problems: they became an important political issue.

Massive strikes called by the newly formed independent Solidarity trade union in August 1980 triggered a huge wave of church construction. The deep state crisis pushed the communist government to make serious concessions to the protesting workers. One of them was a fundamental change in church-building policy. In a situation of massive protests and a multi-level state crisis, church construction was seen by the authorities as a minor problem. Moreover, a policy of granting permits was an awkward win–win solution. For the opposition, every initiation of a church construction was a success – a visible concession from the government. For the government, it gave hope for partial stabilisation: launching a single church construction would tie hundreds of disillusioned workers to the construction site and focus their energy for protest on a place other than the street. As a result, in 1980–81, the government granted over 1,000 building permits to parishes all over the country. Although liberalisation (the so-called 'Solidarity carnival') ended with the introduction of martial law in December 1981, the permits given earlier were not withdrawn. The huge wave of construction initiated in the era of Solidarity ended only in the late 1990s.

The churches built in these two decades reflect the character of the Solidarity movement as well as its achievements. First, churches would

Figure 9.3 The entrance to the Church of the Holy Cross and Our Lady Healer of the Sick in Katowice (1979–1993) by Henryk Buszko and Aleksander Franta. Simply by looking at the patchwork brick façade one can easily recognise the use of bricks from very different sources. Source: Maciej Lulko.

never have been built if not for one of Solidarity's key postulates. During the strikes, the mining unions demanded the introduction of a five-day working week. Gradually freeing Saturday from work gave the workers an immense amount of time to help with the churches. Second, build-ing churches became as much an expression of faith as a form of protest against the communists. Many people, sometimes openly atheist, helped to build their parish church to manifest discontent with the unpopular government. Last, but not least, the churches were built collectively by their future users and the construction sites united people from very different classes of society. The collective building was, again, a reaction to the government's restrictive policy towards church building.

Obtaining a building permit was merely the first step in the long path towards the eventual construction of a parish church. The state controlled the design institutions, the market in building materials and heavy machinery. The construction methods needed to adjust to these limitations. Parish churches were erected by hundreds of volunteers on Saturdays and after work on weekdays. The materials, as well as primitive building machinery, were crowd-sourced from the parish communities. Instead of prefabricated concrete panels, the church builders used leftover materials from the construction of their private houses. Cement was reinforced with mesh fences. Façades were cladded with river stones brought from holidays. Walls were constructed from bricks of different colours and provenance that randomly made their way to the construction sites. Big cement mixers were replaced by dozens of small hand mixers, the work of which was perfectly orchestrated. Wooden scaffolding replaced steel cranes and hundreds of shovels and barrows replaced professional excavators.[5]

These unusual circumstances were strongly reflected in the architectural design. The collective character of the construction completely transformed the role of the architect. In state-run architectural offices (in which designing churches was banned), the design process was aided by modern infrastructure and sophisticated institutional support. Architects could involve in the process any collaborators or design instruments, none of which could have been used when designing a church. On the other hand, the churches were not bound by the limitations of the building industry. Architects were lured to these projects by the promise of unlimited artistic freedom. In the process, though, other limitations appeared: the personal ambitions of hundreds of builders, and the variety of their tastes, skills and expectations. In order to achieve a satisfactory architectural result, the architects needed to learn to manage the competencies and talents of the people building the churches. In other words, in order to be successful, the architects had to share some of the responsibility for the design with their motley crews of volunteers.

This strategy produced unexpected results. The Church of Holy Mary the Queen of Peace in Wrocław was designed by a group of 30-year-old architects, but the construction process was handled by a group of retired stonemasons, who remembered pre-war building methods. As a

Figure 9.4   The Church of Our Lady Queen of Peace in Wrocław (1982–1994) by Wacław Hryniewicz, Wojciech Jarząbek and Jan Matkowski – an unlikely combination of avant-garde geometry and traditional construction methods. Source: Maciej Lulko.

result, the avant-garde geometry of the building (inspired by Japanese postmodernism, which was cutting-edge in the early 1980s) was supplemented with sophisticated brick and stone details. As the local priest, Father Paweł, informed us, the architects of the Church of Divine Mercy in Kalisz used the help of a team of renowned mathematicians to design and build a hyperbolic paraboloid. The Church of St Stanislaus Kostka in Rypin, in the north of Poland, was designed as a frame for gigantic compositions made of stained glass. This radical gesture was a homage by the architect, Jerzy Matusiak-Tusiecki, to the local artists working with this material.

The mechanism of delegating responsibility for the design to the local talents and including their ideas in the project can be found in different proportions in almost every church built in the 1980s. In each case it produced a completely different result, because the talents and skills found in different parishes varied. What connected these cases was a collective method of designing, one in which the architects needed to communicate their ideas on a daily basis and smoothly accommodate their designs to alien elements. The sooner the architects understood these new rules of the game, the sooner they could make them work to the advantage of their projects.

Epilogue

The fall of communism in Poland completely transformed the context in which sacral architecture was built. The construction sites instantly ran out of protest fuel and attracted fewer and fewer volunteers. The introduction of capitalism made machinery and construction materials easily available and commodified labour. It became more logical to simply collect money during Sunday Mass and hire a professional team of builders than to depend on the irregular work of the volunteers. The success of a church development became simply a matter of money. After 1989, successive governments were very favourable to the Catholic Church, which brought an unexpected consequence: moving religion classes from churches to schools made the catechetical rooms in new churches redundant spaces. The cultural role that the churches had played as centres for oppositional activity in the 1980s also decreased.

The radical change of context ignited another fascinating process: the adaptation of collective design and construction know-how into new conditions. New churches show different ways of learning from past experience.

The best-known Polish church, the Basilica of Our Lady of Licheń (the third-biggest Catholic church in the world), is probably the best example of a fully crowd-funded church. The initiator of its construction, Father Eugeniusz Makulski, designed the process of creating the huge building in a very conscious way: for years he had been building a community of motivated pilgrims. Afterwards he ordered a project perfectly tailored to crowd-funding, one that is simple and legible for the masses of pilgrims – traditional, and covered with gold, figurative sculptures and paintings. The Tychy-based architect Stanisław Niemczyk learnt completely different lessons. Each of his churches was fed with the

Figure 9.5   The Basilica of Our Lady of Licheń (1994–2004) by Barbara Bielecka – the third-biggest Catholic church in the world. The distributed means of financing influenced its form: the Basilica's architecture is literal and easily understood by everyone. Source: Igor Snopek.

energy, ideas and labour of parish communities. The architect mastered perfectly the art of communicating his ideas to the parishioners and persuading them to help. The churches designed and built by Mr Niemczyk are among the few that were able to attract big teams of volunteers long after 1989.

Although nearly all Polish church construction after 1945 commenced under the rule of the Communist Party, these churches do not really belong to the communist epoch. Instead, we should treat them as an architectural articulation of the era of transition. Most church constructions were ignited during the 'Solidarity carnival' of 1980–81. The last of them ended as late as the early 2000s, over a decade after the fall of the Iron Curtain. These dates almost perfectly overlap with the economic transition from a centrally planned to a market economy, and the political transformation from autocracy to democracy, a period crowned by Poland's accession into the EU in 2004. The Architecture of the Seventh Day is therefore a unique type of architectural heritage: a tangible legacy of the age of turbulent transition.

Notes

1. This chapter is based on materials we collected while researching for our book, *Architektura VII dnia* (Cichońska, Popera and Snopek, 2016).
2. For two studies of the architecture and social life of Nowa Huta see Lebow, 2013, and Pozniak, 2014.
3. Lipok-Bierwiaczonek, 2015.
4. Basista, 2001.
5. See Cichońska, Popera and Snopek, 2016; the interviews with architects (Wojciech Jarzabek, Jerzy Matusiak-Tusiacki and Stanislaw Niemczyk) took place during research in 2016.

Bibliography

Basista, Andrzej. *Betonowe dziedzictwo: Architektura w Polsce czasów komunizmu*. Warsaw: Wydawnictwo Naukowe PWN, 2001.

Cichońska, Izabela, Karolina Popera and Kuba Snopek. *Architektura VII dnia*. Wrocław: Fundacja Bęc Zmiana, 2016.

Lebow, Katherine. *Unfinished Utopia: Nowa Huta, Stalinism, and Polish Society, 1949–56*. Ithaca, NY: Cornell University Press, 2013.

Lipok-Bierwiaczonek, Maria. *Tychy oczywiste i nieoczywiste: Książęce ślady, dotknięcie sacrum i nowe miasto*. Tychy: Urząd Miasta/Muzeum Miejskie w Tychach, 2015.

Pozniak, Kinga. *Nowa Huta: Generations of Change in a Model Socialist Town*. Pittsburgh, PA: University of Pittsburgh Press, 2014.

10

Post-shtetl: spectral transformations and architectural challenges in the periphery's bloodstream

Natalia Romik

The transformation of the 1990s that followed the collapse of Poland's state socialist regime caused the most recent and still ongoing alteration of the urban tissue of small, peripheral towns, with visible and lasting impact. The architectural chaos takes on the appearance of a liquefied contrast, spawning through the optical disproportions and inequalities between urban centres and peripheries. There is a similar disproportion between metropolitan and peripheral ways of remembering Jewish heritage. Significant buildings, like *mikvahs* (bathhouses) and synagogues, located on the main tourist routes or in former Jewish districts of the larger cities, are being renovated. But less prominent buildings, synagogues or private houses located off the beaten track in the small, frequently depressed, peripheral towns, are left to neglect and decay. Such disproportionate urban regeneration has many causes.

A 2006 report produced by the Polish Academy of Sciences, which discusses the development of small towns, lists several risk factors. In addition to more common ones, such as the location of primary urban functions, trade and entertainment outside of town centres, it lists other elements, among them a lack of respect for urban heritage, often linked to the unresolved ownership status of former Jewish properties. Before the Second World War, many buildings of historical value belonged to the Jewish citizens of these towns. Their current neglect and devastation can be partially attributed to their uncertain legal status.[1] This deterioration is amplified by the misplaced priorities of national heritage policy, which seem to ignore the Jewish heritage of small towns. With the exception of a handful of examples of vibrant community centres (Szczebrzeszyn), libraries (Piotrków Trybunalski) and museums (Świętokrzyski Sztetl in Chmielnik, the Museum of Mazovian Jews in Płock and the Museum in Tykocin), which are located in renovated and well-kept synagogues, Jewish buildings are left without any protection or investment, undergoing slow erosion.

Before I discuss how my urban interventions unveiled and publicly amplified these controversies, I will explain the history and specificity of former shtetls. In Yiddish, *shtetl* means 'small town'. The term connoted a settlement with a large compact Jewish Ashkenazi population, which differed from neighbouring peasant populations in religion, occupation, language, culture and architecture.[2]

Before the Second World War, shtetls spanned the entirety of Central and Eastern Europe (mainly the current territories of Poland, Ukraine, Lithuania, Russia, Belarus, the Czech Republic and Slovakia). In the 1920s and 1930s, shtetls played an important role as local cultural centres, as 'social condensers' of Jewish life in the Eastern European provinces. As such, they hosted small cinemas, youth associations and political parties, libraries and religious facilities. They had an important economic function as centres of agriculture, industry, trade, craft and other services (see Figure 10.1). The unique urban and social reality of the shtetls was destroyed by the Second World War and the Holocaust. After 1945, the former Jewish towns became occupied by new populations, a process which created a specific set of social, urban and architectural problems.

Figure 10.1 Market in Kraśnik, 1939. Courtesy of Tomasz Wiśniewski.

In his widely discussed book *Prześniona Rewolucja: Ćwiczenia z logiki historycznej* ('Sleepwalking through a revolution'), social philosopher and psychoanalyst Andrzej Leder puts forward the notion that Polish post-war urbanisation and the resulting emergence of an ethnically Polish urban middle class were enabled by the social vacuum left after Jewish populations were murdered by Nazis during the Holocaust. This process encompassed a massive property transfer. He points out that:

> Almost all the houses inhabited before the Second World War, with their facilities and furnishings, were inhabited again by new owners. Before 1939 there were three million people who had some form of property: real estate, workshops, plots of land and other goods. After they had been murdered, their property did not disappear, but rather it found new owners.[3]

The Nomadic Shtetl Archive project,[4] discussed here, does not remedy these problems, but rather deals with their consequences for the urban politics of memory in former shtetls. The project emerges in dissent with the current regime of historical amnesia and neglect, which is hegemonic in both official and everyday historical politics in twenty-first-century Poland. Despite a multitude of actions by local enthusiasts and Polish-Jewish NGOs, and localised efforts by a handful of municipalities, the urban memory of former shtetls, the only visible traces of Jewish presence, both secular and religious, is being erased. Or perhaps this memory has never really emerged, and had an opportunity to take material and practical form?

The aim of the Nomadic Shtetl Archive was to contribute to the development of public awareness, discourse and methods that can address the architectural erosion of post-Jewish towns, deal with the suppression of collective memory and tackle the problem of anti-Semitism, while acknowledging and responding to the harsh economic and political conditions of the region. I tested similar methods in my previous participatory-architectural projects, among them JAD (see Figure 10.2), whose name connotes the Hebrew word for 'hand'. In the Judaic tradition, the *jad* serves as a liturgical tool, essentially a rod that ends with a miniature representation of a hand, used for reading the Torah. In my case, JAD was a nomadic machine, in the shape of a big hand with a pointing finger, covered in mirrors, which was deployed to conduct architectural protest and evoke urban remembrance.

The installation was set up in 2012 in various places of architectural erosion in the Silesian Metropolis (Będzin, Bytom, Sosnowiec). In these towns, I selected locations that, before the Second World War, were closely related to the Jewish community, such as houses, hospitals and synagogues. JAD was transported to these locations and used there as a vehicle of 'urban emergency', trying to grasp public attention through its presence, sound, light effects and artificial smoke. We explored the buildings of disused synagogues, and roamed through vacant spaces left after the demolition of other synagogues; we visited private flats, Jewish orphanages, pre-funeral houses, ritual bathhouses, praying rooms, religious schools, cemeteries, and headquarters of youth and political organisations (see Figure 10.3). Currently, the great majority of these places are degraded or used for purposes unrelated to Jewish life or heritage. JAD not only called attention to this situation during live performances, but also was presented in several exhibitions (in Bytom, Katowice and Warsaw), and discussed in the local and national media.

Similarly to JAD, the Nomadic Shtetl Archive attempts to tackle the problems of urban emptiness and the spectral architecture of abandoned post-Jewish properties. The Archive was a piece of mobile architecture, which travelled in 2016 through south-eastern Poland, following the footprints of the former Jewish towns, exploring the layers of urban memory. For ten days we parked the Archive in the main squares of Kock, Piaski, Bychawa, Biłgoraj, Tyszowce, Szczebrzeszyn, Józefów, Krasnobród, Kraśnik and Wojsławice, each of these being towns with

Figure 10.2   JAD CSW. Source: Kronika.

Figure 10.3   JAD CSW. Source: Kronika.

formerly large Jewish populations and now (as in the past), populated by tight-knit communities of no more than 50,000 people.

The main aim of the Archive was to preserve and rejuvenate memory by 'liberating' and making public the archives of the Jewish Historical Institute, the Polish Academy of Science, various NGOs (such as the Grodzka Gate Centre in Lublin) and private individuals. In order to activate these archives in the urban reality of peripheral towns, I chose nomadism as the most appropriate modality of action. This mobility was combined with the participatory openness of the Archive, which grew in the process of collective investigation and animation (through activating oral histories and weaving social connections) to produce the most striking aesthetic and affective form and, hopefully, to provide the most far-reaching results. The Nomadic Archive prompted a mutually beneficial exchange of memory: we displayed archival materials while local amateur historians led guided tours through the towns.

The idea of opening and decentralising the Archive in the process of its nomadic dissemination was directly inspired by Jacques Derrida's analysis of archive, memory and power. In *Archive Fever*, Derrida writes:

> There is no political power without control of the archive, if not of memory. Effective democratization can always be measured by this essential criterion: the participation in and the access to the

archive, its constitution, and its interpretation. ... *There is no archive without a place of consignation, without a technique of repetition, and without a certain exteriority. No archive without outside.* [5]

The notion of the archive's social outside, of vibrant, public processes of memory, informed both the participatory mode of operation of the Nomadic Shtetl Archive and its architectural form (see Figure 10.4). The Archive was built on a mobile trailer 4 metres long, 1.5 metres wide and almost 3 metres high. Its walls and roof were constructed from wood, and covered with plastic mirrors. The main purpose of the mirrors was to play with the notion of disappearance, to merge with the urban surroundings, and to emphasise the importance of unveiled memories (see Figure 10.5).

The unit was equipped with a display system to present archival materials, a centrally located light box, which featured architectural drawings of synagogues, and shelves and other furniture. At the main entrance to the trailer, just above the stairs leading to the Archive itself, hung a red curtain with an embroidered Star of David, resembling a synagogal parochet (the curtain that hangs before the Ark). The Archive contained a small library that consisted of archival materials (for example, maps from *Yizkor* books, literature and poetry related to shtetls, and even a couple of theoretical and historical essays). [6]

Figure 10.4 Nomadic Shtetl Archive. Source: Natalia Romik.

Figure 10.5 Nomadic Shtetl Archive. Source: Natalia Romik.

In every town, the Archive presented a site-related exhibition of archival materials – photos, movies, texts, Yizkor (memorial service) maps and historical information. Immediately in front of the Archive, in the main squares of the former shtetls, we carried out discussions, workshops and screenings. Additionally, the Archive served as a mobile base for architectural interventions and performances, and as a storage for artistic props, designs and materials activated in various public situations.

The local inhabitants did not merely passively absorb the documents we provided but played an active role as co-researchers. They helped us to find new materials, fill in archival gaps, locate original buildings or sites from archival photographs, and find traces of Jewish presence (buildings, polychromes and documents). The conversations in each city were different, but a couple of topics resurfaced continuously, such as problems with the 're-privatisation' of property (some locals feared that the Jews would return to seize their former property), a lack of social knowledge about the history of their 'own' shtetls, the history and present of local anti-Semitism, pogroms during the 1920s and 1930s, and architectural as well as social problems caused by capitalist 'revitalisation' – of former religious buildings, as well as the entire town – during the 1990s and 2000s. In particular, the problems and mechanisms related to the legal status of former Jewish properties were similar everywhere. The spectral presence of Jewish populations enveloped us like a shroud, being everywhere, but visible nowhere. Among the many moments of revelation and laughter, troubling conversations and communal discussions we experienced during our nomadic trip, I am only able to recount a few.

The journey of our 'invisible' Archive began in Warsaw. Together with Aga Szreder, a driver and technician, and Agata Korba, a project researcher, and project coordinator Monika Tarajko, we embarked on our voyage without any major troubles. On the first day, 25 July, we parked the mobile vehicle on the main market square in Kock (current population around 3,500), where in 1939 more than 49 per cent of the population were Jews. Once we arrived, we saw how the nomadic mobilisation of the Archive's social 'exteriority' was tested in practice (see Figure 10.6). We were guided by Maria Kowalewska, one of the town's older citizens, who showed us almost every old house and shop, recalling the professions and surnames of her Jewish neighbours. We went to Rabbi Menachem Mendel Morgenstern's house, also called 'Rabinówka' (see Figure 10.7). Currently, the building is privately owned. The roof is covered with a dark-brown, rusty metal sheeting. The door eaves and the front door have simple ornamental decorations. Before the war, Kock was one of the most prominent centres of Chasidism in Eastern Europe. According to legend, after his religious awakening the tzaddik burnt all his manuscripts and spent the rest of

Figure 10.6 Kock Nomadic Shtetl Archive. Source: Natalia Romik.

Figure 10.7 Mendel Morgenstern's house, 'Rabinówka'. Source: Monika Tarajko.

his life in seclusion in this exact house. In the 1930s the building was turned into the court of the last generation of Kock's tzaddiks – the grandchildren of Menachem Mendel.

The Kock synagogue did not survive the war, and in the cemetery (desecrated in the 1950s) only around thirty *matzevas* (gravestones) remained. Before the war, Kock was a vibrant centre of Jewish life. Similarly to other shtetls visited by us on our journey, it used to have political parties and associations, among them Zionists, communists, Bundists and the Ha-Szomerha-Cair scout movement. There were trade unions, especially active ones led by tailors and purse makers.[7] There are no traces of these activities left. While walking through the town, we talked with our fellow guide and other people, wandering through the landscape filled with Jewish absence/presence. We had similar discussions with visitors to our exhibition, which was welcomed by a local social centre and visited en masse by local people.

In other towns our public programme looked quite similar. Vivid talks about the urban history of each town, private memory-trips to Jewish houses currently inhabited by Polish people, the juxtaposition of current architecture with maps from *Yizkor* books, short lectures on synagogue architecture, and public walks with local historians, enthusiasts and children. Every evening, there was a documentary film showing.

On 27 July we reached Bychawa (population formerly 66 per cent Jewish) (see Figure 10.8). In the early afternoon, during a conversation about the location of the *mikvah*, somebody brought me documents relating to a Jewish pupil, found in the attic of one of Bychawa's houses during its renovation (see Figure 10.9). In the afternoon we went on a trip, during which we compared archival pictures with the current state of the town's architecture. Thanks to the courtesy of Antoni Wieczorkiewicz – the private owner of the synagogue in Bychawa (dated to the nineteenth century) – we had an opportunity to explore the interior, where it is still possible to spot traces of polychrome with motifs featuring musical instruments and inscriptions in Hebrew. The synagogue was sold to Mr Wieczorkiewicz in 2007 by the Foundation for the Preservation of Jewish Heritage in Poland. Despite many questions about the future use of the synagogue, Mr Wieczorkiewicz did not give any concrete answers. A local rumour suggests that an exclusive restaurant is planned, in the 'Jewish' style. The synagogue in Bychawa is an example of the wider process of the privatisation of Jewish heritage, mediated by Jewish foundations legally nominated as custodians of these properties. The process of restitution of Jewish properties has been documented and analysed by the historian Stanisław Tyszka, who provides the following illuminating description:

> According to the 1997 law [on the return of communal religious properties], only individual Polish-Jewish communities and the UJRC [Union of Jewish Religious Communities] are entitled to file restitution clams. ... [I]n June 2000, the WJRO [World Jewish Restitution Organisation] and the UJRC signed an agreement to establish the Foundation for the Preservation of Jewish Heritage (FPJH) as a partnership between the two organizations. The FPJH was registered in Poland in 2002. By creating this foundation, representatives of local communities agreed to allow the WJRO to

Figure 10.8 Market in Bychawa 1918. Source: Tomasz Wiśniewski.

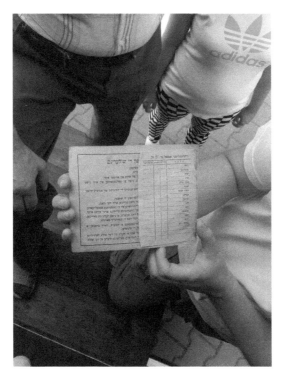

Figure 10.9 Bychawa conversation with local people. Source: Natalia Romik.

benefit from the return of communal property in Poland. ... The FPJH owns and manages returned properties in the remaining twenty-seven districts ... about 60 percent of Poland's territory.[8]

Unfortunately, in the majority of towns visited during our trip, the Jewish communal property has been already sold by the FPJH, who thus relegated its custodianship to private owners without any legal obligations whatsoever, which has resulted in the neglect of this now privatised heritage.

On 30 July we went to Biłgoraj, a town of just under 27,000 inhabitants, which was 60 per cent Jewish before the War, and where Jewish citizens lived together with their Polish and Ukrainian neighbours. Before the War, Jews in Biłograj worked mainly in trade (both local and cross-regional), craft and brewing. At the end of the 1930s, because of the economic crisis, fierce competition with Polish merchants and craftsmen, and rising anti-Semitism, the situation of Jews in Biłgoraj deteriorated. In June 1940, Germans established the Biłgoraj ghetto, to which Jews from surrounding villages were also forcibly displaced. The ghetto was closed in 1943, and all Jews were moved to concentration camps or murdered on the spot. Sixty per cent of the town's inhabitants ceased to exist.[9]

Currently, in Biłgoraj, there are no traces of this tragic past. In fact, 80 per cent of the town itself, including its Jewish architecture, was devastated during the war. There are only a couple of remote traces of this vacuum, and the town itself feels as if it's defined by this spectral, ghostly presence. This situation has peculiar reverberations in the current development of the town's most recent housing establishment, 'the settlement on the route of borderland cultures'. In fact, our Archive's sojourn in Biłgoraj consisted to a large extent of trips to this new development and talks with its initiator. 'The settlement on the route of borderland cultures' is a hybrid estate, which mixes references to the idealised architecture of a small Jewish town with a modern urban structure. It is a private estate in folkloristic style, with a 48-room hotel, restaurants, a car park, a market square with an Orthodox church, a mill, and a spectacular reconstruction of the monumental wooden synagogue from Wołpa (Ukraine), located in the most bizarre, uprooted fashion in the centre of a stylised 'market square' (real synagogues were never located in such a manner) (see Figure 10.10).

All reconstructions of wooden architecture are located near rather luxurious semi-detached houses decorated in 'shtetl-style' (see Figure 10.11). Despite these peculiarities, my ethical and aesthetic opinion about this investment is rather ambivalent, as the settlement – although,

Figure 10.10   Reconstruction of wooden synagogue from Wołpa.
Source: Natalia Romik.

without a doubt, a financially profitable and rather extravagant site of cultural appropriation – remains at the same time a significant site of identification with Jewish architectural heritage in Biłgoraj. It is, in fact, the only visible trace of the town's spectral Jewish presence, not counting a remaining fragment of Jewish cemetery. During our discussions, it became clear that the inhabitants consider this settlement an authentic opportunity to preserve Jewish memory in Biłgoraj, and hope for the chance to establish a dynamically functioning cultural centre there, which may prompt economic development in the town.

On the web page of the foundation established by the investor responsible for the development of the settlement (pithily entitled 'Foundation "Civic Entrepreneurship for the benefit of integration, economic development, culture, tourism and sport, and for preserving [the] traditions of borderland regions – Biłgoraj XXI"'), one can read that the development 'serves as a cultural base, [provides] sports and leisure facilities as well as hotel and catering facilities. Moreover, it acts as the future center of logistics and information for projects related to the development of tourism and recreation in the region'. Indeed, the web page features extensive information on the history and multicultural heritage of Biłgoraj. However, the cultural information is juxtaposed with commercial tabs describing in detail a real-estate stock consisting of apartments in a variety of sizes (33–80 m^2), the architecture of which

Figure 10.11   Biłgoraj, 'The settlement on the route of borderland cultures'. Source: Natalia Romik.

'harks back visually' to the architectural heritage of Jewish Biłgoraj.[10] In one of the press interviews, the settlement's investor and developer Tadeusz Kuźmiński states, 'I decided to preserve this memory from total erasure … It is not a folkloristic park. People can live here normally, in serene surroundings. We have sold six flats already, and during the summer a pizzeria, a hair salon and a grocery will open there.'[11] The national daily newspaper *Rzeczpospolita* estimates the cost of development at 30 million Polish zlotys (approximately £6 million), half of which will be spent on buying land. Eventually, the development will span more than 35 hectares.[12]

The investment is intended to 'bring back' the urban life of nineteenth-century Biłograj. However, there are neither Jews nor Ukrainians in today's Biłgoraj, nor, it appears, are they directly involved in the financing nor implementation of the project. The synagogues were never located in the centres of town squares (or even in other more prestigious locations, which were reserved for Catholic churches), and the wooden shacks of their poor inhabitants did not bear much relation to the sanitised environment of a stylish gated community. Romanticising the past, the Settlement does not deal with its darker side, and is unable to cope with the widespread realities of amnesia and creeping anti-Semitism which permeate both the past and present social life of Biłgoraj.

Mirosław Tryczyk, the author of a controversial analysis of Polish anti-Semitism during the Second World War, has collected several examples of conflicts between Polish nationalists and Jews from the 1930s, including the infamous 'war for trade'. During court proceedings against the far-right Polish National Movement, one of its brochures calling for the boycott of Jewish shops was quoted as saying 'The Polish holdings recede fast, we are getting poorer with every passing minute, our properties are grabbed ingloriously by Jewish hands. Polish towns no longer have a Polish character.'[13] In today's Poland, meanwhile, a political association that directly relates to the heritage of the National Party was officially registered in 2015, with the explicit aim of carrying on its pre-war traditions; it is one of a plethora of far-right organisations reactivated in recent years, among them the National-Radical Camp, registered in 2012, which harks back to the openly fascist and violent traditions of its inter-war namesake, founded in 1934. These are just two instances among many of the contemporary revival of fascism and open anti-Semitism, which creates a backdrop against which such initiatives as the Settlement should be assessed in their inherent ambivalence.

On 4 August 2016, we arrived in Kraśnik (40 per cent Jewish population in 1939) (see Figure 10.12). Together with Mariusz Bieniek (a local history teacher), we went to see the Grand Synagogue (in the care of the Foundation for the Preservation of Jewish Heritage in Poland since 2005) (see Figure 10.13) and the local *beit ha-midrasz* (prayer house). The synagogue was devastated during the Second World War, when it

Figure 10.12   Kraśnik public programme. Source: Aga Szreder.

Figure 10.13 Kraśnik synagogue interior. Source: Natalia Romik.

was adopted as the workshop of a local labour camp. After the War, the building was used as a storage facility and workshop. From the original design only a prayer room with a niche for the Torah ark, and fragments of a polychromy on the eastern wall, have survived.[14] We were astonished by wall paintings portraying the Tablets of the Law, with animal motifs and views of Jerusalem.

Usually, both of these impressive buildings are, unfortunately, closed to visitors. For some of the local inhabitants who came on our tour, it was their first opportunity to visit the interiors. In Kraśnik, just as in other towns on our way, local people frequently complained about the lack of access to synagogues and other Jewish buildings, opened only occasionally for visiting Jewish tours. In the evening, after discussing a couple of archival photographs we had brought with us, the citizens of the town showed us around. We went to the site of a former *mikvah* (now private property) and to the Jewish cemetery. Together we searched for traces of *kuczkas* (temporary shelters used during the week-long Jewish holiday of Sukkot).

We embarked on the last trip of the Nomadic Shtetl Archive in the late autumn, to Wojsławice, a small village with around 1,000 inhabitants. Characteristic wooden buildings with shaded arcades create the atmosphere of this town. People from Wojsławice are also exceptional

Figure 10.14 Wojsławice public programme. Source: Monika Tarajko.

in their devotion to sustaining the memory of their Jewish neighbours (see Figure 10.14). The Panorama of Cultures association (which supported the Archive project) is located in the house of Fawka the Cobbler, who lived there until 1942 (see Figure 10.15). The Archive's visit was announced by a local priest during a Sunday Mass. In the evening we presented and summarised the trip of the Nomadic Shtetl Archive. The meeting, held in the old synagogue (dated to 1903), gathered many people of Wojsławice, with whom we reflected collectively about the possibilities of rejuvenating Jewish heritage. After this meeting, the Senna Collective was commissioned by the local council to design plans for renovating the synagogue as a cultural centre.

The Nomadic Shtetl Archive attempted to cope with the eradication of the memory of former Jewish inhabitants of small towns, which deteriorates alongside their former properties. My designs and interventions were intended to negotiate between the need to commemorate former users and the necessity to respect the rights of the current inhabitants (see Figure 10.16). Still, it is an ongoing investigation, which does not resolve but rather opens up numerous questions. Faced with an urban vacuum of such magnitude as the one left in the former shtetls, what is the appropriate method, scale and goal of a project of this kind? Can architectural intervention retrace lost memories and open up the 'social outside' of the archive? Can the process of commemoration turn into a revival of the

Figure 10.15 Wojsławice house of Fawka the Cobbler. Source: Natalia Romik.

Figure 10.16 Tyszowce public programme. Source: Natalia Romik.

Figure 10.17   Market in Józefów Biłgorajski Nomadic Shtetl Archive –
public programme. Source: Natalia Romik.

Jewish absence/presence? Can 'vernacular architecture' – redefined in a
thoughtful, striking idiom – become an attempt at what I term 'architectural homeopathy' (see Figure 10.17)?

Notes

1. Heffner and Marszał, 2006, pp. 15–16.
2. 'Shtetl', in Kassow, 2010.
3. Leder, 2014, pp. 80–1.
4. The design and construction of the Nomadic Shtetl Archive were executed by the author in
   cooperation with Sebastian Kucharuk, in the framework of the Senna Collective. Senna was
   established in 2013 by myself, Sebastian Kucharuk and Piotr Jakoweńko. Among other projects, it has been commissioned to prepare the adaptation of the nineteenth-century Jewish
   pre-burial house in Gliwice. The Nomadic Shtetl Archive project could not have happened
   without generous support from the 'Panorama Kultures' Association, the Grodzka Gate Foundation, the Cukerman's Gate Foundation, the Jewish Historical Institute in Warsaw and the
   Virtual Shtetl portal. The project was supported financially by the Architecture Research
   Fund – UCL Bartlett School of Architecture, the Koret Foundation, the Taube Foundation. Public programme supported by the Polish Ministry of Culture.
5. Jacques Derrida, 1995, pp. 11 n1, 14.
6. Yizkor books are books published after the Second World War by former Holocaust survivors.
   Very often they included the mind maps of shtetls. Quite frequently they are the only remaining documents that describe the layouts, functions and locations of buildings that were of importance to Jewish communities up to the inter-war era. These maps are usually hand-made
   and focus on the locations of Jewish spaces within the urban tissue of the shtetls, including
   building types like synagogues, *mikwahs* and *heders*.

7. Majuk, 2017, p. 98.
8. Tyszka, 2015, pp. 51–2.
9. Kubiszyn, 2011, pp. 53–8.
10. Fundacja Biłgoraj XII, 2019.
11. Nowicka, 2014.
12. Rzeczpospolita, 2016.
13. Tryczyk, 2017, pp. 72–85.
14. Kubiszyn, 2011, p. 212.

Bibliography

Derrida, Jacques. *Archive Fever: A Freudian Impression*, translated by Eric Prenowitz. Baltimore, MD: Johns Hopkins University Press, 1995.

Fundacja Biłgoraj XXI. 'Biłgoraj XXI'. Accessed 8 August 2019. http://bilgoraj21.pl/.

Heffner, Krystian and Tadeusz Marszał. *Uwarunkowania rozwoju małych miast: Conditions of Small Towns' Development*. Warsaw: Polska Akademia Nauk, 2006.

Kassow, Samuel. *The YIVO Encyclopedia of Jews in Eastern Europe*, 18 October 2010. Accessed 20 April 2017. http://www.yivoencyclopedia.org/article.aspx/Shtetl.

Kubiszyn, Marta. *Śladami Żydów: Lubelszczyzna*. Lublin: Stowarzyszenie Panorama Kultur, Ośrodek 'Brama Grodzka – Teatr NN', Muzeum Historii Żydów Polskick, 2011.

Leder, Andrzej. *Prześniona rewolucja: Ćwiczenie z logiki historycznej* ['Sleepwalking through the revolution: exercises in historical logic']. Warsaw: Wydawnictwo Krytyki Politycznej, 2014.

Majuk, Emil, ed. *Szlakami Sztetli:. Podróże przez zapomniany kontynent*. Lublin: Ośrodek 'Brama Grodzka – Teatr NN', 2017.

Nowicka, Joanna. 'Miasteczko kresowe w Biłgoraju powiększy się za unijne pieniądze', *Kurier Lubelski*, 17 March 2014. Accessed 20 April 2017. http://www.kurierlubelski.pl/artykul/3365711,-miasteczko-kresowe-w-bilgoraju-powiekszy-sie-za-unijne-pieniadze-zdjecia,id,t.html.

Rzeczpospolita. 'Biłgoraj: Miasteczko takie jak dawniej', *Rzeczpospolita*, 11 February 2016. Accessed 20 April 2017. http://www.rp.pl/Zycie-Lubelszczyzny/302119817-Bilgoraj-Miasteczko-takie-jak-dawniej.html.

Tryczyk, Mirosław. 'Sztetl z polską władzą', *Karta* 90 (2017): 72–85.

Tyszka, Stanisław. 'Restitution of communal property and the preservation of Jewish heritage in Poland'. In *Jewish Space in Contemporary Poland*, edited by Erica Lehrer and Michael Meng, 46–70. Bloomington: Indiana University Press, 2015.

11
Eat, pray, shop! The mosque as *centrum* in the Swedish suburbs

Jennifer Mack[1]

Rising along the edge of an elevated highway, a white building – it may be concrete or plaster – appears in the distance, its sedate orange-tiled rooftops nestled into the forest. With a measure of intention from its designers, only one part of the building extends beyond the height of these trees: a slim tower with a square base, becoming leaner and leaner and ending in a small metal sculptural element. With echoes of the Stockholm City Hall, this piece appears to be the decorative topper on the tasteful white cake below it. The building is a new mosque commissioned by the Stiftelsen Stockholms Stora Moské, sited in Järva Field between the neighbourhoods of Tensta and Rinkeby in the northern suburbs of Stockholm. Its architects are from Rashid Engineering in Saudi Arabia, with the Stockholm firm of Tengbom Group acting as project architects; this unusual structure is officially described as 'a meeting between a Muslim formal world and a Scandinavian modernist building tradition'.[2]

In a country said to be increasingly leaning towards atheism in popular domestic and international descriptions, this mosque on the periphery of the Swedish capital is just one of three major mosques planned in the area known as Järva Field, its neighbourhoods created during the Million Programme, the Swedish national housing programme that built 1 million dwelling units between 1965 and 1974.

If and when these three mosques are constructed, they will join existing religious buildings there: a major Syriac Orthodox church and a historic Lutheran church. The groups commissioning these buildings have typically waited many decades to achieve their architectural dreams.

Like many other purpose-built Swedish mosques, these religious 'centres' will be located in the suburbs; they are almost always sited in

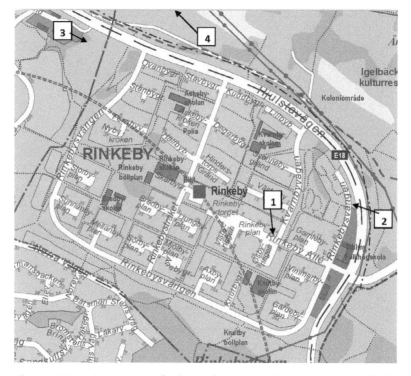

Figure 11.1 Locations of planned mosques in Järva (1. Rinkeby Mosque by Johan Celsing, 2. Multicultural Center by Spridd, 3. Project for the Stockholm Large Mosque Organization by Rashid Engineering and Tengbomgruppen, 4. Delayed). Source: Stockholms Stad.

the supposedly 'segregated' Million Programme neighbourhoods, where newly arrived migrants often find their homes. Even here, the buildings are usually located on the extreme geographical peripheries of areas said to be stagnating under the weight of an ill-fated modernism that has, according to popular understanding, left them with concrete barracks and bad reputations. In other words, if these peripheries are gaining new centres, to whom do they belong, and how do they redefine the social centres of everyday Swedish public life?

Specifically, I consider how original mid-twentieth-century Million Programme notions of public space – especially the *centrum* (town centre) – are transformed through the rise of this new suburban building type: the mosque. As such structures are planned, designed and constructed today, they answer the call, ever increasing in volume, for new gathering spaces for new publics in today's Sweden. Mosques also return everyday religious practice to the social centre of suburban Swedish neighbourhoods, which have long been considered bastions of rationality more than of spirituality.

Remaking a million

As the harsh spotlights of social unrest and resident labour market exclusion have been cast upon Million Programme areas, their architectural forms have often served as symbols of failure or decline.[3] Professional attention from designers has, since such measures began in the 1970s, often focused on retrofitting *housing*, especially on enlivening famously monotonous concrete façades. Yet, as academic research in fields from art history to sociology has outlined, it is critical to the understanding of the initiative at large that the Million Programme's 'new towns' were just that: they comprised entire neighbourhoods. This comprehensive approach to building a modern Swedish society would offer a new everyday domain for an expanded middle class and emphasise socioeconomic equality between citizens through standardised group spaces, activities and products. The Million Programme, in other words, offered much more than mere dwelling units.

Designs conjoined several international models, including CIAM's zoning for work, recreation, dwelling and transport (a model known as the 'functional city') and Ebenezer Howard's 'garden city', which sought to intermingle the best of the country and the city and was famously used in the development of Enskede in southern Stockholm.[4] The Million Programme would blend a new approach to 'rational' urban centres with a suburban pastoral.

When they came to the design of public space for Million Programme new towns, planners relied heavily on the notion of the 'neighbourhood unit' (*grannskapsenhet* in Swedish), especially as articulated in American planner Clarence Perry's 1929 Regional Plan for the City of New York.[5]

From the Social Democratic point of view, this forward-thinking mixture of spatial and social planning complemented ongoing agendas to revolutionise Swedish society, given its focus on linking a defined geography with a discrete social entity. The neighbourhood unit emphasised scientifically determined, walkable distances between its parts. Traffic separation between cars on the one hand and bicycles and pedestrians on the other was also paramount, following not only CIAM but also the recommendations of the 1960s group and model known as SCAFT (Stadsbyggnad, Chalmers, Arbetsgruppen för Trafiksäkerhet).

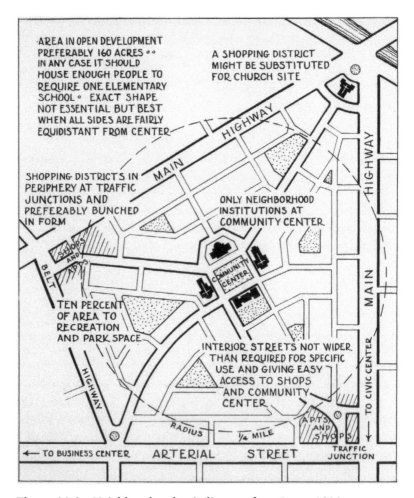

Figure 11.2 Neighbourhood unit diagram from Perry, 1929.

Both symbolically and geographically, the 'town centre' thus served as the key node in this rigidly hierarchical structure; it became known as the *centrum* in Sweden. During the Million Programme, neighbourhood units served as cells from which the new body of the modern nation-state would grow.[6]

Critically, the use of the neighbourhood unit in the distribution of a Swedish planning model to 1 million new dwelling units allowed a redefinition of boundaries between the private and public spheres. Creating a more communal sense of everyday social life in new town communities began with central heating and indoor plumbing and

Figure 11.3 Traffic separation in rendering of Järva Field neighbourhood. Source: *Arkitektur* 5 (1964): 123.

standardised technological innovations such as refrigerators and dishwashers. Likewise, in these neighbourhoods, the *centrum* would serve as the nucleus of the new cell, providing a series of public meeting places and, in effect, becoming a twentieth-century town square to complement or replace the classic public spaces of earlier times. Allowing citizens to have the chance to meet was a key focus of Million Programme designs, so the provision of shops, restaurants, club spaces and other facilities for groups to gather and socialise in was central in the *centrum*.

Despite this, those neighbourhoods were designed to accommodate ideas of modernity from a particular moment in Swedish history, and they often appeared outdated, even as their concrete was drying. Official inaugurations opened *centrum* facilities across the nation during the 1960s and 1970s, with speeches and 'people's parties' (*folkfester*) marking these occasions. Just a few years later, the nuclear families of middle- and working-class Swedes who were meant to occupy them had begun to disappear, and those who had no other options, especially newly arrived migrants, began to take their place. Today, these Million

Programme areas offer new formal manifestations of these now more powerful and well-established migrant groups. Once the *medelsvensson* (average Swede, literally 'middle Svensson') client imagined for workers' associations and meetings of housewives' groups had given way in neighbourhoods like Tensta and Rinkeby to new publics, the need to rethink the neighbourhood structure, the *centrum*, and Swedish gathering space more generally, followed.

The twentieth-century *centrum*

If Million Programme architects and planners sought to retrofit society and reorient practices of community assembly, it is key to note that these had previously been focused on the extended family and, often, the Swedish (Lutheran) Church.[7] Indeed, as in many other European and North American settings, the church often occupied a prominent position in the centre of villages and towns, reminding the public of its social importance through its geographical location. Architectural features such as the clock tower and auditory interventions such as the ringing of the church bells regularly infiltrated everyday life.

Planners of the mid-twentieth century had an entirely different view of how the social centre should be organised in the neighbourhood unit, the Social Democratic agendas of providing 'service' in the new town centres emphasising the offerings of national and local government – such as health clinics and postal services – rather than spiritual ones. In the earliest town centres of the 1940s and 1950s, such as in Årsta, Vällingby and Farsta, the idea that the shopping and service centre had replaced the church dominated planning. The *centrum* was conceived of as primarily a secular civic and commercial space.

Indeed, even when churches found space in the town centres of the Million Programme, they were typically housed in mundane locales, often at the back of the larger *centrum* complex. In other words, for modern Swedish citizens of the booming 1960s, contemporary life circled less around the traditional Sunday gatherings at church and more meaningfully around new secular forms of everyday living: joining the 'study circles' of the local Workers' Educational Association (*Arbetarnas Bildningsförbund*, ABF), booking a time in a new shared laundry room in the apartment building (or a large common laundry with staff on hand), and cooking meals with partially processed food products purchased in the innovative 'self-service' grocery stores where mass production and mass consumption intermingled.[8] These innovations redefined what it meant to gather in Swedish urban space. No longer was a trip to the grocer's merely an opportunity to buy food; the *centrum* made each visit an active practice of citizenship in which the State nearly always trumped the Church.

Rinkeby finds its *centrum*

In the northern periphery of Stockholm, the Järva Field area followed these prescriptions to the letter when the district was planned as part of a larger 1963 proposal for a site that had formerly served as a military training ground. The master plan for its neighbourhood of Rinkeby emerged in 1964 – the year before the Swedish parliament voted to develop the 1 million dwelling units of the Million Programme.

The existing plans for the new E18 motorway, along with the metro line, determined its boundaries. Together with two other areas, dubbed Tensta and Spånga Church (Spånga Kyrka), the plan was 4 kilometres long and 1 kilometre wide, for a total planning area of 460 hectares. The existing Spånga church building remained but was effectively repositioned within the new planning area; the new urban design made the structure literally marginal to its new centres of everyday life.

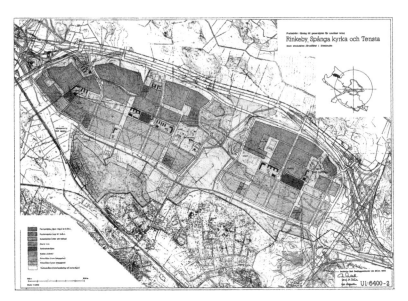

Figure 11.4 Proposal for Järvafältet master plan. Source: *Arkitektur* 5 (1964): 121.

As in other Million Programme zones, Rinkeby's planners imagined the area as the neighbourhood of the future. The urban designers, Igor Dergalin and Josef M. Stäck, presented the 'general plan' (*generalplan*) in nearly identical 1964 articles published in the premier Swedish professional architectural and urban design journals, *Arkitektur* and *Plan*.[9] In these essays, the pair described the possibilities permitted in the context of the nearly unbuilt-on open plain of the Järva Field. Even so, they highlighted that each small parcel of land should be carefully utilised and planned, to allow the designs to meet new demands for higher living standards, including sufficient open space for 'collective services like the subway, schools, shops, and so on and simultaneously the safety and comfort that a dense development can provide'.[10] The regular, rectilinear blocks proposed – which had little to do with the existing topography of the site – would facilitate this. Critically, the article in *Plan* emphasised the importance of a functioning outdoor environment, comprising 'the roads and places in which one moves every day on the way to work, to school, to the town centre'.

In recent urban discourse, however, these same design strategies are often considered to be the source of many of the problems facing Million Programme areas. If Rinkeby and Tensta were faithfully modernist in their mid-twentieth-century urban plans and original architecture, these forms have typically served as the foci for critique more recently. After the public fall of the Programme, from being Sweden's saving grace to being the bane of its cities, which occurred even during its construction, urban planners, architects and politicians began to focus their energies on rehabilitating these areas, including the Järva Field district. From the 1980s to the early 2000s, new plans for these neighbourhoods signalled the strong belief that physical renovations, of housing in particular, such as the many balconies added to façades previously described as monolithic and the addition of colourful paint to reduce visual monotony, would change the entire situation.

Renovations have of course taken place beyond the housing blocks, but they have mostly been through private initiatives. Indeed, today's Rinkeby Centrum, with its open space known as Rinkebytorg (Rinkeby Square), is a lively place where Somali-Swedish women in *hijabs* (headscarves) and basketball players for the Akropol BBK team (originally founded by Greek migrants) cross paths with elderly ladies who moved into their Million Programme apartments when the neighbourhood first opened. Many of the shopfronts offer evidence of this diverse mixture of old and new publics: pizzas and kebabs are purveyed in close proximity to a traditional Swedish Folkets Hus (community centre) and

Figure 11.5 Interior of women's mosque in Rinkeby Centrum, 2013. Source: Jennifer Mack.

the Qaran Express travel agency. The urban planners' emphasis on the provision of cultural and social space has allowed some retrofitted uses. Here, a multi-storey mosque, located just steps from the exit from the metro, is heavily used; its limited size, however, does not accommodate the women in the faith group, who meet at a location at the rear of the square.

Thus, while the standardised *centrum* allows its original spaces to house new services, the ad hoc approach that many occupants have used in their adaptations demonstrates its disadvantages and limitations.[11]

Radical new measures and approaches to gathering space for new Swedish publics are needed. This holds particularly true for religious spaces, which comprised a minor component of Million Programme centres. In today's suburbs, a new architecture is needed for 'new Swedes' (*nysvenskar*), as migrants have come to be labelled in recent discourse, and the three new mosques to be built in Rinkeby–Tensta go well beyond the traditional territory of housing or grassroots renovations.[12] They indicate that significant social changes require new, coordinated planning to renew the material conditions of the existing suburban landscape.

Returning religion to the centre

Journalist Elisabet Andersson writes that 'church building has long been a prestigious assignment for those in the architectural profession. But new churches are seldom built now. Instead, it is Islam that becomes architecture'.[13] Indeed, the rise of the mosque in Sweden as a major commission for architects around the country suggests that the removal of religion from the public sphere – and from public space – was only a temporary condition. The three mosques are, as noted, now being planned in the same area that Dergalin and Stäck developed in 1964 for what used to be Järva Field. As new publics demand these social and cultural spaces beyond the designated *centrum*, they not only reflect the demographic shifts that have occurred since the time of Rinkeby's inauguration but also move well beyond both cosmetic changes to existing buildings and ad hoc measures.

The three planned mosques will cater to diverse clienteles and take divergent forms. Intriguingly, the label 'centre' is frequently used as a synonym for them, explicitly in the case of the architectural firm Spridd's. Even so, only one of them – the one designed by Johan Celsing – is actually located anywhere near the geographical centre of the neighbourhood. This semantic incongruity suggests that a town 'centre' may now be located squarely on the periphery of a community. This development can be considered innovative; these new mosque structures offer both religious and other social functions in a centre far from the geographical middle.

Indeed, as mosques have recently been built or planned in numerous communities around Sweden, their centrality or marginality – spatial or social – has often been to the fore in debates. A widely discussed example is architect Björn Sahlqvist's lavish, 2,000-square-metre Gothenburg Mosque, which opened in June 2011 at a cost of around 67 million Swedish kronor.[14] Its prominence and position in a public park (albeit on the edges of a major highway) led to vehement protests against it. Chauvinist groups launched attacks on the grounds that the group was too peripheral to Swedish society to occupy such a visually central position. Even as the Swedish Church continues to lose members and suffers from low attendance at religious services, it remains relevant to ask whether other kinds of religious structures have returned to the nexus of the Swedish community in the twenty-first century, even if they do not always grow around their physical nuclei. Furthermore, the mosque of today and the church of the past might be said to represent many of the same values. As social centres, they stand as counterweights to the consumerist tendencies found in other *centra*, which have increasingly become mere malls, and their social services instead reflect the conservative dimensions of the religious groups that stand behind them. The symbolic and architecturally iconic presence of these new designs – along with the incredible sums spent on constructing them – indicate their growing importance for everyday community life.

The mosques now being developed draw on this spiritual trend while also providing clues about what happens when a Million Programme neighbourhood outgrows its secular *centrum*. Changes in demographics and the very 'idea of Swedishness', here apply at the scale of the neighbourhood. In this sense, the use of plots that work against the original designers' rectilinear ideal offers insight not only into how the social structures of the community are being altered for the 'new Swedish' programmes of the present, but also into how the neighbourhood is being remade from structural and physical points of view.[15] These projects offer new ideas about how to retrofit the supposedly monolithic Million Programme neighbourhoods of the past for the Sweden of the present and the future.

Intriguingly, such buildings comprise many of the elements included in the Million Programme town centres built during the project's heyday: shops, gathering spaces for community activities, educational facilities, athletic facilities, and places for food preparation and consumption. As an article featured in the local Järva paper, *Norra Sidan*,

Figure 11.6   Rendering, Multicultural Center. Source: Spridd AB.

argued explicitly, each mosque is 'more than [a] place for prayer'.[16] For example, Spridd's features shops along its front façade, a café, and a women's area that includes a sauna and exercise equipment in a mosque of 1,900 square metres.

Over five storeys, the new building for the Stockholm Large Mosque Organisation includes 7,875 square metres of space and will offer a restaurant, shops, library, educational facilities and offices. Celsing's will include offices, a gym, and a recreation centre for children (*fritidsgård*). The projects thus question whether the traditional town square – the public space par excellence of the nineteenth century, later transformed into the *centrum* of the modernist Million Programme – requires the emphasis on open space that Dergalin and Stäck highlighted in their 1964 articles. Rather than the suburban typology of the open square surrounded by 'residential service' (*boendeservice*), these new facilities are all contained in one large building.

New mosques – designed by Swedish architects – are often reminiscent of the *Kulturhus* ('cultural houses' or 'centres') designed in central Swedish urban zones during the modernist era.[17] They recall the notion of the 'social condenser', but in its Koolhaasian 'distortion' that privatises the concept 'whose publicness … constitutes its very kernel'.[18] In other words, these planned 'megastructures' offer similar forms of service to their *Kulturhus* predecessors, yet they radically shift their geographies from urban to suburban Sweden and reconstitute one of the essential architectural representations of new modern life in the 'Middle Way' as a space for private use.

Here, from the scale of urban planning to that of architecture, the 'production of [community] space' creates the town centre needed in the New Sweden, using as its parallel and paradigm a different inherited model, the Cultural House. Lefebvre's notion of 'dialectical centrality' is useful here, where centres are 'full or empty … infinite or finite' at the same time.[19] Mosques are located squarely in peripheries, where they remain out of view to the majority of society, yet they are also centres, both as points in geographical space and as social condensers. Following Lefebvre, then, mosques suggest 'simultaneity' and show how centrality is movable.[20]

Furthermore, these projects engage in an intriguing dialogue with the universalist tendencies of their forebears, which assumed that a *centrum* was a non-exclusive place for all citizens. The name 'multicultural centre', which was originally used for the Spridd project, implied an intentional openness to visits from anyone and everyone in the Rinkeby community and beyond.

Figure 11.7 Model, Multicultural Center. Source: Jennifer Mack.

The reality is that one congregation of Somali-Swedish Muslims has commissioned it, and that others in larger Rinkeby may feel – if not in explicit terms or regulations – unwelcome. To address this concern, the group has also proposed the inclusion of a youth centre on the edge of the structure. There, teenagers who are not members of the congregation could (at least in theory) come to interact with others in their age group without having to travel through the space of the mosque itself. The faith group believes that this will enable a larger use of the structure among members of the community who are not Somali, not Muslim, and perhaps not even aware of the identity of the primary use of the building. Likewise, the shops along the front façade of the structure will enable the sale of Somali and other goods, which may certainly have an appeal to customers beyond the limits of those who come specifically to pray.

At the same time, the inclusion of multiple functions in their designs lends these mosques another kind of flexibility that may, in a certain respect, mirror that of the earlier Million Programme town centres. The sizeable, open prayer spaces suggest that they could easily be used for other purposes, or that other groups could potentially use their shops and restaurants in the future. As architectural historian Johan

Mårtelius argues, 'a mosque is more than most other religious edifices a public space that at its foundation has a great universality … easily converted to other purposes'.[21] This inbuilt programmatic flexibility signals that the Million Programme town-centre prototype may have met a particularly conducive contemporary counterpart in the form of these new mosques.

Moving against the grid

Another shift in the perception of acceptable community space concerns the urban form of the blocks. Dergalin, Stäck and their contemporaries designing other Million Programme new towns across Sweden privileged the rectilinear block as part of a comprehensive, holistic neighbourhood design. These 'rational' forms made internal subdivisions legible and articulated an urban structure that functioned as one complete mass. The Rinkeby designers espoused such aims openly, writing:

> The regular block pattern makes it easier to achieve a high utilisation and a dense, urban character within the built areas, something that is judged to be worth striving for and that is included as an

Figure 11.8 Rendering, Johan Celsing's Rinkeby Mosque. Source: Celsing Arkitektkontor AB.

Figure 11.9 Pictogram of a mosque in the skyline of a Million Programme neighbourhood. Source: Spridd AB.

essential part of the goals laid out for the work on the general plan. The regular blocks can be adapted relatively easily to needs during further planning.[22]

Celsing's project, located at the heart of the original neighbourhood, uses the existing block structure as its outer perimeter, yet turns diagonally to allow worshippers to face Mecca.

The mosque for the Stockholm Large Mosque Organisation ignores the grid entirely in an open field surrounded by grass. Rather than

Figure 11.10 Rendering, Multicultural Center. Source: Spridd AB.

attempting to integrate their neoclassical mosque into the existing assembly of urban components or, conversely, to position the building as a serenely bucolic contrast to them, the architects incorporate elements of both. Finally, the Multicultural Centre is located where the grid crashes dramatically against the highway that bounds the neighbourhood, leaving an asymmetrical space in between.

This plot of land, which was previously deemed nearly impossible to use for anything but an industrial function, has paradoxically allowed the architects to develop a unique and potentially iconic architectural form.

In short, the three new mosques rethink the place of religion in Swedish suburbs, filling gaps in their social and material worlds while revising the rules of the original plans. Mosques function as new *centra*, offering new approaches to religious spaces, neighbourhood-level community structures and geographies, and, most importantly, Swedish public space.

New centres, new peripheries

Indeed, if the classic Million Programme *centrum* has, over time, adapted to new users and new uses, the mosques that will soon appear in stucco, brick, concrete and stone in the neighbourhoods of Rinkeby and Tensta comprise many of the elements that architects and planners included in town centres built in the project's heyday. The *centrum* of the 1960s offered local residents shops, gathering spaces for community activities, educational facilities, sports centres, and places for food preparation and consumption. In so doing, they served as the cornerstone of social programmes linking citizenship in the modern Swedish welfare state to a 'rationalised', modernist built environment.

The future public spaces that Celsing, Rashid with Tengbom, and Spridd have designed as mosques for specific groups offer operationally significant and architecturally iconic places for prayer, as one might expect. Simultaneously, however, these buildings provide a panoply of services: restaurants, cafés, shopping, youth centres, offices, libraries and other gathering spaces. In this sense, they both complement and potentially replace the traditional functions that the Million Programme *centrum* was meant to include. The new mosques seek to attract members and non-members, men and women, and everyone from the very elderly to small children, to use them.

Furthermore, while most purpose-built and planned mosques in Sweden are located in urban edges, open fields, or industrial zones, these buildings will nonetheless return religion to the centre of everyday neighbourhood life in areas like these, founded on secular rather than religious principles. Despite this change, the mosque has simultaneously become the 'multicultural' *centrum* of the neighbourhood at large: a place to eat, pray and shop. As designers and residents adapt the infamously rigid formal and social frameworks outlined in the original Million Programme plans and realised for the metropolitan Sweden of the 1960s and 1970s, new solutions to old problems emerge. Here, either turned from the grid towards Mecca, through an unusual *mélange* of the highway pastoral, or in the interstices, new Swedish public spaces meet new Swedish publics.

Notes

1. All translations from the Swedish are by the chapter author.
2. City of Stockholm, 2011.
3. Hall and Vidén, 2005.
4. Rådberg, 1972, 1994. Also Svedberg, 1980.
5. Hall, 1991.
6. Franzén and Sandstedt, 1981.
7. Mårtelius, 2012, pp. 155–6.
8. Cf. Mattsson, 2015.
9. Dergalin and Stäck, 1964a, 1964b.
10. Dergalin and Stäck, 1964a.
11. Cf. Mack, 2013, 2017.
12. Svanberg and Tydén, 2005, p. 383.
13. Andersson, 2013.
14. *GT*, 'Nya moskén invigd I Göteborg' 17 June, 2011. Accessed 9 January 2014, http://www.expressen.se/gt/nya-mosken-invigd-i-goteborg.
15. Mack, 2013.
16. Djalaie, 2012.
17. Cf. Grafe, 2010.
18. Murawski, 2017, p. 375.
19. Lefebvre, 1991.
20. Lefebvre, 1991.
21. Mårtelius, 2012.
22. Dergalin and Stäck, 1964b.

Bibliography

Andersson, Elisabet. 'En moské blir till', *Svenska Dagbladet*, 5 May 2013. Accessed 30 May 2013. http://www.svd.se/kultur/titta-in-i-modellen-av-stockholms-forsta-moskebyggnad_8143752.svd.
City of Stockholm. 'Kvalitetsprogram för gestaltning gällande KV LACKES 2, TENSTA', May 2011.
Dergalin, Igor and Josef M. Stäck. 'Generalplan för Rinkeby, Spånga kyrka och Tensta', *Arkitektur* 64, no. 5 (1964a): 119–24.
Dergalin, Igor and Josef M. Stäck. 'Rinkeby, Spånga kyrka och Tensta', *Plan* 3 (1964b): 101–7.
Djalaie, Rouzbeh. 'Ny moské ska bli mer än böneplats', *Norra Sidan/StockholmDirekt*, 10 April 2012. Accessed 23 September 2019. https://www.stockholmdirekt.se/nyheter/ny-moske-ska-bli-mer-an-boneplats/Dbbldj!IGSjPec8K3hJI90nnaf2cg/.

Franzén, Mats and Eva Sandstedt. *Välfärdsstat och byggande: Om efterkrigstidens nya stadsmönster i Sverige*. Uppsala: Arkiv förlag, 1981.

Grafe, Christoph. 'People's palaces: architecture, culture and democracy in two European post-war cultural centres'. PhD thesis, Delft University of Technology, 2010.

Hall, Thomas, ed. *Planning and Urban Growth in the Nordic Countries*. London: E. and F.N. Spon, 1991.

Hall, Thomas and Sonja Vidén. 'The Million Homes Programme: a review of the great Swedish planning project'. *Planning Perspectives* 20, no. 3 (2005): 301–28.

Lefebvre, Henri. *The Production of Space*, translated by Donald Nicholson-Smith. Oxford: Blackwell, 1991.

Mack, Jennifer S. 'New Swedes in the new town'. In *Use Matters: An Alternative History of Architecture*, edited by Kenny Cupers, 121–37. London: Routledge, 2013.

Mack, Jennifer S. *The Construction of Equality: Syriac Immigration and the Swedish City*. Minneapolis, MN: University of Minnesota Press, 2017.

Mårtelius, Johan. 'Minareternas sång.' In *Stockholm global stad* (Sankt Eriks årsbok), 154–7. Stockholm: Langenskiöld, 2012.

Mattsson, Helena. 'Where the motorways meet: architecture and corporatism in Sweden 1968'. In *Architecture and the Welfare State*, edited by Mark Swenarton, Tom Avermaete and Dirk van den Heuvel, 155–75. London: Routledge, 2015.

Murawski, Michał. 'Introduction: crystallising the social condenser', *Journal of Architecture* 22, no. 3 (2017): 372–86.

Råberg, Per G. *Funktionalistiskt genombrott: Radikal miljö och miljödebatt i Sverige, 1925–1931*. Stockholm: Norstedt, 1972.

Rådberg, Johan. *Den svenska trädgårdsstaden*. Stockholm: Statens råd för byggnadsforskning, 1994.

Svanberg, Ingvar and Mattias Tydén. *Tusen år av invandring: En svensk kulturhistoria*. 3rd edn. Stockholm: Dialogos, 2005.

Svedberg, Olle. 'Funktionalismens bostadsprogram – en bakgrundsskiss'. In *Funktionalismens genombrott och kris: Svenskt bostadsbyggande 1930–80*, 41–63. Stockholm: Arkitekturmuseet, 1980.

Part IV
Looking upward: power verticals

12
Verticality and centrality: the politics of contemporary skyscrapers[1]

Stephen Graham

Spike in the sand

February 2015. Twenty kilometres north of the ancient city of Jeddah, on the shores of the Red Sea, lies an unprepossessing building site (Figure 12.1). Its cluster of cranes, geometric concoctions of steel girders, and busy groups of bonded South Asian workers are common sights across the region's fast-expanding cities. The building site abuts hundreds of miles of dusty desert. It's hard to imagine that there could ever be sufficient demand from businesses, residents, tourists or investors for a super-tall tower in such a location. Certainly, anyone schooled in the traditional geographical ideas that it is intense competition for prestigious sites at the centres of large cities that drives skyscraper development would laugh at the prospect. And yet, by 2023, the building under construction on this site will stretch vertically upwards for over a kilometre to be – at least for a time – the tallest skyscraper in the world.

This fact is even more remarkable when it is realised that this tower has actually been downsized. A combination of the 2009 financial crisis and in-depth geological excavations meant that an earlier design – completing the full vertical mile to mimic Frank Lloyd Wright's designs for 'The Illinois', a tower in Chicago in 1956 – was *reduced* in scale.

Anchoring a major new city, like most Saudi megaprojects, the $1.2 billion tower is being directly driven forward by the Saudi royal family. Prince Alwaleed bin Talal, nephew of the late King Abdullah, is chairman of the company building the tower. At least in part, Bin Talal is clearly building 'his' tower – a gateway to the holy Islamic cities of Mecca and Medina – in a personal bid to outdo Sheikh Mohamed bin Rashid Al

Figure 12.1 Construction of the Kingdom Tower in Jeddah, February 2015. Source: Ammar Shaker (CC BY-SA 4.0).

Maktoum's Burj Khalifa skyscraper in Dubai. Jeddah's Kingdom Tower symbolises perfectly how the geographies and politics of the world's tallest skyscrapers have been revolutionised over the last few decades.

Once, the tallest of such towers clustered only at the centres of the world's most important business, corporate and finance capitals in the capitalist heartlands of the Global North. Vertical symbols of the dominance of major corporations and capitalist business elites, they fed off extreme competition for sites, super-high land values and struggles to materialise corporate prestige in stone, steel, aluminium and glass.

By linking the real-estate industry both to speculators and to extending subterranean mining operations across the world to provide construction materials, the rising towers of New York and Chicago, in particular, created a new type of volumetric city where previously only a small area above the surface could be commodified and let. Air, in other words, could itself be monetised and enclosed into rising towers, a process that architecture academic Eric Höweler called a 'new speculative terrain of vertical extension'.[2]

Improved and safety-braked electric or hydraulic elevators and steel-frame construction technologies, brought in from the mining industry, were central to the emergence of skyscrapers as a building form. Just as important, though, was the new super metal of aluminium, which allowed the higher parts of the super-tall towers built from the 1930s onwards to be light enough to be borne safely by the structure and foundations below.[3] 'The modern skyscraper', the industry body the Aluminum Association claims, 'would not have been possible without aluminum'.[4]

The rising clusters of downtown skyscrapers in cities such as Chicago and New York, in turn, acted as powerful signifiers on the symbolic plane. In cinema, skyscrapers were widely portrayed metaphorically as symbols of career advancement 'up' within deeply hierarchical corporate organisations. Indeed, corporate skyscrapers were carefully designed to materialise physically the 'vertical' structure of the large corporation.

'The height of the building is a concrete metaphor of the company turnover', Italian journalist Marco D'Eramo emphasises. The luxury offices of CEOs look down from the highest floors in the heavens, the corporate minions slave away down near the ground, and career advancement can literally be measured by the physical ascent to be 'on top of the pile'.[5]

Crucially, also, corporate skyscraper headquarters became imbued as a symbolic representation of the power, reach and identity of corporations themselves.[6] Architects, developers and corporations searched hard for unique building forms which could be used to distinguish them from their competitors as cultural signifiers. They sought larger and taller structures to symbolise the financial and economic power of the tenant. And they worked to project 'their' building as an icon of the established and continuing power of their corporation.

'This is a discourse of stature, status, stability, establishment and estate', urban theorist Kim Dovey stresses. 'And [it] shares with these words the Greek root *sta*: "to stand".'[7]

The prolonged skyscraper 'race' between New York and Chicago dominated the building form in the twentieth century. Above all, the new towers were symbols of the aggressive, centripetal pull of capitalist urbanism, and of the growth of corporate headquarters organised to remotely control disparate and widely spread manufacturing, marketing and distribution.

As new building, materials and elevator technologies combined with the massive growth of the power and reach of corporations, insurance companies, airlines, retail operations, telegraph companies, banks and conglomerates, rising skyscrapers embodied a period of intense 'Manhattanism' – the structuring of a few dominant central cities based on skylines made up of clusters of skyscrapers.[8]

'All Manhattan's tall buildings had been content to confront each other in a competitive verticality', French philosopher Jean Baudrillard wrote in 2002, 'and the product of this was an architectural panorama reflecting the capitalist system itself – a pyramidal jungle, whose famous image [of Manhattan] stretched out before you as you arrived from the sea.'[9]

Just as the skyscraper-skyline emerged as the dominant symbol of the central US city, so skyscrapers loomed large as images of modernity and futurity within fiction, cinema, comic books, art, architecture and urbanism.[10] 'The skyscraper is not only the building of the century', the *New York Times*'s legendary architecture critic Ada Louise Huxtable wrote in 1984, 'it is also the single work of architecture that can be studied as the embodiment and expression of much that makes the century what it is.'

Skyscrapers, she continued, were key symbols of the power of consumer and corporate culture; they romanticised power and the intensity of the twentieth-century metropolis; they were literal embodiments of the promise of modernity, technology and 'progress'; and they were powerful icons of the most powerful nation on Earth. To Huxtable, 'the tall building probes our collective psyche as it probes the sky'.[11]

Crucially, it was the combination of the vertical skyscraper and the horizontal street grid that came to symbolise US urbanism in the second half of the twentieth century. Rem Koolhaas, in his extravagant 1978 paean to New York's skyscrapers *Delirious New York*, revelled in the ways 'the Grid's two-dimensional discipline also creates undreamt-of freedom for three-dimensional anarchy'. The street grid, he argued, 'defines a new balance between control and de-control in which the city can be at the same time ordered and fluid, a metropolis of rigid chaos'.[12]

To feminist critics, skyscrapers of twentieth-century Chicago and Manhattan, symbols of a muscular and heroically masculinised notion of US modernity, also inevitably reeked of an extreme, phallocentric patriarchy. 'The twentieth century urban skyscraper', architectural commentator Leslie Kanes Weisman writes, 'a pinnacle of patriarchal symbology, is rooted in the masculine mystique of the big, the erect, the forceful – the full balloon of the inflated masculine ego'. Urban skyscrapers, she believed, 'compete for individual recognition and domination while impoverishing human identity and the quality of life'.[13]

To symbolise such masculinised competition, New York skyscraper architects even paraded at balls dressed in effigies of their own towers. The buildings' designers were also not slow to celebrate their structures in highly sexual terms.[14] Architect Louis Sullivan, often called the 'Father of the Skyscraper', described a building by his colleague Henry Hobson Richardson – built using Sullivan's innovation of the girder box surrounded by non-load-bearing walls – as follows. 'Here is a *man* for you to look at', Sullivan gushed:

> ... a virile force – ... an entire male. It stands, in physical fact, a monument to trade, to the organized commercial spirit, to the power and progress of the age, to the strength and resource of individuality and force of character. ... Therefore have I called it, in a world of barren pettiness, a male; for it sings the song of procreant power, as others have squealed of miscegenation.[15]

And yet, not all twentieth-century skyscrapers emerged as powerful icons of the imagination. On the one hand, architect Minoru Yamasaki's twin World Trade Center towers, completed on Manhattan's tip in April 1973, were almost universally loathed. The towers, built by the Port Authority of New York and New Jersey as what they called a 'vertical port' to directly parallel the Authority's horizontal infrastructure of ports and airports,[16] quickly emerged as overbearing symbols of the crass extremes of domineering and destructive capital. They particularly came to symbolise both the destruction of street life by monolithic modernist structures and the growing economic monoculture of Fordist corporations in New York in the 1970s, with their concentration of corporate headquarters specialising in finance, insurance and real estate.

Marshall Berman lambasted the towers as 'brutal and overbearing ... expressions of an urbanism that disdained the city and its people'.[17] He especially decried the destruction of large swathes of older streetscapes in Downtown Manhattan which was necessary to build them as a 'manifestation of terrorism ... a destructive act'. In an eerie parallel with the mechanism of the towers' demise nearly three decades later, other critics of the project condemned their construction as a brutal act of 'urbicidal' violence – that is, violence against the city.[18] Sixteen acres of dense streetscape – including a thriving Middle Eastern neighbourhood – were erased to clear the ground for the construction of the Twin Towers.[19]

Figure 12.2 Construction of New York's World Trade Center, 1971. Public domain.

By startling contrast, 1930s icons like the Empire State and Chrysler buildings have often attracted extraordinary adulation and mythology.[20] 'Even at its inception', Toronto philosophy professor Mark Kingwell writes of the Empire State Building, 'the building was a strange palace of dreams, a heaven-seeking tower made of solid metal and stone, and serving the needs of business. Standing so firm, technology's latest last word, it appears nevertheless to shimmer and shift before our eyes.'[21]

The site of countless movies, the Empire State Building is a site of intense cinematic memory. As part of the rising skyline of twentieth-century Manhattan, it has long acted, with other towers, as a key symbol to migrants across the world of the opportunities offered by America. And as a (now historic) symbol of the future, the tower has also had huge global cultural and architectural impact. 'As with so many parts of New York', Kingwell suggests, 'even if this is your first visit, you know you've been here before.'[22]

Gigantic logos: nowhere into somewhere

Corporate headquarter-skyscrapers have, of course, not disappeared completely. However, processes of globalised urbanisation over the last few decades have led, in cities like Jeddah, Riyadh and Dubai, to the growth of the super-tall skyscraper as urban or national brand.

Such structures are being brought into existence by super-rich national elites as attempts to quickly manufacture sites and cities that matter, and that have a new degree of centrality, within contexts of the intense globalisation of leisure, tourism, finance, business and real estate. Real-estate specialist William Murray puts it succinctly. 'Supertall buildings are gigantic logos', he writes. They are 'brand identifiers for the countries that built them. They create a skyline, a marker and a recognizable shape that help us to remember, relate to and form positive associations about a place.'[23]

Changes in the technologies used in financial and corporate services, meanwhile, have made large towers less appropriate to the headquarters of many large corporations. Many such firms now occupy lower, boxier structures in downtowns or on the edges of big cities in order to house the boxy structures of contemporary trading flows and financial services complexes.

Both remaining and new corporate towers in the centres of New York and Chicago, meanwhile, are less and less marked as the symbols of large corporations. Indeed, in the aftermath of 9/11, many such corporations have increasingly sought more anonymous real estate; their efforts to build symbolic capital now relate less and less to the building of physical structures. Many of the largest skyscraper-users in the twentieth century have also been swept away by economic changes.

'Visibility is no virtue in the late capitalist society', writes architectural theorist Kazys Varnelis, perhaps overemphasising the demise of the skyscraper as corporate symbol:

The first outrageously tall skyscraper of the twentieth century, the 792' tall Woolworth building, completed in 1908, emptily symbolizes a chain of discount stores that closed in 1997, mainly due to competition from Wal-Mart which replaced the now-empty symbolic value of the towering corporate headquarters with the real economic utility of a computer database reputedly second in size only to that of the Pentagon.[24]

In addition, some central office towers in London and New York have, in turn, been converted to now more profitable residential use; most new towers in these cities are also residential towers built for the super-wealthy.[25]

Beyond the cores of older global cities, skyscraper construction has a different logic. Driven less by escalating land values and corporate semiology, the new skyscrapers are often material embodiments of contemporary dynamics for circulating the vast capitalist surpluses of oligarchs, oil sheikhs and global financial and super-rich elites. Since 1996, when the Petronas Towers opened in Kuala Lumpur, the tallest towers have been developed in the Middle East and Asia – the first time since the building of Europe's Romanesque and Gothic cathedrals that the world's tallest structures have not been in the West.[26]

Indeed, geographer Andrew Harris now identifies what he sees as a 'vertical fix' in the fast-moving political economies of capitalism.[27] By building highly vertical structures carefully orchestrated to emerge as the centre of huge cycles of hype, spectacle, branding and advertising, the new super-tall towers work to transform complex debt, investment and speculation into lucrative real-estate assets more powerfully than do other, less visible or less vertical structures. The new towers can thus emerge pretty much anywhere where such surpluses become grounded within ambitious megaprojects backed by hubristic local elites. The argument, these days, is very much 'if we build it, they will come'.

Most arguments that the new skyscraper towers are necessary to improve urban densities, reduce sprawl, increase 'sustainability' and so on are almost entirely specious. French urbanist Jean-Marie Huriot sees such discourses as little more than a smokescreen for the powerful symbolism of extreme, vertical architecture.[28] He emphasises the much higher build and operational costs of very tall compared with conventional buildings.

Calling the new towers 'deplorable symbols', Huriot concludes that, beyond the camouflaging rhetoric, the main reason for their proliferation can be found simply in 'the intimately linked symbolisms of *performance*, *prestige* and *power*' (italics original).[29] Questioning the lust for height as a de facto objective of planning policy in many contemporary cities, Huriot questions the motives of the radical verticalisation of cities in the name of 'urbanity' or 'iconicity'. 'One *must* build higher, ever higher', he writes. But with what societal goal? 'To sell, to speculate, to generate profit at the expense of truly urgent social issues? These towers are nothing but deplorable symbols ... Decision-makers, get your feet back on the ground and desecrate these towers and all that they symbolise!'[30]

The fact that a growing proportion of the height of super-tall sky-scrapers is so narrow that it is 'vanity height' – little wider than the lift shafts and therefore completely unlettable – adds further weight to Huriot's arguments. If the new towers were really a response to the need to house booming populations, increase urban density or improve 'sustainability', why design them so that large portions of the building are little more than unused monuments to the hubris of developers or the super-rich?

In 2013, the *ArchDaily*'s James Taylor-Foster calculated the proportion of new skyscrapers made up of unusable 'vanity' height around the world. In the UAE, the country with the largest proportion of vanity height, he found that, on average, 19 per cent of the height of skyscrapers was completely unlettable and unoccupiable. Of the combined height of the ten tallest skyscrapers in the world in 2013, moreover, 27 per cent was entirely superfluous 'vanity height'.[31] Fully 85 floors of Jeddah's 1 km Kingdom Tower – to be complete in 2023 – are too narrow to be lettable in any way whatsoever. Such statistics powerfully reaffirm architecture critic Deyan Sudjic's conclusion that 'There is of course something ludicrously childish about the irrational urge to build high, simply for the sake of being the world's highest'.[32]

It is clear that the new super-tall towers act as key anchors within the wider construction of what Mike Davis and Dan Monck have called 'dreamworlds of neoliberalism',[33] enclaves of largely unregulated capitalism organised around the production of speculative, fantasy landscapes for leisure, consumption, investment, finance and tourism. In a world of extending, identikit suburbs and transnational urban regions stretching to, and beyond, the horizon, the towers are engineered in ways that allow extreme verticality to signal (at least ambitions of) significance, power and centrality.

The competitive and much-hyped 'race' to build the tallest skyscraper only adds to the search for centrality, spectacle and symbolic capital in a struggle to evidence 'national arrival' on the world stage.[34] The Council for Tall Buildings and Urban Habitats, which is based in New York, calculates that in May 2019 there were twenty-three 'super-tall' skyscrapers over 400 m high in the world and three 'mega-talls' over 600 m – a category that didn't even exist a few years ago. Widespread debate, research and design efforts are already underway, moreover, for the next generation of 'ultra-talls': towers higher than 1.6 kilometres.

It is important not to neglect the political aspects of contemporary skyscraper development. Anthropologist Aihwa Ong emphasises the ways in which the building of spectacular vertical megaprojects can be seen as part of an effort by Asian and Middle Eastern states and their associated elites to attract speculative capital while asserting a self-assured sovereignty in the face of extremely mobile flows of finance, people and imagery. The frenzied building of spectacular structures, Ong stresses, works to leverage real-estate values while also raising hopes among many local stakeholders about urban and national futures. It helps build a world in which competition between rival cities and states becomes indexed and fetishised through the relative size and scale of vertical urban forms and spectacles.

Here, as with the skyscrapers in Chicago and New York in the late nineteenth century, mega-tall buildings gain their power through their inspiration of wonder, awe and terror, a technological sublime that makes it easy to connect them, in some putative vertical 'race', with similar structures around the world. 'This is the sublime terror of the abyss and the peak', business theorist Martin Parker writes, 'of elevation and descent'.[35] Above all, the structures work to offer what Ong calls 'promissory values about the geopolitical significance of the city and the country' within the changing geo-economics and geopolitics of global capitalism. In other words, 'a skyscraper … made nowhere suddenly into somewhere'.[36]

In such a context, the new super-tall towers tend to house little or no commercial space. Much more important are hotels, restaurants, leisure attractions, viewing platforms and extremely expensive super-luxury apartments from which owners and investors can look over their new domains.[37] In 2000, only five of the world's twenty tallest skyscrapers were mixed-use; by 2020, only five won't be.[38] Such a shift symbolises and reflects wider transformations of many cities from landscapes of production to centres of consumption and leisure.

Crucial to the success of the new towers is the way the buildings themselves become the focus for a myriad of symbols and marketing drives to represent the places that they spring from – and associated commercial and elite capital. 'The symbolic function of the iconic sky-scraper in the contemporary metropolis is to define the presence of the city on a world stage', UCL's Michele Acuto emphasises. Importantly, too, Acuto stresses how the towers emerge as dominating of aspiration and status locally, as symbols of the 'aspiration of local political, planning and real-estate elites on the world stage, and, as shorthand to signal and represent the locality in myriad of adverts, product placements and tourist and investment drives'.[39]

Also important for the rise of the new towers are the complex ways in which their ascent is lauded by a myriad of supine, superficial and boosterist media and architectural commentary. These endlessly reinforce discursive formulations that simplistically equate vertical height with power, wealth, importance, quality or modernity.

'Our vision for Kingdom Tower is one that represents the new spirit of Saudi Arabia', Adrian Smith, one of the Tower's Chicago-based architects, and a key designer, as part of the SOM practice, of super-tall towers across the world, stated in 2011. Not surprisingly side-stepping the House of Saud's truly execrable record of human rights abuses and its global promotion of terrorist violence, Smith continues:

> This tower symbolizes the Kingdom as an important global business and cultural leader, and demonstrates the strength and creative vision of its people.' … With its slender, subtly asymmetrical massing, the tower evokes a bundle of leaves shooting up from the ground – a burst of new life that heralds more growth all around it.[40]

Gordon Gill added, 'We're thrilled to be working with His Highness [Prince Alwaleed bin Talal] and Jeddah Economic Company to help define this path for the Kingdom.'[41]

Visitors to the viewing platform at the summit of the Burj Khalifa (Figure 12.3) are obliged to sit through a powerful audiovisual show before they can access the viewing platform and gaze down at the stunning panorama. Accompanied by spiritual ambient and oriental music, the video juxtaposes images of Rashid Al Maktoum's tall form and the building and claims that the tower 'is our symbol and our shield for the future progress of our land and children'.

Brazilian pastor René Breuel reflects, in a blog entry titled 'The tallest god in the world', that the experience 'felt more than anything like a religious atmosphere. To our surprise, we felt that we were walking into a temple, a temple dedicated to the greatness of that building.' The show finishes by giving the final word to the building itself – as though the edifice itself was excitedly proclaiming its own magnificence and agency in the world. 'A chill went down our spines as we read those tall,

Figure 12.3 Burj Khalifa, Dubai, anchor for a huge real-estate development. Public domain.

commanding, divine words', Breuel recalls. 'They were the words of a god.' Engraved on a wall in English and Arabic, those words were:

> *I am the power that lifts the world's head proudly skywards, surpassing limits and expectations.*

> *Rising gracefully from the desert and honouring the city with a new glow, I am an extraordinary union of engineering and art, with every detail carefully considered and beautifully crafted.*

> *I am the life force of collective aspirations and the aesthetic union of many cultures. I stimulate dreams, stir emotions and awaken creativity.*

> *I am the magnet that attracts the wide-eyed tourist, eagerly catching their postcard moment, the centre for the world's finest shopping, dining and entertainment and home for the world's elite.*

> *I am the heart of the city and its people; the marker that defines [developer] Emaar's ambition and Dubai's shining dream.*

> *More than just a moment in time, I define moments for future generations.*

> *I am Burj Khalifa.*[42]

To explain the contemporary fetish for 'iconic' tall towers and their super-fast elevators from a broader perspective, geographer Maria Kaika draws important links between the hypermobility of the world's corporate and super-rich elites and the often craven efforts to brand new skyscrapers as easily identifiable everyday objects. Here, London's new range of skyscrapers – nicknamed the 'Gherkin', the 'Shard', the 'Cheesegrater', the 'Walkie Talkie', and so on – offer especially powerful examples (Figure 12.4).

Kaika calls such structures, appropriately, 'autistic icons' or 'serial objects'. She links their proliferation to the hypermobility of global elites, and the ways in which such groups no longer tend to link their identities and financial fortunes to growth coalitions within one specific city (as did the likes of Guggenheim or Rockefeller in the twentieth century). Instead, those in control of the processes of neoliberal globalisation now seek to operate within networks of key global cities while not being limited – or indeed responsible – to one of them.

By developing strings of obviously identifiable toy-like skyscrapers, which quickly become crassly packaged as 'iconic', the so-called 'transnational capitalist class'[43] of occupiers, developers, rentiers and investors

Figure 12.4 The most (in)famous of London's supposedly 'iconic' crop of new skyscrapers: The Shard, left, and, across the river, the Walkie Talkie and the Gherkin, viewed from South London. Source: Daniel Chapman (CC BY 2.0).

benefits from the construction of extremely lucrative 'premium' products that saturate global media circuits.

Local planners and politicians, Kaika emphasises, in turn support the increased development of super-tall structures as necessary so that they are 'not left behind' in some putative 'race' between global cities. In global financial cities like London, the stress falls on the ways in which the new buildings will ostensibly become emblematic of the status of their cities as powerful and instantly recognisable 'global' hubs. Caught in the pincer between these forces, and the growing privatism and elitism of many urban planning regimes in neoliberalising cities, the city's resident population, Kaika argues, is often left to deal with arrogant landscapes of power made up of strings of poorly designed, highly secured and unreachable 'object[s] of desire' that are inaccessible to all but the elite or wealthy few.[44]

To compound matters still further, concerns about 'security' are now widely used to justify the fortification of the new skyscrapers – with their interior gardens, expensive roof-top restaurants and penthouse terraces – and their removal ever further from the wider public and the wider city. Such a process only aids the aura of extreme exclusivity and enigma that surrounds the new towers. In London, 'public spaces' around the base of the new towers are actually highly secured and privatised plazas, patrolled by private security forces who prohibit even photography.

Kaika emphasises:

> Even if the next skyscraper to be erected in London's or New York's skyline does not relate to anything that Londoners or New Yorkers can identify with, the city's public is nevertheless bombarded by so many expert opinions on its significance, sublime design, and aesthetic value, that when it is finally erected, all that's left to do is 'kneel down' and admire it, hoping that the subsequent ritualisation of the building into the city's everyday life might justify this belief.[45]

Worse still, the hyping of new towers often works to override already squeezed traditions of democratic accountability in urban planning. Maria Kaika emphasises how the public enquiry over the 'Walkie Talkie' tower completed in late 2014 in central London – and memorably described by the *Guardian* as 'bloated, inelegant and thuggish'[46] – was dominated by promises that the structure would emerge as 'iconic'. Francis Golding from the developer Land Securities exemplified this attitude when he prophesied that '[the] "Walkie Talkie" tower [will] become as iconic a part of London's skyline as the ... "Gherkin"'.[47]

Renzo Piano's 'Shard' on London's South Bank, meanwhile, was widely lionised within messianic discourses about the future of London before it was even constructed. 'Something … significant [is] simmering south of the Thames', gushed *The Independent*. 'Something that transcends iconic architectural statements, and is poised to deliver a key step-change in vertical city planning. We're talking size, and we're talking clumps. The Shard, designed by the brilliant Renzo Piano, may prove to be a building of the highest quality and drama.'[48]

Fallen towers: 'destructural works'

Players of the hugely popular *Battlefield 4* urban warfare video game, meanwhile, are already desperate to incorporate the Burj Khalifa into the simulated cityscapes within which they continually do virtual battle. 'As someone who lives in Dubai and sees this tower everyday', one exhorts, 'I would love to see Dubai as a map in Battlefield 4. Destroying the Burj Khalifa would be an awesome sight!'[49]

The destruction of skyscrapers has, indeed, long been a preoccupation within popular culture. Manhattan's towers have been brought to the ground so many times and in so many ways that a book of several hundred pages has been necessary to encompass the myriad of devastations within cartoons, films, novels and video games.[50]

Just as the erection of New York's towers became the cliché of rampant modernity and futurity, so their rapid and violent demise has long been the signifier par excellence of rapid and apocalyptic Armageddon. A swathe of post-apocalyptic films have so shaped the collective culture of urbanism that a stock response to the all-too-real 9/11 catastrophe was that it was 'just like a scene in a movie!' The 9/11 attacks 'were organised as epic horror cinema with meticulous attention to the *mise-en-scéne*', urban critic Mike Davis writes:

> The hijacked planes were aimed to impact precisely at the vulnerable border between fantasy and reality… . Thousands of people who turned on their televisions on 9/11 were convinced that the cataclysm was just a broadcast, a hoax. They thought they were watching rushes from the latest Bruce Willis film.[51]

Of course, the perpetrators of the 9/11 attacks were interested in much more than the chain of apocalyptic media events that their violence set off and their resonances with Western popular culture. Their actions were a careful and premeditated strategy of attacking the connections between extreme vertical modernism, aerial mobility and the geo-economic power of the West – while also bringing a real-time spectacle of death and mayhem to the heart of metropolitan power.

'A great tower is … vulnerable', theologian Lilli Nye stresses. 'By virtue of its height and its hubris, it is inevitably precarious; it's always exposed – to instability, to attack, to forces greater than itself, such as the downward pull of gravity.'[52]

Detailed research into the background of Mohamed Atta, the leader of the 9/11 attackers and the pilot of the first plane to hit the World Trade Center, destroying the north tower, suggests that targeting the most vertical and extreme examples of modernist verticality – out of the full gamut of possibilities of Metropolitan America – was no accident.

Atta was a graduate in architecture from Cairo University and a master's graduate in urban planning from Hamburg-Harburg Technical University. Already radicalised, he completed a research dissertation in Hamburg in 1994 on the tumultuous architectural changes then emerging in the ancient city of Aleppo, Syria (a long-standing research focus of Dittmar Machule, Dean of the Department, and a city since massively damaged in the Syrian civil war).

Atta's thesis, 'City planning in the Syrian town of Aleppo', lambasts the local employment of Western planners in the modernisation of the city and decries the destruction of traditional neighbourhoods and ancient, labyrinthine souks with raised flyovers, fast-food outlets and ramparts of high-rise modernist housing blocks and hotels. Atta argued that high-rise modernising buildings in Aleppo – and elsewhere – needed to be destroyed because they both desecrated traditional Islamic townscapes and symbolised the invasion of Western culture into Islamic heartlands.

In order to restore traditional Islamic culture, Atta earmarked all the accoutrements of Western modernism for demolition with his suggested planning scheme. They were to be replaced once again by the dense, finely woven souks and neighbourhoods of what he called the 'Islamic-oriental city'. Such a process would, Atta stressed, also remove all non-Islamic kufrs and tourists.[53] 'The traditional structures of the society in all areas should be re-erected', Atta wrote. Enclosed housing along traditional lines would be used to incarcerate woman so as not to 'engender emancipatory thoughts of any kind', a development which he views as 'out of place in Islamic society'.[54]

Atta met some of his fellow hijackers through an Islamic student group that he founded in Hamburg. Further radicalised at Hamburg's al-Tauhid Mosque, Atta deepened his loathing of Western skyscraper and modernist architecture both during trips to his fast-changing home city of Cairo and during professional work at the Hamburg architectural firm,

Plankontor. Arriving eventually at a jihadi training camp in Afghanistan, Atta became committed to martyrdom. He became bent on apocalyptic violence.[55]

Once selected by Osama bin Laden to lead the 9/11 strikes, Atta did not personally select the World Trade Center as the main target of his attacks. This decision fell to Khalid Sheikh Mohammed, a mechanical engineer by background, whose nephew Ramsi Yousef had attempted but failed to level the buildings with a truck bomb in 1993. Indeed, the two had long looked through illustrated books of US skyscrapers, looking for targets.[56]

The Twin Tower targets – attacked by repurposing Western systems of vertical and aerial mobility – were certainly in keeping with Atta's broader views. Representing modern, Western, verticalised urbanism, they were obvious targets for Wahhabist ideologues mobilised against the globe-spanning economic and cultural power of Western modernity. A perceived affront to God Himself in their verticality, they were the culmination of a Manhattan skyline that itself symbolised, to the attackers, all the decadence and immorality of Western urban culture.

Constructed to force people to take notice of their height and bulk, the towers by their destruction would kick off the ultimate global media spectacle – in real time. 'The modern city', philosophers Avishai Margalit and Ian Buruma write,

> representing all that shimmers just out of our reach, all the glittering arrogance and harlotry of the West, has found its icon in the Manhattan skyline, reproduced in millions of posters, photographs, and images, plastered all over the world. You cannot escape it…. It excites longing, envy, and sometimes blinding rage.[57]

The attacks were clearly designed to represent divinely inspired retribution against the ways in which extreme vertical modernism symbolised the concentration of wealth and power within the geopolitical heartlands of the dominating Western metropolis. Given Atta's lack of formal religious training, US novelist Jarett Kobek, who has written a semifictionalised account of Atta's life, emphasises strongly that 'looking at 9/11 architecturally makes a lot more sense than looking at it through the lens of religion'.[58]

Osama bin Laden, a trained civil engineer himself, applauded the atrocities in New York in September 2001, citing the vertical elevation of the targeted structures as an affront to his fundamentalist cosmographic conception of an all-powerful Islamic God controlling a ground-based humanity from the heavens. 'There is America, hit by God in one of its softest spots', he said in a speech on 7 October 2001:[59]

> Its greatest buildings were destroyed, thank God for that. There is America, full of fear from its north to its south, from its west to its east. Thank God for that.... . To America, I say only a few words to it and its people. I swear by God, who has elevated the skies without pillars, neither America nor the people who live in it will dream of security before we live it in Palestine, and not before all the infidel armies leave the land of Muhammad, peace be upon him.

What Osama bin Laden would have made of the rapid skyward growth of the 'pillar' of the Kingdom Tower in Jeddah, a city with a revered Islamic history in which he lived for long periods as a child and student, can only be imagined. His comments, though, leave us with a startling paradox. For the huge construction company established by Osama bin Laden's father in 1931 – now one of the largest of global construction corporations – is both a key investor and main constructor in the building of Jeddah's Kingdom Tower.[60]

There is also irrefutable evidence that various members of the Saudi royal family – along with their litany of Wahhabist religious clerics – were the principal financiers of al-Qaeda and the Taliban in the 1990s, in the run-up to the 2001 attacks as part of their long-standing support for Islamist jihad across the world. It has been estimated that between 1921 and 1991 Saudi royal and religious elites spent between \$100 and \$200 billion exporting the Wahhabist ideology that is at the root of the Islamist violence of the Taliban, al-Qaeda and ISIS. Fifteen of the eighteen hijackers were also Saudi nationals.[61]

The profound and unsettling links between the creation and destruction of vertical towers within the past two decades become clear and darkly ironic at this juncture. As ever, the politics of creation and destruction connect seamlessly. Social and architectural theorist Ben Bratton has drawn close parallels between the operation of al-Qaeda as a kind of 'transnational firm' or 'figurative corporation' bent on what he calls architectural 'destructural works' and Osama bin Laden's father's immense construction conglomerate.

Bratton writes:

> It is not surprising that this New Economy transnational firm [al-Qaeda] would be led by the son of one of the most powerful public works engineers in all of Saudi Arabia, of the man who literally built that kingdom, and would subcontract urban planners, like Mohammed Atta, to carry out its plans.

Reflecting on such a situation, he continues, 'it's not just fitting skills to tasks, nor ironic coincidence, it is a spiritual politics of space'.[62]

And yet, as we saw with our earlier discussion of the construction of the World Trade Center, the profound parallels between skyscraper construction and skyscraper terrorism run deeper still. Unusually, Eric Darton, author of *Divided We Stand: A Biography of New York's World Trade Center*, directly compares the figures of the Towers' prime destroyer – Mohamed Atta – and its creator – Japanese architect Minoru Yamasaki – at a metaphysical level.

Darton identifies what he calls 'a kindred spirit linking the apparently polar realms of skyscraper terrorist and skyscraper builder'.[63] He argues that the enormous physical forces necessary to both create and destroy skyscrapers can only succeed though extreme and violent levels of abstraction – what he calls 'daydreams of domination'.

Both construction and violent erasure entail the use of the professional and calculative power of architects and engineers. This is used on the one hand to push up an immense and abstract set of modernist towers against the forces of gravity and on the other to 'unbuild' them through calculating the structural properties of the target and the capabilities of the truck bomb or the velocity and power of the impacting aircraft.[64]

'We are creatures of the earth and air', Darton concludes, 'capable of functioning with our heads in the clouds so long as our feet remain on the ground.'[65] He finishes, however, by drawing metaphysical connections between the hubris that raises vast towers, and that which brings them down. 'Rising toward the stratosphere', Darton writes, 'we feel we have broken free of gravity. When that illusion possesses us, it is not long before our ascent finds its opposite number in the terror of the fall.'[66]

Notes

1. This chapter is adapted from a paper published in *City* 20, no. 5 (2016): 755–71.
2. Höweler, 2003.
3. See Sheller, 2014.
4. See Aluminum Association, 2019.
5. D'Eramo, 2003, p. 86.
6. Dovey, 1991, p. 286.
7. Dovey, 1991, p. 286.
8. Koolhaas, 1978, p. 291.
9. Jean Baudrillard, 2002, pp. 42–4.
10. See, for example, Schleier, 2009; Sanders, 2001, pp. 4–6.
11. Huxtable, 1984, p. 11.
12. Koolhaas, 1978, p. 20.
13. Weisman, 2000, p. 1.
14. Weisman, 2000, p. 1.

15. Sullivan, 1979, pp. 29–30.
16. Darton, 2001.
17. Berman, 2002.
18. Huxtable, 1970.
19. See Smith, 2006, chapter 5.
20. Daniel Libeskind, in pushing through his designs for the 'Freedom Tower' – later renamed '1 World Trade Center' – on the site of the World Trade Center towers, often talked of his new skyscraper as a way of restoring the 'spiritual peak' of New York. See Kamin, 2010, p. 36.
21. Kingwell, 2006, p. 14.
22. Kingwell, 2006, p. 28.
23. Murray, *Council for Tall Buildings and Urban Habitat,* 2012.
24. Varnelis, 2005.
25. See Barton and Watts, 2013.
26. Sudjic, 2006, p. 356.
27. Harris, 2015.
28. Huriot, 2012.
29. Huriot, 2012.
30. Huriot, 2012.
31. Taylor-Foster, 2013.
32. Sujdic, 2006, p. 319.
33. Davis and Monk, 2011.
34. Currently, 'super-tall' skyscraper projects in Azerbaijan, China and Qatar are at various stages of development in the struggle to top Dubai's Burj Khalifa's current record of 830 m. They may even surpass the 1 km height of Jeddah's Kingdom Tower. See Ong, 2011.
35. Parker, 2015, p. 218.
36. Sudjic, 2006, p. 358.
37. Fully 160 floors of the Kingdom Tower's total of 200 will be used for apartments, hotels and viewing platforms; the tower's largest penthouse will have its own private exterior gardens 3,000ft (915m) up in the air.
38. Risen, 2013.
39. Acuto, 2010, p. 274.
40. *Architecture and Design*, 2011
41. *Architecture and Design*, 2011.
42. Breuel, 2013.
43. Sklair, 2001, pp. 5–6.
44. Kaika, 2011, p. 986.
45. Kaika, 2011, p. 983.
46. Moore, 2015.
47. Clift, 2007. Clift's title suggested that the Walkie Talkie would become a loved symbol of London. Instead, this execrable building has merely generated anger, bewilderment and satire. Indeed, in 2015, it was 'awarded' the Carbuncle Cup award for the UK's worst new building of that year.
48. 'Architecture: the sky's the limit', *Independent*, 11 February 2008, p. 12.
49. Battlefield 4 discussion forum, 2013.
50. Page, 2008.
51. Davis, 2002, p. 5.
52. Nye, 2011.
53. The term from the Qur'an for non-believers or infidels; see Brook, 2009.
54. Brook, 2009.
55. See Raban, 2002.
56. As well as being highly symbolic prestige targets, skyscrapers were relatively easy to see from the air amidst the complex landscapes of cities. See McDermott, 2005, p. 167.
57. Buruma and Margalit, 2002, p. 4.
58. Wedell, 2012; see Kobek, 2011.
59. Bin Laden, 2001.
60. See Mawani, 2011.
61. Summers and Swan, 2011; Hubbard and Shane, 2015.
62. Bratton, 2009.
63. Darton, 2001.

64. It must be stressed here that there is no evidence that Atta and his colleagues had any way of predicting, let alone planning, the final collapse of the buildings once they were struck by the two aircraft.
65. Darton, 2001.
66. Darton, 2001.

Bibliography

Acuto, Michele. 'High-rise Dubai urban entrepreneurialism and the technology of symbolic power'. *Cities* 27, number 4 (2010): 272–84.

Aluminum Association. 'The modern skyscraper: made possible with aluminum'. Accessed 27 July 2019. http://www.aluminum.org/modern-skyscraper.

Architecture and Design. 'World's next tallest tower – being built by Bin Ladens', *Architecture and Design*, 5 August 2011. Accessed 27 July 2019. https://www.architectureanddesign.com.au/news/industry-news/world-s-next-tallest-tower-being-built-by-bin-lade#.

'Architecture: the sky's the limit', *Independent*, 11 February 2008.

Barton, James and Steve Watts. 'Office vs. residential: the economics of building tall', *CTBUH Journal* 2 (2013): 38–43. Accessed 13 November 2019. http://global.ctbuh.org/resources/papers/download/255-office-vs-residentialthe-economics-of-building-tall.pdf.

Battlefield 4 discussion forum post (online). Accessed 13 November 2019. http://www.reddit.com/r/battlefield_4/comments/1g83ob/wouldnt_a_part_of_dubai_be_a_great_map_for_bf4, 2013.

Baudrillard, Jean. *The Spirit of Terrorism and Requiem for the Twin Towers*, translated by Chris Turner. London: Verso, 2002.

Berman, Marshall. 'When bad buildings happen to good people'. In *After the World Trade Center: Rethinking New York City*, edited by Michael Sorkin and Sharon Zukin, 1–12. New York: Routledge, 2002.

Bin Laden, Osama. Untitled speech. *Al Jazeera TV*, 7 October 2001. English translation accessed 23 September 2019. https://www.theguardian.com/world/2001/oct/07/afghanistan.terrorism15.

Bratton, Benjamin H. 'Figures of destructuration: terrorism, architecture, social form', *bratton.info*, November 2009. Accessed 27 July 2019. http://www.bratton.info/projects/texts/figures-of-destructuration-2001–02/.

Breuel, René. 'The tallest god in the world', *Wondering Fair*, 21 October 2013. Accessed 27 July 2019. https://wonderingfair.com/2013/10/21/the-tallest-god-in-the-world/.

Brook, Daniel. 'The architect of 9/11', *Slate*, 10 September 2009.

Clift, Patrick. 'Walkie Talkie would become "loved symbol of London"', *EGI News*, 8 March 2007. Accessed 27 July 2019. https://www.egi.co.uk/news/walkie-talkie-would-become-loved-symbol-of-london/.

Darton, Eric. 'The Janus face of architectural terrorism: Minoru Yamasaki, Mohammad Atta and the World Trade Center', *openDemocracy*, 8 November 2001. Accessed 27 July 2019. https://www.opendemocracy.net/en/article_94jsp/.

Davis, Mike. *Dead Cities, and Other Tales*. New York: New Press, 2002.

Davis, Mike and Daniel Bertrand Monk, eds. *Evil Paradises: Dreamworlds of Neoliberalism*. New York: New Press, 2011.

d'Eramo, Marco. *The Pig and the Skyscraper: Chicago: A History of Our Future*, translated by Graeme Thomson. London: Verso, 2003.

Dovey, Kim. 'Tall storeys: Corporate towers and symbolic capital', *EDRA* 22 (1991): 285–94.

Harris, Andrew. 'Vertical urbanisms: opening up geographies of the three-dimensional city', *Progress in Human Geography* 39, no. 5 (2015): 601–20.

Höweler, Eric. *Skyscraper: Designs of the Recent Past and for the Near Future*. London: Thames and Hudson, 2003.

Hubbard, Ben and Scott Shane. 'Pre-9/11 ties haunt Saudis as new accusations surface', *New York Times*, 4 February 2015. Accessed 10 August 2019. http://www.nytimes.com/2015/02/05/world/middleeast/pre-9–11-ties-haunt-saudis-as-new-accusations-surface.html.

Huriot, J.-M. 'Towers of power', translated by Oliver Waine, *Metropolitiques.eu*, 25 January 2012. Accessed 19 August 2019. http://www.metropolitiques.eu/Towers-of-Power.html.

Huxtable, Ada Louise. *Will They Ever Finish Bruckner Boulevard? A Primer on Urbicide*. New York: Macmillan, 1970.

Huxtable, Ada Louise. *The Tall Building Artistically Reconsidered: The Search for a Skyscraper Style*. New York: Pantheon Books, 1984.

Kaika, Maria. 'Autistic architecture: The fall of the icon and the rise of the serial object of architecture', *Environment and Planning D: Society and Space* 29, no. 6 (2011): 968–92.

Kamin, Blair. *Terror and Wonder: Architecture in a Tumultuous Age*. Chicago: University of Chicago Press, 2010.

Kingwell, Mark. *Nearest Thing to Heaven: The Empire State Building and American Dreams*. New Haven, CT: Yale University Press, 2006.

Kobek, Jarett. *Atta*. Los Angeles: Semiotext(e), 2011.

Koolhaas, Rem. *Delirious New York: A Retroactive Manifesto for Manhattan*. New York: Monacelli Press, 1978.

Margalit, Avishai and Ian Buruma, 'Occidentalism', *New York Review of Books*, 17 January 2002. Accessed 10 August 2019. http://sites.math.rutgers.edu/~sussmann/papers/occidentalism.html.

Margalit, Avishai and Ian Buruma. *Occidentalism: The West in the Eyes of its Enemies*, London: Penguin, 2005.

Martin, Ian. 'The city that privatised itself to death: "London is now a set of improbable sex toys poking gormlessly into the air"', *Guardian*, 24 February 2015. Accessed 27 July 2019. https://www.theguardian.com/politics/2015/feb/24/the-city-that-privatised-itself-to-death-london-is-now-a-set-of-improbable-sex-toys-poking-gormlessly-into-the-air.

Mawani, Vrushti. 'Kingdom Tower by Bin Laden group will be the world's tallest building', *Industry Leaders Magazine*, 5 August 2011. Accessed 27 July 2019. https://www.industryleadersmagazine.com/kingdom-tower-by-bin-laden-group-will-be-the-worlds-tallest-building/.

McDermott, Terry. *Perfect Soldiers: The 9/11 Hijackers: Who They Were, Why They Did It*. London: Politico's, 2005.

Moore, Rowan. 'Walkie Talkie review – bloated, inelegant, thuggish', *Observer*, 4 January 2015. Accessed 27 July 2019. https://www.theguardian.com/artanddesign/2015/jan/04/20-fenchurch-street-walkie-talkie-review-rowan-moore-sky-garden.

Murray, William. 'Selling tall: The branding and marketing of tall buildings'. In *Asia Ascending: Age of the Sustainable Skyscraper City*, edited by Antony Wood, Timothy Johnson and Guo-Qiang Li, 302–7. Chicago: Council on Tall Buildings and Urban Habitat, 2012. Accessed 27 July 2019. http://global.ctbuh.org/resources/papers/download/261-selling-tall-the-branding-and-marketing-of-tall-buildings.pdf.

Nye, Lilli. 'Axis Mundi: The meaning of towers'. Sermon, Theodore Parker Unitarian Universalist Church, West Roxbury, 11 September 2011. Accessed 27 July 2019. http://www.tparker-church.org/sermons/20112012/11-0911Axis%20Mundi.htm.

Ong, Aihwa. 'Hyperbuilding: Spectacle, speculation, and the hyperspace of sovereignty'. In *Worlding Cities: Asian Experiments and the Art of Being Global*, edited by Ananya Roy and Aihwa Ong, 205–26. Chichester: Wiley-Blackwell, 2011.

Page, Max. *The City's End: Two Centuries of Fantasies, Fears, and Premonitions of New York's Destruction*. New Haven, CT: Yale University Press, 2008.

Parker, Martin. 'Vertical capitalism: skyscrapers and organization', *Culture and Organization* 21, no. 3 (2015): 217–34.

Raban, Jonathan. 'Rebels with a cause', *Guardian*, 4 March 2002. Accessed 27 July 2019. https://www.theguardian.com/theguardian/2002/mar/04/features11.g2.

Risen, Clay. 'The rise of the supertalls', *Popular Science*, 15 February 2013. Accessed 27 July 2019. https://www.popsci.com/technology/article/2013–02/rise-supertalls/.

Sanders, James. *Celluloid Skyline: New York and the Movies*. New York: Alfred A. Knopf, 2001.

Schleier, Merrill. *Skyscraper Cinema: Architecture and Gender in American Film*. Minneapolis: University of Minnesota Press, 2009.

Sheller, Mimi. *Aluminum Dreams: The Making of Light Modernity*. Cambridge, MA: MIT Press, 2014.

Sklair, Leslie. *The Transnational Capitalist Class*. Oxford: Blackwell, 2001.

Smith, Terry. *The Architecture of Aftermath*. Chicago: University of Chicago Press, 2006.

Sudjic, Deyan. *The Edifice Complex: How the Rich and Powerful – and Their Architects – Shape the World*. New York: Penguin, 2006.

Sullivan, Louis H. *Kindergarten Chats and Other Writings*. New York: Dover Publications, 1979.

Summers, Anthony and Robbyn Swan. 'The Kingdom and the towers', *Vanity Fair*, 30 June 2011. Accessed 27 July 2019. https://www.vanityfair.com/news/2011/08/9–11-2011–201108.

Taylor-Foster, James. 'Vanity height: How much of a skyscraper is usable space?', *ArchDaily*, 6 September 2013. Accessed 27 July 2019. https://www.archdaily.com/425730/vanity-height-how-much-of-a-skyscraper-is-usable-space.

Varnelis, Kazys. 'A brief history of horizontality: 1968/1969 to 2001/2002'. *Pasajes de Arquitectura y Critica*, March 2005. Accessed 23 September 2019. http://kazys.varnelis.net/articles/horizontality.

Wedell, Noura. 'Jarett Kobek's portrait of a hijacker', *BOMB Magazine*, 8 March 2012. Accessed 27 July 2019. https://bombmagazine.org/articles/jarett-kobeks-portrait-of-a-hijacker/.

Weisman, Leslie Kanes. 'Women's environmental rights: A manifesto'. In *Gender Space Architecture: An Interdisciplinary Introduction*, edited by Jane Rendell, Barbara Penner and Iain Borden, 1–5. London: Routledge, 2000.

13

Partitioning earth and sky: vertical urbanism in post-socialist Mumbai

Vyjayanthi Venuturupalli Rao

In considering what might be gained from a re-centring of urban scholarship, I am prompted to ask: what *is* the centre? Or, more precisely, what is *at* the centre? In a city like Mumbai, the answer somehow lies with the high-rise built form, newly emergent and rapidly normalising across the city. But one area in particular – the textile mill district – has become an intense focus for high-rise construction. Not accidentally, it is also a historically significant neighbourhood, whose character was vital to the city's cosmopolitan image in its industrial age. It is thus through the lens of the textile mill district that these brief reflections consider the centrality of the high-rise building and, more generally, the meanings of architecture for both its practitioners and its consumers, and different ways in which architecture relates to centrality.

Mumbai is a city full of reclamations. For many centuries, 'reclamation' was used for the practice of converting interstitial zones between earth and sea – neither earth nor sea – into solid ground and then into land. Reclamation, in reality, was an inherently generative act, an act of defiance and accumulation. Today, the word might refer to a different interstitial zone, that between earth and sky. This is a space in which an intense air rights game is being played in contemporary Mumbai. This battle has recently intensified, as the municipal corporation frames and sanctions its next twenty-year land-use plan. The protagonists in this battle are groups who proclaim hyper-dense vertical development as the solution to asymmetric urbanisation and others who advocate different urban forms to achieve the same goals.

For over twenty years now, affordable housing for various groups of people has been linked to the redistribution of air rights, and that means not only opening up occupied land for commodification but specifically extending upward. The high-rise, once the built form of the elite and the privileged, has now inundated the city. But in this place, vertical urbanism is not really monumental in the sense that inspired an analogy with sacred architecture in early twentieth-century New York: the Woolworth building in Lower Manhattan was likened to a 'cathedral of commerce' – a bold and very telling analogy. Georges Bataille, in his laconic observations on architecture, described it in this way:

> In practice, only the ideal being of society, that which orders and prohibits with authority, expresses itself in what are architectural compositions in the strict sense of the term. Thus, the great monuments are raised up like dams, pitting the logic of majesty and authority against all the shady elements: it is in the form of cathedrals and palaces that Church and State speak and impose silence on the multitudes. It is obvious, actually, that monuments inspire socially acceptable behaviour, and often a very real fear.[1]

Mumbai's contemporary high-rises are not, in this sense, monumental: they are too recent and too mediated to 'inspire socially acceptable behaviour'. As derivative forms mirroring cities elsewhere, they invoke instead Aldo Rossi's sense of urban artefacts, monuments to the passage of time and the persistence of patterns of socioeconomic organisation through time.[2]

One of Mumbai's earliest laboratories of vertical urbanism, the textile mill district in central Mumbai, housed around 160 working textile mills until the early 1980s. For over a century their numbers grew steadily, at their peak invoking comparisons with Manchester. Occupying large parcels of land in what is now the geographical centre of Mumbai, and surrounded by tenement buildings housing mill workers and their families, these mills were iconic in constructing an image of the city both for itself and for the world. In the 1970s, with new technologies and restrictive labour laws that prevented mill owners from upgrading and from making workers redundant, the mills gradually accumulated massive losses but continued to hold large numbers of formally employed workers on their payrolls. When payments could not be met, a year-long workers' strike in 1982 hastened the demise of the industry.

Alongside this collapse, the rising tide of economic liberalisation was sweeping India, forcing the government to open up its restricted, autarkic national economy. Although the rhetoric of socialism prevailed in political circles, India's political economy was a curious, tense coexistence of protectionism for industrialists and industrial workers, and massive exploitation of other sectors of the economy. The latter included large floating populations of informal workers, what Jan Breman has called 'footloose labour',[3] constantly forced to move, sometimes between city and countryside and often within the city itself. Liberalisation focused its early attention on cities, and with the promise of new economic opportunities cities began to experience intensified housing and office space shortages at the same time that many heavy industries concentrated in cities began to lose ground to newer industrial technologies. This may seem to create the conditions for a classic case of post-Fordist restructuring, and though it could be read as such it may be more productive to view what followed as a curious case of the restructuring of rights, specifically the restructuring of air rights. As elsewhere in the world, architecture became, as we shall see, a key tool in generating value.

In Mumbai, extremely restricted development laws and land-use plans calculated and envisaged a city of much lower densities and a much smaller population. Such restrictions had two effects: the massive growth of informal and unauthorised settlements, and the desire for large land parcels which would yield large volumes in the existing context of uniform, low floor-area ratios (FARs) across the city. There remained no district where development could legitimately take place without breaking through these FAR restrictions, and thus a single formula was born that structured the many projects commodifying land for new purposes: for every family resettled from a building or structure targeted for 'redevelopment', private real-estate actors received air rights as incentives. This formula involved the creation of exchange value for land, not through its sale and purchase, but rather through the displacement of its occupants, whether they were poor or not, in search of homes or places of work.

This resulted in a city in which the formal–informal exchange algorithm generated an assembly of self-organising patterns, volumes and effects from an extremely limited set of parameters. Among the notable effects of this kind of formulaic parcelling of air rights was the exclusion of the demands of those being resettled. Furthermore, the places where these air rights would land were not exactly predictable in advance, which resulted in a huge market in transferable development rights, distributed to landowners and builders in the form of certificates, whose inflation and deflation corresponded to speculative demands for real estate products.

These displacements of people – sometimes on the same parcel of land, at other times great distances away from their original places – created a form of currency exchange between spatial allotments and high-rise construction. Architecture, the intentional practice of building, is thus a reflection of this formula, a structuring practice that produces a social experience not just from space but from the invisible, intangible economy of exchanges. It is useful to return to an imaginary dialogue between Aldo Rossi and Georges Bataille. Rossi's contribution, when viewed favourably, is his insistence on moving beyond the functionalism of architecture. Similarly, Bataille attacked the central metaphysical assumption of modern capitalist economies, that of utility. As Jean Baudrillard puts it, Bataille's critique was to see the manner in which

> [a]ll economics are founded on that which no longer can, no longer knows how to expend itself …, on that which is incapable of becoming the stake of a sacrifice. It is therefore entirely residual, it is a limited social fact; and it is against economy as a limited social fact that Bataille wants to raise expenditure, death, and sacrifice as total social facts.[4]

Located between these critiques of functionalism and utilitarianism, the high-rise is a curious figure of both excess and withholding. It restricts or blocks the flow of vital energies from circulating through society. In Mumbai, the textile mill district is significant because it was the first and earliest iteration of this formula of exchange and continues to feature prominently on Mumbai's real-estate heat map as high-rises grow taller and acquire greater prestige: the lives of those working in the interstitial zones between mill compounds are exchanged for air rights, turning the already agonistic field of worker–owner relationships into something different.

For a brief moment, this turning of the field flared with revolutionary prospects. During an interview with me, Datta Isvalkar, the charismatic leader of the GKSS (Mill Workers' Action Committee), gave me a memoir of the organisation he had prepared for its twenty-fifth anniversary in 2014. The memoir chronicled the struggles of this community in the years following the strike of 1982, when 250,000 formally employed workers lost their jobs. Like his father before him, Datta worked in the mills and lived in a tenement house owned by the Modern Mills. When it was clear that it was futile to agitate for the reopening of the mills, and that mill owners were already being given permission to sell their land parcels for development surreptitiously, the group changed its tactics to agitate instead for housing for the workers. Agreements between the mill owners and the state culminated, first in 2001 and again in 2014, in the state housing board handing over the keys of hundreds of resettlement apartments to former mill workers, who were chosen by lottery. The exact numbers are not known but it was in the region of 68,000 workers, according to Datta.

Since the GKSS was founded in 1989 in the long aftermath of the strike and the mill closures, high-rises have grown in the mill district, reaching even greater heights, now vying to be properly called *skyscrapers*. What they are *scraping*, however, is air rights, the anabolic energy of transferable development rights and incentive development rights granted to mill owners and developers in exchange for allowing the state to sell affordable units in the vicinity of the super-talls to working-class families. When I asked him where the agitation would move next, Datta, who impresses his visitors as a wise and pragmatic figure, said of course that it would move into development planning; at the time debates were raging between the Municipal Corporation and activist groups about the Mumbai 2034 Development Plan, which would reserve lands for particular uses and would set the template for Mumbai's future for the next twenty years. As always, Datta's stories, which are building stories, or ones built on grounded observations, were rooted in having an answer to the question 'what next?' I noticed that he never engaged in retrospective speculation, nor asked the question 'what if?' His lack of interest in that question stems from a confidence about what the right thing to do would be in that situation.

It was grounded, moreover, in his memories of what appeared to be a 'good city': a city where he would walk to work, his children to school and his aged mother to the doctor; a place that was not planned but nevertheless functioned efficiently; a place that was self-sufficient but did not foreclose encounters with the wider city. These thoughts were prompted after I'd returned to his office from visiting another GKSS activist, who had received a housing board allotment flat in one of those new towers. She in turn had taken me to a few other resettlement buildings where the same formula had been applied to individual buildings rather than to the housing board development of twenty-four towers at the site previously occupied by the New Hind Mills, on the eastern edge of the mill district. In my interpretation, this was Datta's way of realising that architecture contributes to the imaginary of a stable physical world through which we may move and within which we may act, and of asking what happens when the air-rights game starts to undermine even the basic laws that are the conditions of possibility of a stable physical world.

Air rights accelerate certain forms of energy exchange: it is the air itself that is exchanged when the slowness or inertia of the traditional building envelope is replaced with rapidly deteriorating materials that hasten death of all kinds by building up toxicity in the very medium of existence and exchange. In today's Mumbai, polluted air has become the medium of urban exchanges, rather than flows on the ground through streets and public spaces; the thickness of social exchange is obscured by the hyper-density of the high-rise. Its sectional isolation vis-à-vis the ground plan generates new paranoias of penetration from the outside, which is so proximate and yet so distant. From the outside, which is also the ground plane, the high-rise appears like a walled void, a world entirely interior to itself. The high-rise can only grow through the virtuosity of the designer, who adjusts the elevation to take in the play of light and shadow, but this high-rise, born of the air-rights game, takes nothing else into account: first it battles those forms different from itself, while later it has to battle others like itself. But the key feature of the high-rise's ability to centre is that it is utterly Janus-faced. Viewed from one side it may perhaps appear to be totally domineering, but viewed from another side, the process that brought it into being – the socioeconomic and political 'envelope' that configures its form and that of its companion, the resettlement building – is nakedly visible.

Elsewhere I have argued that the key transition in this landscape may be the loss of a dialectical sense of the future, one in which 'the present contains, in the form of a contradiction, a potential that history is necessarily destined to resolve'.[5] It is from this resolution that a social form free of violence and poverty will emerge. But, viewing the air-rights game as it is played out across this former industrial landscape, one sees clearly that the present contains endless potential that might be captured by creative construction represented in the dispersal of speculative energy across the field of the city, not just in the spectacle of the high-rise but in the landscape within which it is set. Centrality, or the story that the city may tell itself about itself, is intimately connected to these emerging verticals.

Notes

1. Bataille, 1997, p. 21 (entry for 'Architecture' for the unfinished *Documents* dictionary).
2. See Rossi, 1982.
3. Breman, 1996.
4. Baudrillard, 1991, p. 136 (original published in French in 1976). The connection between the idea of use-value, the gift and the total social fact is explored at length in Murawski's contribution to this volume, and in Murawski, 2019, chapter 2.
5. Rao, Krishnamurthy and Kuoni, 2015.

Bibliography

Bataille, Georges. 'Architecture'. In *Rethinking Architecture: A Reader in Cultural Theory*, edited by Neil Leach, 21. London: Routledge, 1997.

Baudrillard, Jean. 'When Bataille attacked the metaphysical principle of economy' (translated by D. J. Miller). *Canadian Journal of Political and Social Theory* 15, no. 1–3 (1991): 135–8.

Breman, Jan. *Footloose Labour: Working in India's Informal Economy*. Cambridge: Cambridge University Press, 1996.

Murawski, Michał. *The Palace Complex: A Stalinist Skyscraper, Capitalist Warsaw, and a City Transfixed*. Bloomington: Indiana University Press, 2019.

Rao, Vyjayanthi Venuturupalli, Prem Krishnamurthy and Carin Kuoni, eds. *Speculation, Now: Essays and Artwork*. Durham, NC: Duke University Press, 2015.

Rossi, Aldo. *The Architecture of the City*. Cambridge, MA: MIT Press, 1982.

14
Vertical horizons: the shadow of The Shard

Tom Wolseley

During my year-long stint as Leverhulme Artist-in-Residence at UCL's Urban Lab, 2015–16, I worked in the geography department with Andrew Harris, interviewing, researching and creating a film called *Vertical Horizons: The Shadow of the Shard*. I have interviewed ex-City Planning head Peter Rees, Savills Head of Global Research, The Shard's project architect and a range of other academics and individuals, from engineers to local café owners. I have also been working with a group of psychotherapists. I have tried to get a sense of what The Shard is in these different arenas. Over this time I have also written a lot about what this topic means to me, and how it relates to my life in London, which has been my home for twenty-five years.

The film is made up of a series of slow 360° panning shots from different locations. It juxtaposes views of The Shard from different points around South London with contrasting narratives about the building and my own response to living in its shadow. It asks questions about the relationship between the individual and the larger global dynamics that are manifesting themselves in a changing city such as London. The film explores whether showing that London is 'open for business' produces buildings that are less products of global capital than embodiments of conservative political ideologies of the future, which themselves are predicated on nostalgic national and personal modes of identification. It speculates on how The Shard represents a re-functionalising of the built environment, from cities understood as places to live, to containers for insecure financial assets.

My interest in The Shard began with my project Sentient City,[1] which was based around a thirty-minute tracking shot between Hoxton,

Figure 14.1 'Atlas 2009'. C-Type print, 355 x 254 cm (14 x 10"). One of a series of thirty images of the orientation maps commonly found at the boundary of social housing projects in London, part of an installation in the Cabinet, 2010. Source: Tom Wolseley.

where I worked, and Walworth, where I lived. The route passed London Bridge and The Shard. In that essay film, I was particularly interested in how the dynamics of capital shaped the city and my experience of this. How do these trajectories – both personal and financial – delineate the horizon of the possible in the city?

I had previously worked on the relationship between fossil fuels and post-war modernity in my work *Atlas*, which I carried out together with geographer Mark Jackson.[2] This is a series of photographs of the orientation maps of post-war social housing projects, which highlighted territoriality, power and the aesthetics of rationalism – geometry and symmetry – in the high modernist aesthetic.

One aspect of the *Atlas* project that particularly interested me was the apparent transcendence of the material into the mental and rational, into a modernism that was predicated on the massive energetic excess of fossil fuels, in a number of different and interesting ways: mechanically, it was fossil fuels that enabled the clearing of the old city, that enabled the mining and transport of building materials and thus the construction of the new city in its place. It was fossil fuels that enabled the separation and zoning of the city by making public transport possible; it was fossil fuels that enabled the urban imaginary of modern architect-demiurges, such as Le Corbusier; and finally, it was money from the extraction of fossil fuels that funded a large part of post-war social housing construction. For an ideology strongly linked to a transcendence of the material, modernism seemed entwined with the notion of 'geological agency'. Fossil fuels enabled the modernist city, not just materially but also mentally and culturally; they changed the material, personal and cultural horizon within which the urban condition of the twentieth century took form.

One of the major sources for the spatial as well as the intersubjective aspects of my art practice is my experience of fifteen years of psychotherapy. A second source is some useful ideas I have developed from my reading of psychotherapeutic theory, such as transitional space, relational space and mutually constructed space. A third, especially important in the actual making of an artwork, is the therapy session as a space that contains a variety of processes: what is said, unsaid and inferred, the impact of the physical environment, the constant relationship between the event and the context within which it is happening. Most of all, the relationship between what is said explicitly and implicitly, the foregrounded appreciation for what is not said, denied and compensated for, have been inspirational for my work. This has come to influence my films, which are

Figure 14.2 '36 Images of The Shard. Ambition Waterloo', 2017.
Source: Tom Wolseley.

constituted by a mixture of what is directly said (by me, the narrator) and what is shown via the medium of film. I use some of these tools to explore my subject, to reflect on some of the desires for visibility, identification and power that surround The Shard.

I have lived and worked in London for twenty-five years. I have raised a family and bought a flat. My kids are growing up, they are changing, I am changing, the city is changing. I have made a film that tracks these trajectories of change – of the city and of the living subjects and material objects that inhabit it – through their relation to each other and their tendency towards monolithic modes of identification. I have chosen to focus on The Shard, and its relation to the city I live in, as a central focus, an anchor for this piece. I live and work in the shadow of The Shard, and the film explores my and the city's tendencies to strive towards a more authoritative self-identification. Where do these tendencies come from, how are they situated – in the city and in my own life? In the city, there is a tendency to verticality; in my son, there is a tendency to admire superheroes.

As the project has progressed, it has become more about our need, individual and collective, for images of centrality and authority.

My first interest in The Shard was as a product of dynamics that brought together very different arenas: from the material agency of the fossil fuels that funded it, to the dynamics of capital and the aesthetics of modernity, then neatly back to the specificity of the power station in the basement of the tower, supplied with Qatari gas.

The film has become increasingly horizontalist, as it literally *pans*, slowly, across the city, and in its insistence on a flattening out – of authority, information, my personal neurosis and the latest planning regulations. Each of these is portrayed as having an equal or at least a commensurable significance. I try to put my subjective experience of The Shard, and the different arenas of its production, spectacle and dissemination, resolutely side by side. One reason for doing this is not to determine, but to suggest, transformative vectors, pathways, tangents (of interpretation as well as of causality), across very different scales and dimensions. My small subversive act is this insistence on relational horizontality, on a levelling between myself and the building. My challenge is how to form a relationship with this object that tries so hard to appear separate from the scale of the individual, from the city, from gravity and time – to domesticate its transcendental aspirations.

The high-rise has been rationalised in different ways in different places, in terms of density, efficiency and finance.[3] An aspect of The Shard that I find difficult to unravel is its functionality, especially the

Figure 14.3 '36 Images of The Shard. St Saviours Estate', 2017. Source: Tom Wolseley.

relationship of its interior function to its spectacular presence in the city. It seems to me that the primary functionality of the high-rise is, increasingly, as a symbol to be manipulated.

A pivotal interview I conducted about The Shard was with the head of a major international property management company. She said that The Shard, contrary to expectation, was not really an object of global business, but was largely a political object, precipitated by political will. She said that it should not so much be considered as an object manifesting the power of global finance, as is often assumed, but as a fossil of an old-fashioned idea of global business inherited from Manhattan, the dominant player of the twentieth century. The world, it seems, is still mimicking this obsolete model, the alpha male of the twentieth century. The Shard is a product, then, of the retro-conservative nostalgia of identification held by our politicians. The Shard, she said, is a great billboard signalling that London is 'open for business', a leftover from an old-fashioned mode of identification, and partly catalysed by a fear of the imminent threat of China, particularly Shanghai – a place in the East, perceived as making a giant leap out of historical contingency into the future, leaving 'us' behind.

Shanghai is often mentioned in connection with The Shard, as if to put it in context, to make it seem more 'reasonable'. But it turns out

Figure 14.4 '36 Images of The Shard. Southwark Bridge', 2017.
Source: Tom Wolseley.

that the high-rises of Shanghai were also not born of a business decision, but of a political one made by the authoritarian communist leadership; they were a communist experiment in the financial iconography
of the high-rise. This decision also capitalised on the historical context of
Shanghai, on a sense that Shanghai's fantastic futurism of the 1930s, as
one of the global cities of the late colonial era, had been foreclosed by the
Japanese invasion and communism.[4] Shanghai's high-rises were therefore intended to bring the old Shanghai back to life; they were a prop in a
nostalgic rerun of early twentieth-century modernism.

I question some of these larger narratives within my own personal
This was a welcome justification to lever open The Shard, from the
perception of its being a simple artefact of the contemporary capitalist
'real', to it being something that was more complex: the product of a
number of human decisions, driven by a variety of desires, within a number of overlapping contexts.

I question some of these larger narratives within my own personal
ones: my impending mid-life crisis, my aspirations on coming to the city
from the hills of Exmoor, my social class. I look at how my role as an
artist has changed (twenty-five years ago people would ask how I earned

Figure 14.5 '36 Images of The Shard. St Thomas St.', 2017. Source: Tom Wolseley.

my living; now they ask me if I am 'famous'). I see myself, my personal psychological process, as, to an extent, just another arena of the larger cultural and material process I live within, and therefore another prism through which I can interrogate the contemporary space or condition of a seemingly much larger phenomenon, like The Shard.

I see global tendencies manifest in my own proclivities to identify myself in certain ways, and I see those personal tendencies manifested outside of myself. Do my own tendencies towards hierarchical, fortified, authoritative modes of identification, in the face of fear and insecurity, reflect similar political tendencies in the West, which emerge in relation to the perceived threat of globalisation?

If there is a political act in this piece, it is to refuse the aspirations of The Shard to separate itself from the present into the future, and from the individual into the sublime. I try to achieve this by my relentless demonstration of the manner in which it is complicit in my own life. I try to refuse the transcendence of this object above and beyond its own contingencies, in our culture, geology and life.

Figure 14.6 '36 Images of The Shard. Southwark St.', 2017. Source: Tom Wolseley.

Figure 14.7 '36 Images of The Shard. Funeral parlour', 2017. Source: Tom Wolseley.

Figure 14.8 '36 Images of The Shard. 22 Amelia St.', 2017. Source: Tom Wolseley.

Figure 14.9 '36 Images of The Shard. Elephant and Castle shopping centre', 2017. Source: Tom Wolseley.

Figure 14.10   '36 Images of The Shard. Arnold Estate' 2017. Source: Tom Wolseley.

Notes

1.   'Sentient City' by Architrope, Tom Wolseley. Accessed 13 November 2019. https://vimeo.com/80786950.
2.   Architrope, Atlas. Accessed 13 November 2019. http://www.architrope.com/architrope_vs_3/architrope_atlas_cover_page.html.
3.   Graham, 2016.
4.   Greenspan, 2014.

Bibliography

Graham, Stephen. *Vertical: The City from Satellites to Bunkers*. London: Verso, 2016.
Greenspan, Anna. *Shanghai Future: Modernity Remade*. London: Hurst and Company, 2014.

Part V
Looking outward: hinterlands, diffusions, explosions

15
New geographies of hinterland

Pushpa Arabindoo

Hinterland

Pronunciation: /ˈhɪntəland/
1. The remote areas of a country away from the coast or the banks of major rivers:
   the hinterland of southern Italy
2. The area around or beyond a major town or port:
   a market town serving its rich agricultural hinterland
3. An area lying beyond what is visible or known:
   the strange hinterland where life begins and ends[1]

Between the 1950s and the 1970s, it was common practice for international development organisations such as the UN, the World Bank, USAID and the Ford Foundation to commission studies into what were then perceived as problems of the cities of the developing world.[2] Western scholars participated actively in the preparation of reports by these institutions as well as producing academic publications on what came to be broadly considered Third World urbanisation.[3] It mostly comprised enquiries into the challenges of a rapid and uncontrolled urbanisation, often presented as over-urbanisation and emphasised through population growth rates, rural-to-urban migration, and pressures on land, housing, transport, water and sanitation, leading to exacerbated conditions of urban poverty and unemployment. Driven by a strong development-studies bias based on a narrow (economic) theory of growth, an ethos of development followed decolonisation, modelled on Western guidelines of modernisation, and set loose by a burgeoning international industry of bilateral, multilateral, private and academic agencies.[4] Here, despite the alleged urban bias of the development, cities were treated uncritically as sites of developmental action.[5] Stressing sectoral issues such as housing, health, education, and gender that were largely, but not exclusively, urban issues, the place of the urban question in global policy making, as a result, became a poorly understood vein of historical enquiry.[6] The ensuing development logic, moreover, hinged on a clunkily and rigidly reinforced idea of a rural–urban dichotomy which was, in fact, based on anti-urban sentiments, where urban problems in the developing world might have gained some prominence in the international imaginary in the early 1970s but were short-changed by an understanding of 'development in cities' rather than the role of 'cities in development'.[5] Against an awkwardly and axiomatically defined urbanisation–development nexus, scholars were thus slow to question the neatness of such categories as the rural–urban binary imposed by the positivistic orthodoxy of a development rationale.[7] Acknowledgement eventually came of the increasing spatial interdependencies and complex livelihood strategies between the urban and the rural, revealing more of a continuum with no discernible land-use pattern or development behaviour distinguishing the two.[8] Amidst a realisation that this implies neither an urbanisation of the rural condition nor a ruralisation of the urban setting, there is a recognition that more sophisticated conceptual filters are required to understand this phenomenon, especially given the rise of a 'global urban agenda' calling for a paradigmatic refreshing of the idea of 'the urban' in global thinking.[9]

Peri-urban: more than a periphery?

Initially, widely popular debates of metropolitanisation and regional urbanisation were considered sufficient to explain the new configuration of social, economic and political life, blurring the transition from urban to rural, as, after all, they had been successful in making sense of suburbanisation and sprawl in Western cities.[10] Apart from the fact that diverse urban processes in different politico-economic and sociocultural realms make generalisations difficult, more specific lenses are needed to unpack the interplay between the urban and the rural, especially in the context of developing cities where the urban–rural interface continues to be calibrated from a developmental vantage point. In this context, a notion of peri-urbanisation emerged prominently to define not only spatially, but also socially, economically and politically, a geographical area in which an agriculture-dominated, labour-intensive, dispersed rural overlapped with a more concentrated form of capital-reliant, non-farming-oriented urban in the Global South.[11]

Peri-urbanisation was, to begin with, largely interpreted as a process of peripheral urbanisation, with a focus on illustrating the urban periphery as a problematic condition, relying on reductivist portrayals of 'degenerated peripheralization' highlighting a dominant narrative of marginality, poverty and exclusion.[12] This has been rectified somewhat through an enquiry of the peri-urban area as more of a heterogeneous mosaic of 'natural' ecosystems, 'agro' ecosystems and 'urban' ecosystems producing a varied social composition of small farmers, informal settlers and migrant workers, industrial entrepreneurs and urban middle-class commuters, and whose sociocultural overlap weaves an intricate condition of heterogeneity and segmentation, creating new forms of segregation, polarisation and fragmentation.[13] But even before one can get a grip on the complexity of this condition, peri-urban interactions have been further complicated by their exposure to explicit globalising imperatives where the heterogeneity created by the presence of various social groupings including the 'real-estate developers, global investors, liberalizing government officials, bourgeois urbanites, and peasants with de facto land rights', not to mention the already existing as well as incoming rural migrants, has posed new challenges.[14]

In spite of these clarifications, peripheries continue to be pitted in a dialectical relationship with the centrality of the city where it is seen as expanding primarily due to forces exerted by the city's economic hegemony, even if it might reciprocally produce conditions that, in return, impact ebbs and flows emerging from the centre. There is a simplified assumption of centrifugal and centripetal forces at work here, one that belies the intricacy of these interactions. This is seen even in Holston and Caldeira's well-developed sense of peripheral urbanisation emphasising the need for a dynamic apparatus to define urban peripheries.[15] Interrelations between its various political, legal, social, economic and infrastructural components are constantly changing, yet Holston and Caldeira seem to think of centres and peripheries as being in a relationship of mutual dependence to each other, one that is difficult to uncouple. This is not for lack of trying, as seen in Simone's description of a 'negative potentiality' between the periphery and the centre, as he finds that even though peripheries are imbued with a sense of insufficiency and incompletion that is remaining in need of the largesse and guidance of a centre, they are 'never really brought fully under the auspices of the logic and development trajectories that characterise a centre, and therefore embodies an instability that is always potentially destabilising of that centre'.[16]

Thus, even though peri-urbanisation has so far been useful in dissolving a sharply set rural–urban dichotomy, it is high time that we rethought its conceptualisation, and allied notions such as the edge, fringe or transition zone, one that opens some productive new perspectives on the urban.[17] For even though, in recent years, arguments have emerged for rethinking peripheral urbanisation in a processual manner, more as a mode of making cities and producing the urban than as a literal interpretation of outwards spatial expansion, its associated sense of centrality and marginality remains a rigid proposition. The starting point of the question here is not what is urban versus rural but what is urban and what is non-urban, as what lies beyond the urban is key to our understanding of the process of (capitalist) urbanisation.[18]

Hinterland: urban and non-urban

It is in this context of a need for a better interpretive vocabulary to describe the urban without an outside that the hinterland emerges as a more suitable axiom than the periphery.[19] Its differentiation and variegation, distinct from the elaborateness of the peri-urban which is still hinged to the urban, is one that is systemically connected to the urban as a process, and is mediated through a broad array of institutional, political, social and environmental factors.[20] Organised at a range of spatial scales, hinterland involves an assortment of morphological forms and settlement typologies including the urban, the suburban, the peri-urban, the rural, and even the wilderness. As hinterland becomes central to our reconceptualisation of the urban, we need to understand that what we are undertaking is a simultaneous rereading of the hinterland, which as a lexicon itself has been around for a while.

In fact, during the very decades of development discourses that triggered our fascination with urbanisation in the developing world, the city and the hinterland were frequently invoked as a de facto binary, especially when an extended sense of the city as a region was being considered. For instance, when a prominent conference at the University of California, Berkeley, deliberating the nature of India's urbanisation resulted in an edited volume, *India's Urban Future*, a significant contribution proved to be Richard Ellefsen's five cities survey (Bombay, Delhi, Madras, Hyderabad and Baroda), which provided specific observations on the nature of city–hinterland relationships as a way of understanding the unfolding nature of urbanisation.[21] The intention of this exercise was, by using demographic and economic data, to delineate a regional transformation of cities using factors measuring the degree of urbanisation (such as density, sex ratio, literacy, non-agricultural occupation, and the proportion of persons dependent on commerce). While Ellefsen's postulation that the hinterland is more than an urban periphery is intriguing, it is not really unpacked or clarified, as his exercise concentrated on developing a methodological approach to hinterland studies in underdeveloped countries. If we are to open the hinterland to new analytical horizons, we need to focus on its hyper-reality, one that dissolves any static binary (centre–periphery or urban–rural) and goes beyond a modernist development agenda.

Hinterlands, in their current version, signify a territorial form of urbanisation whose new economic geography of extraction, production and circulation can no longer be seen through the idiom of twentieth-century agglomeration processes.[22] What we are facing here is a strategic shift to a focus on the land question as an intrinsic aspect of the urban question, with land (and its embeddedness within the term hinterland) emerging as a key element outlining the emergent landscapes of a salient yet still indeterminate planetary form of urbanisation.[23] This contemporary version of the hinterland is characterised by a land regime that, in a context of mostly informal set-ups of inhabitation, occupation and tenancy, employs property market logics and its contingent techniques of cadastralisation to make land available for private development.[24] This is aided and abetted by a land reform routine which relies not just on aggressive modes of land acquisition, but on more brutal forms of land grab, whereby lands that were once subject to agrarian regulatory modes are now forced to make way unrelentingly for the urban.[25] The ensuing land conversion is highly controversial, exacerbating inefficient land uses and creating a black market in land sales, corruption at the local state level and multiple scales of real-estate speculation. And the irony here is that through its own set of autonomous networks the 'new' hinterland rejects any sort of relationship with the city, choosing instead to subvert and circumvent the city. Instead, this hinterland implies a vantage point from elsewhere, a resource hinterland that is not contiguous with the metropole but is defined by its distance, measured in miles and otherness from both the centre and any kind of urban, thriving instead on the fact that the 'new' hinterlands are scattered and beyond in a new articulation of territories, landscapes and ecologies.

Chennai's hinterland: logics and logistics

This can be seen in the Indian city of Chennai, where efforts to officially expand its metropolitan area have foundered. In 2012, planners at the Chennai Metropolitan Development Authority (CMDA) reviewed proposals to expand the metropolitan area from 1,189 km^2 (first red-lined in 1975) to either a modest 4,400 km^2 or a more ambitious 8,800 km^2, but made little headway in this direction. Five years later, in July 2017, the state government finally announced that a mega urban region of 8,878 km^2 would be formed, comprising Chennai district and fully engulfing its adjoining Thiruvallur and Kancheepuram districts, as well as additional taluks in further-out Vellore district. A total of 1,709 villages were to be annexed to the region in this scheme, including the municipalities of Chengalpattu in the south and Tindivanam to the north. A Government Order to this effect was issued in January 2018, though it has been suspended following a hostile public consultation process and the filing of a Public Interest Litigation (PIL) in the High Court that challenges the expansion. While it is very likely that the outcome will be a scaled-down expansion, a major reason this mega enlargement was sought in the first instance is the simple fact that the hinterland has been experiencing (through deliberate as well as unanticipated policy decisions) higher economic growth rates than the city. Chennai metropolitan area currently comprises three districts, a core 176 km^2 of Chennai district, surrounded by 637 km^2 of Thirvuallur district to the north and west and 376 km^2 of Kanchipuram district to the south and west (Figure 15.1). While the gross district domestic product of Chennai grew at a compounded annual rate of 4 per cent from 2006 to 2012, Thiruvallur and Kancheepuram districts registered much higher rates, of 9 per cent and 14 per cent respectively. There is a rapidly emerging industrial landscape of global capital flows and foreign direct investments, located in the hinterland districts beyond the metropolitan area, that accounts for this phenomenal growth. Taking the shape of zones and corridors, nondescript places such as Sriperumbudur (in Kancheepuram District) have emerged as India's Shenzhen and convey an investment fetish with the hinterland, one that requires it to remain not just outside the city but outside the region as well.[26]

The operational landscape of this 'new' hinterland is based on a megalogistical collective and its attendant 'urbanism of logistics':[27]

> In contrast to historically inherited hinterlands, in which various 'free gifts' of nature embedded in the land (materials, energy, labour, food, water) are appropriated to produce primary commodities, operational landscapes involve the industrial redesign of agricultural, extractive and logistical activities to engineer the most optimal social, institutional, infrastructural, biological and ecological conditions for (generally export-oriented) capital accumulation.[28]

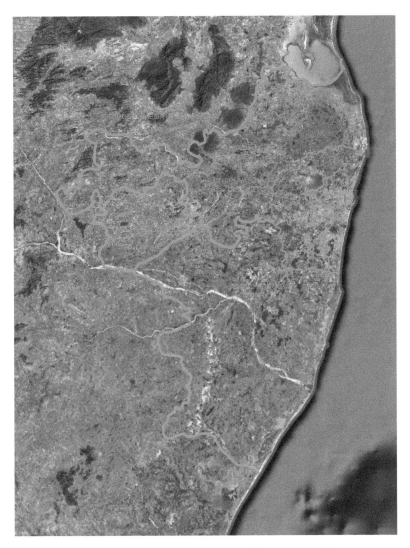

Figure 15.1 Chennai: proposed expansion from metropolitan area to mega urban region. Base: Google Maps.

Characterised by new industrial forms based on global supply chains, and vast territories given over to the shipment, staging and delivery of goods, the resulting landscape is neither a concentrated nor an extended form of urbanisation, but a distributed model criss-crossed by indistinguishable generic forms that hardly constitute the urban.[29] (See Figure 15.2.) Such an overture relies on a good amount of extrastatecraft,

Figure 15.2 Hinterland as the non-urban. Source: Christophe Delory.

where persistent concretion, articulation and speculation of logistics takes precedence in a territorial neo-colonisation of the hinterland that results in what Roy has described as the dis/possessive collectivism.[30] There is an optimisation logic here around distribution and delivery, consumption and convenience, and accommodation disposal, where the hinterland is not just about abstract grids and networks, but also involves tangible efforts, mostly in the form of physical infrastructure to bypass the city.[31] Most often, these are projects that are co-opted by the situatedness of the hinterland as seen in the case of the Outer Ring Road (ORR) in metropolitan Chennai. This 60-km road infrastructure project was originally proposed as part of the first master plan (1971–91) to decongest the city but remained a drawing-board exercise for several decades. It found renewed favour in the twenty-first century when public and private interests converged, and the ORR became a central feature of a 'bypass urbanism' in the hinterland's new terrain of speculative politics (see Figures 15.3 and 15.4).[32] The ORR involves connecting hinterland zones and corridors of capital accumulation from the south and the west as quickly and directly as possible to the port operations in the northern part, in an attempt to bypass large swathes of the city's everyday, gritty reality. There are unforeseen, and serious, consequences

Figure 15.3   Outer Ring Road, Chennai. Source: Christophe Delory.

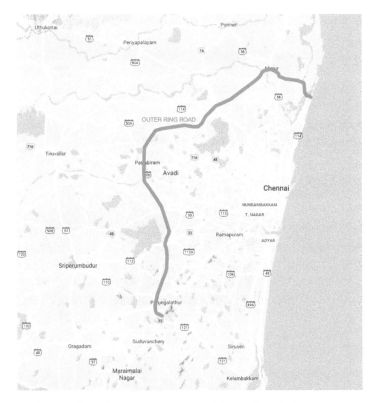

Figure 15.4   Outer Ring Road, Chennai. Base: Google Maps.

Figure 15.5 Hinterland as spectre. Source: Christophe Delory.

to such an urbanism's overt territorial focus, as witnessed during the 2015 floods, when the completed first phase of the ORR proved to be an unmitigated ecological disaster.[33]

Amidst a temptation to use the hinterland as a conceptual filter, one that provides an overarching theorisation of the urban, we need to ensure that it is subjected equally to a rigorous empirical scrutiny.[34] Embodying new forms of uneven capitalist development underpinning unprecedented forms of creative destruction, its pathways of urbanisation remain unpredictable where exclusive gated communities or high-end residential developments might fail to take off and are reduced to ghost towns while haphazard developments from low-end developers thrive (see Figure 15.5). Discerning a meaningful pattern within this vagary is a difficult task and risks being limited to crude forms of analysis. What might help at this point would be to find appropriate methodologies that go beyond current visualisation techniques involving aerial satellite imagery to develop a series of toolkits for the analysis of its 'multiple sites of peripheralisation' at various territorial scales.[35]

Notes

1. Oxford Dictionaries.
2. Lubell, 1984.
3. Abu-Lughod and Hay, 2007;. Drakakis-Smith, 2000; Gilbert and Gugler, 1982; Potter and Lloyd-Evans, 2014.

4. Sylvester, 1999.
5. Lipton,1977; cf. Byres, 1979; Harriss and Moore, 1984.
6. Parnell, 2016.
7. Davis, 2016; Turok, 2014.
8. Harriss and Moore, 1984; Champion and Hugo, 2016; McGranahan and Satterthwaite, 2014.
9. Allen, 2003; Parnell, 2016.
10. Arabindoo, 2009. See also Laquian, 2005.
11. Simon, 2008.
12. Kundu, Pradhan and Subramanium, 2002; Dupont, 2007.
13. Allen, 2003; Friedmann, 2006.
14. Roy, 2003, p. 144.
15. Holston and Caldeira, 2008.
16. Simone, 2007, p. 469.
17. Mabin, Butcher and Bloch, 2013.
18. Caldeira, 2017.
19. Brenner, 2016.
20. Brenner and Schmid, 2013.
21. Ellefsen, 1962.
22. Topalovic, 2013.
23. Brenner, 2016.
24. Roy, 2016.
25. Steel, van Noorloos and Klaufus, 2017.
26. Neilson, 2012; Easterling, 2014; Homm and Bohle, 2012.
27. Luke, 2003.
28. Brenner, 2016, pp. 125–6.
29. Waldheim and Berger, 2008.
30. Easterling, 2014; Roy, 2017.
31. Waldheim and Berger, 2008.
32. Sawyer and Schmid, 2015; Bhattacharya and Sanyal, 2011.
33. It is difficult to elaborate on this argument within this short-essay format. For a somewhat oblique discussion of this argument around regionalisation of disasters, see Arabindoo (2016).
34. Brenner, 2016.
35. Kanai, 2014.

Bibliography

Abu-Lughod, Janet and Richard Hay, Jr, eds. *Third World Urbanization*. London: Routledge, 2007.
Allen, Adriana. 'Environmental planning and management of the peri-urban interface: perspectives on an emerging field', *Environment and Urbanization* 15, no. 1 (2003): 135–47.
Arabindoo, Pushpa. 'Falling apart at the margins? Neighbourhood transformations in peri-urban Chennai', *Development and Change* 40, no. 5 (2009): 879–901.
Arabindoo, Pushpa. 'Unprecedented natures? An anatomy of the Chennai floods', *City* 20, no. 6 (2016): 800–21.
Bhattacharya, Rajesh and Kalyan Sanyal. 'Bypassing the squalor: new towns, immaterial labour and exclusion in post-colonial urbanisation', *Economic and Political Weekly* 46, no. 31 (2011): 41–8.
Brenner, Neil. 'The hinterland urbanised?', *Architectural Design* 86, no. 4 (2016): 118–27.
Brenner, Neil and Christian Schmid. 'Towards a new epistemology of the urban?', *City* 19, no. 2/3 (2015): 151–82.
Byres, T.J. 'Of neo-populist pipe-dreams: Daedalus in the Third World and the myth of urban bias', *Journal of Peasant Studies* 6, no. 2 (1979): 210–44.
Caldeira, Teresa P.R. 'Peripheral urbanization: autoconstruction, transversal logics, and politics in cities of the global south', *Environment and Planning D: Society and Space* 35, no. 1 (2017): 3–20.
Champion, Tony and Graeme Hugo, eds. *New Forms of Urbanization: Beyond the Urban–Rural Dichotomy*. London: Routledge, 2016.

Davis, Diane E. 'Reflections on the relations between development and urbanization: past trajectories and future challenges', *International Journal of Urban Sciences* 20, no. 1 (2016): 1–14.

Drakakis-Smith, David. *Third World Cities*. 2nd edn. London: Routledge, 2000.

Dupont, Véronique. 'Conflicting stakes and governance in the peripheries of large Indian metropolises: an introduction', *Cities* 24, no. 2 (2007): 89–94.

Easterling, Keller. *Extrastatecraft: The Power of Infrastructure Space*. London: Verso, 2014.

Ellefsen, Richard A. 'City–hinterland relationships in India'. In *India's Urban Future*, edited by Roy Turner, 94–115. Berkeley: University of California Press, 1962.

Friedmann, John. 'Four theses in the study of China's urbanization', *International Journal of Urban and Regional Research* 30, no. 2 (2006): 440–51.

Gilbert, Alan and Josef Gugler. *Cities, Poverty, and Development: Urbanization in the Third World*. Oxford: Oxford University Press, 1982.

Harriss, John and Mick Moore, eds. *Development and the Rural–Urban Divide*. London: Frank Cass, 1984.

Holston, James and Teresa Caldeira. 'Urban peripheries and the invention of citizenship', *Harvard Design Magazine* 28 (2008): 18–23.

Homm, Sebastian and Hans-Georg Bohle. '"India's Shenzhen" – a miracle? Critical reflections on New Economic Geography, with empirical evidence from peri-urban Chennai', *Erdkunde* 66, no. 4 (2012): 281–94.

Kanai, Juan Miguel. 'On the peripheries of planetary urbanization: globalizing Manaus and its expanding impact', *Environment and Planning D: Society and Space* 32, no. 6 (2014): 1071–87.

Kundu, Amitabh, Basanta K. Pradhan and A. Subramanian. 'Dichotomy or continuum: analysis of impact of urban centres on their periphery', *Economic and Political Weekly* 37, no. 50 (2002): 5039–46.

Laquian, Aprodicio A. *Beyond Metropolis: The Planning and Governance of Asia's Mega-Urban Regions*. Washington, DC: Woodrow Wilson Center Press, 2005.

Lipton, Michael. *Why Poor People Stay Poor: A Study of Urban Bias in World Development*. London: Temple Smith, 1977.

Lubell, Harold. 'Third World urbanization and international assistance', *Urban Studies* 21, no. 1 (1984): 1–13.

Luke, Timothy W. 'Global Cities vs. "global cities": rethinking contemporary urbanism as public ecology', *Studies in Political Economy* 70, no. 1 (2003): 11–33.

Mabin, A., Siân Butcher and Robin Bloch. 'Peripheries, suburbanisms and change in sub-Saharan African cities', *Social Dynamics* 39, no. 2 (2013): 167–90.

McGranahan, Gordon and David Satterthwaite. *Urbanisation Concepts and Trends*. London: International Institute for Environment and Development, 2014.

Neilson, Brett. 'Five theses on understanding logistics as power', *Distinktion: Scandinavian Journal of Social Theory* 13, no. 3 (2012): 322–39.

Parnell, Susan. 'Defining a global urban development agenda', *World Development* 78 (2016): 529–40.

Potter, Robert B. and Sally Lloyd-Evans. *The City in the Developing World*. London: Routledge, 2014.

Roy, Ananya. *City Requiem, Calcutta: Gender and the Politics of Poverty*. Minneapolis: University of Minnesota Press, 2003.

Roy, Ananya. 'What is urban about critical urban theory?', *Urban Geography* 37, no. 6 (2016): 810–23.

Roy, Ananya. 'Dis/possessive collectivism: property and personhood at city's end', *Geoforum* 80 (2017): A1–A11.

Sawyer, Lindsay and Christian Schmid. 'Bypass urbanism'. In *Jahrbuch 2015: Departement Architektur, ETH Zürich*, 213–15. Zurich: gta Verlag, 2015.

Simon, David. 'Urban environments: issues on the peri-urban fringe', *Annual Review of Environment and Resources* 33 (2008): 167–85.

Simone, AbdouMaliq. 'At the frontier of the urban periphery'. In *Sarai Reader 07: Frontiers*, edited by Monica Narula, Shuddhabrata Sengupta, Jeebesh Bagchi and Ravi Sundaram, 462–70. Delhi: Centre for the Study of Developing Societies, 2007.

Steel, Griet, Femke van Noorloos and Christien Klaufus. 'The urban land debate in the global South: new avenues for research', *Geoforum* 83 (2017): 133–41.

Sylvester, Christine. 'Development studies and postcolonial studies: disparate tales of the "Third World"', *Third World Quarterly* 20, no. 4 (1999): 703–21.

Topalovic, Milica. 'Introduction'. In *Architecture of Territory – Hinterland: Singapore, Johor, Riau*, edited by Milica Topalovic, Martin Knüsel, Marcel Jäggi and Stefanie Krautzig, 17–21. Zurich: ETH Zürich DArch and FCL Singapore, 2013.

Turok, Ivan. 'The urbanization–development nexus in the BRICS'. In *The Routledge Handbook on Cities of the Global South*, edited by Susan Parnell and Sophie Oldfield, 122–38. London: Routledge, 2014.

Waldheim, Charles and Alan Berger. 'Logistics landscape', *Landscape Journal* 27, no. 2 (2008): 219–46.

16

De-escalating the centre: urban futures and special economic zones beyond poststructuralism's neoliberal imaginations

Patrick Neveling

In his 1977 book on *The Urban Question*, Manuel Castells pointed out that there was no such thing as the 'urban' and the 'urban condition'. This was because the pre-industrial rural–urban divide no longer existed. Thus, to speak about something distinctively urban means to fall victim to ideology and to obfuscate how, under capitalism, the urban is nothing but a concentration of a proletarian labour reserve.[1] Indeed, this analysis can be extended in history as it pre-dates the advent of capitalism.

From a critical theory vantage point, 'the urban' as a comparatively large-scale agglomeration of humans in particular space-times has always captured humanity's imagination. This is because the allure of the urban has generated numerous mythologies, from the Tower of Babel in antiquity, to the medieval German saying '*Stadtluft macht frei*' ('city air makes you free'), and to the seven cities of gold that the Spanish conquistadors hoped to find in the Americas. Such mythologies invoke marvellous multiculturalism, unseen liberty and amazing riches, to name but a few features. However, there is mostly nothing to them. '*Stadtluft macht frei*', for example, was only true for a few decades at the beginning of the second millennium and only in some parts of Europe, when bonded labourers under feudal rule could become free persons if they managed to escape to the cities. Such liberation was an option because the cities lacked labourers. But soon the counts and petty kings controlling the vast spaces around the cities put an end to this loss-causing liberation business.[2] Similarly, there were no seven cities of gold in the Americas, and the world-changing bullion that the Spanish and Portuguese recovered from their New World possessions with considerable violence was silver, instead.[3] Thus, world historical analysis often leads to other results than the fetishisation of world historical ruptures that informs many theories in the social sciences and humanities. This is especially true for one current articulation of that mythical imagination of the urban as the centre of the human (coming) condition.

That mythology of the urban/centre/future is the special economic zone (SEZ). Such zones are commonly considered to be neoliberal variants of spaces of exception, Agambian *'nomos* of the postmodern', we may say.[4] One leading poststructuralist thinker concerned with SEZs is Keller Easterling. To her, an SEZ is a rhizome-like structure, constantly breeding its own iteration, especially so since the global spread of zones escalated in the late 1970s, when the People's Republic of China opened four coastal cities to foreign investors and therewith created Shenzhen and other future megacities of the twenty-first century.[5]

Yet Easterling backdates the origins of the zone model to antiquity, more precisely to European antiquity, when the Roman Empire opened an alleged free port in Delos.[6] The model kept popping up in the late medieval Hanseatic League city ports, and expanded globally during the early days of imperialism, when European powers opened free ports in Hong Kong, Shanghai and elsewhere.[7] Today, with the zones breeding and being a 'spatial software of extrastatecraft', the whole world is going to be a Shanghai, a Shenzhen, or similar, and Easterling illustrates that claim with numerous virtual excursions to web pages that promote SEZ cities in the planning stage, such as the King Abdullah Economic Zone currently being built by the Saudi monarchy on the shores of the Red Sea.[8]

Certainly, SEZs are particular articulations of capitalism and have had a huge impact on the world system's bifurcation for several decades. However, the origin of today's 4,000 zones can be traced no further back than to the neoliberalisation of development policies in the US dependency Puerto Rico in 1947. I have shown this in detail with a view to the zones' role in the decades of the Cold War and decolonisation, when the rise of socialist and anti-imperialist independence movements rattled the foundations of the geopolitical condition and forced Western former colonial powers and their bourgeoisies to reconsider the organisation of global capitalist exploitation. In this conjuncture, SEZs (back then often labelled free-trade zones or export-processing zones) offered a handy set of standardised features to sustain capitalist exploitation and, at the same time, were advertised as policy measures that would deliver

Figure 16.1 Not Shenzhen: 1970s foundation stone of the Coromandel Industrial Estate with some occupied and some derelict factory buildings in the background, Mauritius Export Processing Zone. 2012. Source: Patrick Neveling.

post-colonial economic growth. The extended sales pitch was that zones attracted the relocation of advanced capitalist manufacturing industries from Western capitalist heartlands to newly independent states in the Third World.[9]

On the surface, this looked like a win for newly independent nations now taking a higher share of global manufacturing output and hoping for technology transfers from this. Yet it turned out to be – in the great majority of cases – sweatshop labour in garments and electronics factories that would relocate to the next zone as soon as wages increased, taking all their knowledge and market share with them. In fact, tax and customs waivers for investors, universal across SEZs, and lack of controls by national governments and local publics turned SEZs into epiphenomena of the neoliberal era.[10]

Easterling, instead, shows little concern for the historical fixes in global capitalism and previous modes of production. Her history of SEZ origins in Greco-Roman antiquity has a striking resemblance to Eurocentric notions of ancient Greece and Rome as the cradles of democracy, reason and advanced civilisation. What is more, this history overlaps with the mythologies that leading institutions in global SEZ promotion, from the World Bank to the World Economic Processing Zones Association (WEPZA), have proposed. The latter is a self-proclaimed 'association of leading practitioners, government officials, consultants, and academics engaged in evaluating, developing, promoting, and improving special economic zones … globally'.[11] This statement is no exaggeration, for indeed several of WEPZA's officers and board members hold influential positions in international organisations.[12] One member of the advisory board, Thomas Farole, is, at the time of writing, a leading World Bank economist for East Africa. More important is his authorship and editorship of various recent publications by the World Bank, more precisely the International Finance Corporation (IFC), which is a subsection of the World Bank.[13]

Founded in the 1950s, the IFC was supposed to act as a lender guarantor for private-sector investment in the Global South. As research by two journalist fellows of the Centre for Investigative Journalism shows, the IFC has since moved into the pole position as regards capital turnover of the World Bank, with a good share of its securities and loans going not where they are supposed to, to the much-fetishised small and medium-sized enterprises that will save the world, but to shadowy families owning corporations, such as the Schwarz family, the owners of the German discount supermarket chain Lidl.[14] In his earlier capacity as Senior Economist at the IFC Farole published a now widely cited book on special economic zones in Africa, which also has a thirty-page world history of SEZs. The historical origin of special economic zones offered there is the same one that Easterling published a year later – the Roman 'free' port in Delos.[15] How do we explain this unconventional convergence of neoliberal pseudo-academic writing from the World Bank with supposedly critical poststructuralist theory?

In my view, Easterling here uncritically embraces a neoliberal myth that wrongly backdates a contemporary capitalist practice to Greco-Roman antiquity, and the fact that she does so is a symptom of a world-historical turn in the social sciences and humanities. Whereas for several decades all master narratives of world history were rejected, now social scientists are suddenly supposed to think in *longue durée* categories such as the Anthropocene. This way, academics with little or no expertise in *longue durée* hook up on enticing narratives that the International Finance Corporation/World Bank serves to them and are attracted to a 2,500-year genealogy of a central articulation of capitalist exploitation in the present.

Yet it is of central importance to the social sciences and humanities how the history of SEZs is assessed, especially if we wish to end the exploitation of around 100 million workers producing the world's garments and light consumer electronics in more than 4,000 zones across more than 130 nations. Billions are made in zone enterprises, and it is surely no wonder that a World Bank institution such as the IFC has an interest in making us believe that ever since human history began in earnest – and where else would it begin but in Greek and Roman antiquity, the cradle of Western civilisation? – we have been setting up special economic zones. However, while backdating today's manifestations of inequality in world history may be central to the neoliberal project, to embrace such narratives from a supposedly critical, emancipatory, poststructuralist angle is a different ballgame, and it is important to uncover this as a shortcoming of academic research and theorising.

Certainly, Shenzhen turbo-morphed from a sparsely populated rural region on the Iron Curtain border with British Hong Kong in the 1970s to a world-leading and future-making megacity of the twenty-first century – and it certainly did so because it was one of the PRC's first SEZs. Yet to assume that Shenzhen is a current variant of Delos port policies under Roman rule around 167 BCE, as Easterling does, means to embrace a line of argument that equates the glamour of such zones with the 'ordinary' operations of capitalism. This is most evident in the portrayal of the zones as an exception, something that lies outside the normal and the centre and may yet tell us what the shape of the future will be. When Easterling labels the zones as 'extrastatecraft' in the title of her book – as something outside the masterful management of state affairs – she denies the very fact that states and their leadership create and manage the zones and have a vested interest in attributing their turbo-capitalist operations to an outside, to fictional market forces and the necessities they create. Easterling thus aligns poststructuralist reflexes with Carl Schmitt's misleading depictions of sovereignty and states of exception.

Exceptionalisers such as Easterling study and theorise special economic zones exactly the way that capital wants us to look at them, as 'special' and 'different', while they are as much the bread and butter of capitalism as the political economies that surround the zones. Thus, there is no need to follow Easterling's sensationalist assumptions that all urban futures are made in such megaprojects as the King Abdullah Economic Zone. Instead, it is important to keep in mind that it is a fairly trivial undertaking to plan a city and that most new cities or zones of the past decades never came anywhere near the rapid development of Shenzhen.

Figure 16.2 Shenzhen: view of civic centre from Lianhuashan Park, 2013. Source: Patrick Neveling.

Now, how does this impact on academic reflections on centrality and centres? If an understanding of the formation of centres in history also considers them as projects that were central to world-historical futures at the moment of their formation, then I suggest we move beyond research on past and present urban geographies and geopolitical hierarchies and towards an analysis of the productions, manifestations and articulations of such hierarchies. Cities rise and fall, centres come and go. What defines a centre, and whether it could hold in a given era of world history, lies in the capacity of a ruling class to collect tributes from humanity's production of wealth and to control how this is shared out. Centres and centrality are thus defined by the particular historical organisation and regulation of labour power/production *and* by the circulation of humans, goods and money in a given era. A critical world history considers the specificity of such organisation and regulation; in recent centuries this requires attention to how capital is accumulated, how means of production are appropriated, and how labour is exploited. My plea is thus for a return of focus to the continuities and differentiations of the obvious.

In the above I have argued one example for such a focus and discussed one of the most pronounced phenomena in late-modern capitalism:

the global spread of special economic zones. Such zones emerged when the geopolitical economy changed after 1945, and now their number stands at 4,000, with more than 100 million zone workers. Few nations do not have zone programmes, and many dream of zones that would trigger rapid, large-scale, industry-driven urbanisation, and create new centres like Shenzhen. Yet Shenzhen is exceptional not because it is an SEZ, but because it is a rare case of rapid development among thousands of SEZs that never delivered this and never will. Along with this mundane exceptionality comes a mythical exceptionality that goes all the way from zone origin-stories to allegedly foolproof development-policy toolkits for the creation of successful zones that never succeed. Social scientists and humanities scholars such as Keller Easterling are not immune to the allure of those myths. Instead, and here we go back to Castell's insights on the urban as a concentration of proletarian labour reserves, when Easterling delivers the poststructuralist equivalent of an World Bank-sponsored Eurocentric myth of SEZ origins, she also delivers a possible poststructuralist ideological backing that might help populate the King Abdullah SEZ and other such high-flying urbanisation projects with the precarious, proletarian labour reserve for the twenty-first century.

Notes

1. Castells, 1977.
2. Mitteis, 1952.
3. Frank, 1998.
4. Ong, 2006.
5. Easterling, 2012.
6. For details of why the port was anything but free, see Neveling, 2015b.
7. Easterling, 2012.
8. Easterling, 2014.
9. Neveling, 2015a.
10. Neveling, 2017.
11. See http://www.wepza.org (accessed 26 May 2017).
12. See http://www.wepza.org/officers/ (accessed 26 May 2017).
13. Farole, 2011.
14. Kennard and Provost, 2015. Also Kennard and Provost, 2016.
15. Farole, 2011.

Bibliography

Castells, Manuel. *The Urban Question: A Marxist Approach*, translated by Alan Sheridan. London: Edward Arnold, 1977.
Easterling, Keller. 'Zone: the spatial softwares of extrastatecraft', *Places Journal*, June 2012. Accessed 18 October 2018. https://doi.org/10.22269/120610.
Easterling, Keller. *Extrastatecraft: The Power of Infrastructure Space*. London: Verso, 2014.

Farole, Thomas. *Special Economic Zones in Africa: Comparing Performance and Learning from Global Experiences*. Washington, DC: World Bank, 2011.

Frank, Andre Gunder. *ReOrient: Global Economy in the Asian Age*. Berkeley: University of California Press, 1998.

Kennard, Matt and Claire Provost. 'Burma's rush for economic growth leaves its villagers homeless and jobless', *Independent*, 12 April 2015. Accessed 23 July 2019. https://www.independent.co.uk/news/world/asia/burmas-rush-for-economic-growth-leaves-its-villagers-homeless-and-jobless-10170113.html.

Kennard, Matt and Claire Provost. 'How aid became big business', *Los Angeles Review of Books*, 8 May 2016. Accessed 23 July 2019. https://lareviewofbooks.org/article/aid-became-big-business/.

Mitteis, Heinrich. *Über den Rechtsgrund des Satzes 'Stadtluft macht frei'*. Münster: Böhlau, 1952.

Neveling, Patrick. 'Export processing zones, special economic zones and the long march of capitalist development policies during the Cold War'. In *Decolonization and the Cold War: Negotiating Independence*, edited by Leslie James and Elisabeth Leake, 63–84. London: Bloomsbury Academic, 2015a.

Neveling, Patrick. 'Free trade zones, export processing zones, special economic zones and global imperial formations 200 BCE to 2015 CE'. In *The Palgrave Encyclopedia of Imperialism and Anti-Imperialism*, edited by Immanuel Ness and Zak Cope, 1007–16. Basingstoke: Palgrave Macmillan, 2015b.

Neveling, Patrick. 'The global spread of export processing zones, and the 1970s as a decade of consolidation'. In *Contesting Deregulation: Debates, Practices and Developments in the West since the 1970s*, edited by Knud Andresen and Stefan Müller, 23–40. New York: Berghahn Books, 2017.

Ong, Aihwa. *Neoliberalism as Exception: Mutations in Citizenship and Sovereignty*. Durham, NC: Duke University Press, 2006.

17
Explosion, response, aftermath

Joy Gerrard

Introduction

My work is about explosive events – protests, marches and riots – occurring in monumental spaces in the centres of large cities: Cairo, Kyiv, Chicago and elsewhere. In large black-and-white canvases, I try to capture and reflect the human and affective power which condenses – and explodes – in these architecturally framed spaces. I do this to ask questions about witnessing, mediation and collective fate. In this chapter I also reflect upon the unstable distinctions that exist between 'natural' and 'human' events, between our constructed environments and 'the environment' as a frame for political agency and lived experience.

So, what is an explosion? On one level, it is an outward force, a burst of artificially produced energy. But our sense of what an explosion denotes is also shaped by mediated representations. As an idiom of terror, explosion expresses absolute enmity and a relation to others with no possibility of dialogue. But equally, the idea that something is 'explosive' – a piece of theatre or literature – suggests a generative, productive force. Something is opened up and exposed; a truth is revealed. In reflecting on representation and mediation, my paintings foreground the precarious conjunction between the generative, the destructive and the explosive.

Archive and (re)images

As an effort to manage social and political differences, democratic processes always exist in tension with the desires and beliefs they express, even produce. The outcomes of such processes – sometimes only narrowly

Figure 17.1 Protest crowd, Kyiv, Ukraine, 2015. Japanese ink on linen, 130 x 190 cm. Source: Joy Gerrard and John Gerrard.

Figure 17.2 Protest crowd, Moscow, 2015. Japanese ink on linen, 165 x 255 cm. Source: Joy Gerrard and Dean Hotel.

Figure 17.3 Protest crowd, Charlotte, NC, USA, Black Lives Matter
(2016), 2017. Japanese ink on linen, 195 x 360 cm. Source: Joy Gerrard.

won – are frequently resisted, protested and critiqued. Visual-cultural
forms have the power, as the writer Rebecca Solnit puts it, to 'make injury
visible'.[1] As a spectacle of resistance, public protest has a long history and
persists as a powerful form, but is increasingly inextricable from its representation in real time, 'citizen-enabled' global media.

My working processes and the final product reflect the volatility and
unpredictability of the crowd – and, conversely, the permanence of the
architectural site within which it gathers. In the studio, I present protesting crowds, viewed from above, contained by the physical and social
architecture of cities. This work is based on painstaking archiving of
media images of crowds over many years, generally the quickly passed-
over ephemera of new reportage. I then make these images the subject of
large paintings. I think about aftermath: where might these images bring
us? The events that brought us the images often still affect us in many
and unexpected ways. How do we respond?

Explosion

Events such as the Brexit referendum and the Trump victory have been
widely experienced as unforeseen 'shocks'. Media discussion has drawn
on the terminology of natural events – a 'political firestorm' of protest

Figure 17.4 Protest crowd, Chicago, USA, Trump rally 2 (2016), 2017. Japanese ink on linen, 195 x 300 cm. Source: Joy Gerrard and Arts Council, Ireland.

in response to the US presidential election (CNN), recurrent references to 'disaster', a 'Trump storm'.

I am unexpectedly struck by the odd continuity between my current crowd images and a series of paintings I made several years ago, depicting tornadoes. They too were monochrome, ink on paper. At the time, I was making work that explored the structure of the 'event'. Tornadoes, typhoons and hurricanes are nearly always violent entities. At their peak, they are incredibly strong, and have a treacherous solidity made up of whirling detritus. This detritus is formed of thousands of objects, dust, earth and water. They cannot be physically stopped or their presence in time predicted. Their paths and consequences are unknowable. They confront us with the limits of our power. Witnessed as impersonal, another mediated visual sequence among a multitude, these processes are already naturalised, an 'environment' in which we can only hope to exist. Economic 'globalisation', for example, is presented as an irresistible fate to which we can only adapt. When it collapses in financial crisis, this might as well be a natural disaster, enveloping us, denying us agency, shaping our fate in ways we have no hope of controlling. In such a condition, the idea of resistance becomes hugely potent, the currency of a populism which, for those it minoritises, discriminates against and disadvantages, might just as well be a rising tide.

An event causes a rupture, an interruption, a break in lived experience. But it also demands interpretation and response. Mediation in language and image initiates and shapes this. Are we reconciled to the meaning of the event? Do we simply 'move on'? As 'events', these moments are detached from the processes that produce them.

What might happen immediately after an explosion or a violent natural cataclysm?

People who have survived being at the epicentre of an explosion sometimes describe a moment of pure silence immediately after impact, and many of us have seen this depicted visually in film. The world becomes pale and misty, dust and detritus whirl and float; there is a kind of awful, dreamlike beauty to the scene. And then, suddenly, noise, objects falling, screaming, fast movement. Shock. There is a realisation of reality; this is no dream. There are multiple different responses to an explosion. Survivors involved or at the centre flee outwards, as far away from the fulcrum of risk as possible. Responders and rescuers move inwards, urgently seeking to give emergency aid and also immediately seeking evidence and explanation. There is a constellation of trajectories of movement, but of course there is also total stillness. There will be still bodies, forever trapped at the centre of the constellation.

Figure 17.5   Protest crowd, Chicago, USA, Trump rally 1 (2016), 2017. Japanese ink on linen, 130 x 220 cm. Source: Joy Gerrard and Arts Council, Ireland.

Figure 17.6   Details from protest crowd, Kyiv, Ukraine, 2015. Japanese ink on linen, 130 x 190 cm. Source: Joy Gerrard.

Response 1: fear

When the meaning of events is uncertain, the power to interpret, mediate and communicate is extraordinary. Entrepreneurs of meaning compete with alternative visions of what we should be most afraid of. Refugees and immigrants flee from violent events in their own countries. Those to whom they flee see that danger adhering to them, as though carried in their skin and hair. I am struck by the continuity between my paintings and UKIP's now infamous image (used during the Brexit campaign) showing a refugee crowd and photoshopped to include mainly brown, bearded men, waiting to invade from a Europe to which they don't belong.

De Cauter analyses this particular fear in *The Capsular Civilization: On the City in the Age of Fear*. He geologises and separates contemporary fears into six strata,[2] at the base of which is demographic fear, or fear of overcrowding. By 2050, the world population will be 9 billion people. He posits this knowledge as a kind of sociological unease, of which we are all subconsciously aware, the simple fact of there being too many people on the planet. Migration becomes the obvious face or scapegoat of demographic fear and leads to De Cauter's fourth

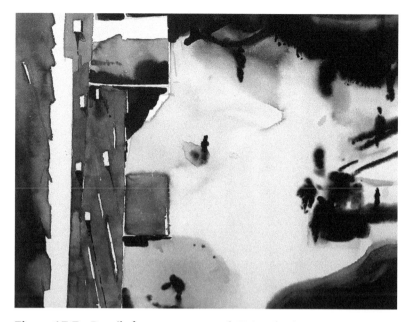

Figure 17.7 Details from protest crowd, Kyiv, Ukraine, 2015. Japanese ink on linen, 130 x 190 cm. Source: Joy Gerrard.

stratum, which is xenophobia, or fear of foreigners. This is rooted in a fear of change or disintegration of society as it stands. De Cauter's sixth fear is terrorism, which is of course distinguished by the deliberate pursuit of mediation and communication. De Cauter is, however, more concerned with American governmental response to terrorism in the form of rampant militarisation, technological militarisation and the notion of pre-emptive strikes, rather than the harm terrorism itself might inflict.

Response 2: protest

And then the response to the event moves outwards into the world. The event becomes news. News is narrative. Narrative requires characterisation. There are perpetrators, victims, survivors, witnesses. In every story there are heroes and villains, and sometimes these are reversed, depending on your location, viewpoint, position or politics. A crowd may form, to witness and mourn and sometimes to change the story and how it ends.

Trump's election and inauguration were two such moments. His election prompted both shock and awe, not unlike a physical event. And the protests that immediately followed were intensely visible expressions of resistance. The numbers attending his inauguration were set in simple visual comparison with the numbers at the Women's March, on the following day in the same location. The meaning of the event, its truth, became part of a bigger truth on which his election rested, or not. This 'digital multitude',[3] it seemed, could be re-counted, or recalibrated according to whim. The mainstream media, of course, also responded to the physical appearance of these huge crowds in civic spaces all over the world. Pictures flowed over us in a glorious, unfettered stream. There seemed to be a dominant triumvirate of visuals, the first showing the crowd from the air, the second the range of hand-painted and -produced signs and banners that people carried above them. And third, a range of 'confrontational' images, where there is a symbolic face-off, between protester and supporter, or protester and police officer. A kind of ping-pong of analysis emerged. Does protest work? What happens next? How does the appearance of resistance in the street translate to actual opposition inside the political system?

Figure 17.8 Installation view. 'Shot crowd' at the RHA gallery, Dublin. Joy Gerrard. Photograph by Ros Kavanagh.

Figure 17.9 Installation view. 'Shot crowd' at the RHA gallery, Dublin. Joy Gerrard. Photograph by Ros Kavanagh.

Aftermath 1: studio

I spend a great deal of time collecting and looking at these images of protesting crowds. In my studio work, I have concentrated almost completely on these images for a decade. I have thought about architectural and urban forms for almost my whole art career; but now, I am held in the embrace of an angry, protesting crowd. Except, I'm not actually held in the embrace of the crowd; instead I look at the crowd from above, constantly informed by media viewpoints. From here the crowd is always contained by architecture, and with this viewpoint we can see both the pull to the centre and the splintering that occurs at the edge of the crowd. It is a milling, moving force. We watch these crowd scenes unfolding from high buildings, helicopters and drones.

Using Japanese Sumi ink on canvas, I always paint in monochrome. There is a starkness that comes from the translation to black and white. There is also a relationship with photography; I am preoccupied with exposure. The blacks are burnt into the canvas, while the whites are made of nothing. They are simply the absent, naked ground of the canvas. And between black and white is a huge range of expressive greys. The material itself is volatile; the ground Sumi ink is precarious, never quite controlled, and has a life to it. I mix it with water to produce grey washes. Into these wet washes I drop the pure ink, and manipulate it, pulling out figures and shadows. The paintings must be made on the horizontal, so the canvas is laid flat on a working table. If it was placed

Figure 17.10 Installation view. 'Shot crowd' at the RHA gallery, Dublin. Joy Gerrard. Photograph by Ros Kavanagh.

on the perpendicular, the ink would simply run away, leaving just a trace or a shadow of the original placement.

With these paintings I need to be able to place the upper part of my body above the canvas, and work on small areas, one patch at a time. Eventually, these small areas combine into a singular image. Like all artists, I find the production of the image both a physical and mental chore. Most importantly, while working, I seek a transformative translation from the scopic moment of the original photographic image. Of course, this original photograph provides the exact time and location of the protest and shows architectural constraints and composition. But the process and volatility of the material alters the horizontal plane. Thousands of tiny, minute decisions and deliberations play out. And, finally, at the end of the making, there is often a grand gesture; a large area is darkened, a section disappears, a building is flattened.

Aftermath 2: gallery

The work I make is exhibited in public spaces in both London and Dublin. Here, too, meaning is pursued and imposed after the process, after the precarious, vertiginous moment of generative freedom, of both the civic space and the studio. From a distance, the paintings are intense and feel more figured. As you draw closer and enter the gallery, the image is formless, liquid and ambiguous. Then the viewer pulls away and the image comes back into sharp focus; the soft blacks become shadows of figures; square white shapes are distinct banners and placards.

Figure 17.11 Installation view. 'Shot crowd' at the RHA gallery, Dublin. Joy Gerrard. Photograph by Ros Kavanagh.

Vulnerable and contained, the crowd also holds a promise of renewal and change. We are changed by events, even if we experience that change as powerlessness. Confronting the schema in which events are presented, painting in permanent monochrome what passes in ephemeral colour, is a certain power not made present? The lens of history is both wide and narrow, obscured and focused. Right now, we still stand between past and future, time and image constantly unfolding.

Notes

1. Solnit, 2016, p. xiv.
2. De Cauter, 2004, p. 118.
3. Boal, Clark, Matthews and Watts, 2005.

Bibliography

Boal, Iain, T.J. Clark, Joseph Matthews and Michael Watts. *Afflicted Powers: Capital and Spectacle in a New Age of War*. London: Verso, 2005.
De Cauter, Lieven. *The Capsular Civilization: On the City in the Age of Fear*. Rotterdam: NAI Publishers, 2004.
Solnit, Rebecca. *Hope in the Dark: Untold Histories, Wild Possibilities*. Edinburgh: Canongate Books, 2016.

Part VI
Things fall: (after)lives of monumentality

18

Domestic monumentality: scales of relationship in the modern city

Adam Kaasa

Of all the urban projects that the Mexican architect and urbanist Mario Pani completed in his life, perhaps the largest single exercise that combined the restructuring of urban spaces, transport infrastructure, housing and services was the *Conjunto Urbano Nonoalco Tlatelolco* (Nonoalco-Tlatelolco) developed as an idea and built between 1949 and 1964 in Mexico City. At its opening on 20 November 1964,[1] it was a collection of 102 buildings capable of housing 100,000 people. Yet this monumental scale was just a portion of what was planned. In Pani's words:

> We wanted to continue with more projects, to expel all those who were living in poor neighborhoods, we wanted to build more and more housing complexes. I was planning on building five or six Tlatelolcos, with an extension of over 3 million square meters, two million square meters of gardens, and a capacity for 66,000 families.[2]

Monumental in terms of its built scale, its social programme, and its narrative promise for the Mexican nation state, Nonoalco-Tlatelolco was the end point of a series of larger and larger urban interventions led by Pani throughout the 1940s and 1950s.[3] And yet, like much post-war architectural and urban production, it is made up of, and responsive to, the domestic. While a definitive history of the development of the Nonoalco-Tlatelolco site has yet to be written, particularly one that brings together its social, political, architectural, material and visual manifestations, this chapter turns to the productions of a specific set of materials from the Taller de Urbanismo, an urban research studio founded by Mario Pani.

In doing so it demonstrates that foundational to the concept of the city and its new modernist monumentality was the domestic. In analysing this large state-funded modernist housing estate project in Mexico City, I work towards a concept of domestic monumentality, that is, the standardisation of the family and the place in which the family lives, in order to make possible through scales of relationship the concept and idea of the city itself.

The urban object

In preparation for the VII Pan American Congress of Architects in Havana from 10 to 16 April 1950, the Taller de Urbanismo centred on the development of an idea that would form the core of an urban approach to housing the urban poor in Mexico City, and would be used to justify the approach and logic of Nonoalco-Tlatelolco. On 6 March 1950, the then president of the Society of Mexican Architects and of the Colegio Nacional de Arquitectos de México Guillermo Zárraga wrote to President Miguel Alemán informing him of the upcoming congress, and given that several high-ranking diplomats and governmental representatives from across the Americas would be in attendance, he requested to be an official representative of the Mexican state. Zárraga also announced that the VIII Congress was selected to take place in Mexico City in 1952.[4] On 27 March 1950, Zárraga was officially granted permission to represent Mexico at the Congress.[5] The Mexican delegation included Guillermo Zárraga, José Luis Cuevas, Mario Pani, Carlos Contreras, Raúl Cacho, Héctor Mestre and Alonso Mariscal.[6]

The title of their presentation in Havana gives a good description of its intentions: 'Experimentos concretos de dispersión organizada y de concentración vertical para el mejoramiento de la habitación de la clase trabajadora en la capital de la República Mexicana' (Concrete experiments of organised dispersion and vertical concentration for the improvement of the housing of the working class in the capital of the Mexican Republic). Pani and Cuevas's study marks a distinct shift from the one produced a decade earlier by the German émigré and CIAM member Hannes Meyer. Theirs turned to a theory connecting working-class housing with the regeneration of what they termed the 'central hovel areas'. In short, the argument presented in Havana was as follows: as people move into new housing units, they vacate their older homes, which are then occupied by people from even lower classes, who vacate their homes. This housing ladder continues until the lowest-quality housing is vacated, so that 'the

authorities can freely dispose of these slums, once emptied, transforming them, for example, into magnificent sports fields'.[7] On 15 April 1950,
the Office of the President received a letter of praise from Benito Coquet,
the ambassador of Mexico to Cuba, about the Mexican participation in the
Congress, noting the extraordinary press coverage in Havana, with one
paper commenting on the relationship between modern architecture and
the revolutionary movement in Mexico.[8]

The visual materials analysed in the two sections below stem
from this presentation at the VII Pan American Congress of Architects
in Havana, which were published in *Arquitectura/México*,[9] and original presentation boards based on the study for the Congress from the
Archivo Pani in the Faculty of Architecture at the National Autonomous
University of Mexico (UNAM).[10] In the first section, I examine the visual
in terms of how it allows the translation of scale from the whole (city) to
the part (domestic apartment). Scale as a geographical and urban concept has a long history, as does the relationship of the whole to the part.
Latour suggests that the whole should be considered less than its parts,
and explores the implications this could have for theorising the aggre-
gate in social and physical relations.[11] In some ways, the 'operational concept', to use Certeau's words, worked to create a whole (Mexico City in
the 1950s and 1960s) that privileged a new understanding of the parts
(the domestic interior).[12] That is to say, in working to confront the urban
problem of Mexico City as a whole, there first needed to be the legitimation of the scale of the intervention, one which worked between the
apartment block and the neighbourhood unit. In what follows, I look at
some of the visual representations of Mexico City from the part to the
whole, to try and uncover ways in which the visual itself contributes to
the legitimacy of its scalar concept.

Scales of relationship

In 1961, Mario Pani's Urban Studio published a diagram showing the city
of Mexico from whole to part as it *is*, and as it *should be*.

On the right of the diagram, Pani's studio interprets Mexico City as
it is, with drawings of geographical units descending from the scale of
the metropolis, to the city, to the quarter, to the sector, to the *barrio*, to
the block, and to the house. The left of the diagram proposes a new order,
beginning still with a drawing of the metropolis, but then moving to an
urban community, to the neighbourhood unit (see below), to the superblock, to the group, and then to the house. Arrows draw us down from

the large scale of the urban to the small scale of the home. By identifying scales of relationship between parts of the city and their aggregates, this diagram creates the justification for intervening in them. By constructing the city from house to group to superblock to neighbourhood unit, this diagram positions the neighbourhood unit as a legible and legitimate scale of intervention. The Nonoalco-Tlatelolco project was defined at precisely this level.

The work presented at the Congress in Havana gives evidence of how visualisations of these scales can create links that do the work of assembling the parts into the whole. The research studio was using the terminology of the 'neighbourhood unit' or *unidad vecinal* as the organising principle for the city. That is, the neighbourhood should be a unique and self-sustaining part of the city as a whole, and therefore more needs to be considered in its planning than just housing. The neighbourhood unit should contain other public, commercial and social services, becoming a micro-city within the city.[13] The first thing one notices in a cursory overview of the document is that the visual register allows the authors to jump scales very quickly. The visual allows mental leaps of scale whose connection is not at all clear, by being able to contain the whole, the map of Mexico City, on one page, for example, and a part of that whole, a neighbourhood unit, on another. It moves from broad statistical information and mapping of the entire city of Mexico, to smaller models of a neighbourhood unit, to the individual house, complete with architectural drawings of interior rooms including details like house plants, and a person sitting cross-legged and reading a book. To the contemporary reader used to Google Earth flyovers, popular images of satellite photography zooming in to smaller and smaller parts, this may seem natural. However, the ability of the visual to produce such convincing scalar representations *produces* a relationship between the various scales which is such that things that may or may not be related do relate. A living room and a map of Mexico City, by way of their being within the logic of zooming in become, not just relational, but subject to a logic of aggregation. A change to the parts, the argument goes, will therefore have an effect on the whole.

The domestic made monumental

In the productions of these studies by Pani's Taller de Urbanismo, the living room *is* the house, *is* the unit, *is* the neighbourhood, *is* the zone of the city, *is* the city itself, not because they appear in the same publication, but because they are represented through the same visual logic linked through scalar relationships. They become analogically related through their shared method of visual representation. The notion of scale in the urban is meaningful precisely at the movement between two or three or four scales, a movement that produces the city as a fluid assemblage of aggregates made visible and articulable at certain distances to and from the object of the urban itself. The city is made to appear to the viewer only at certain intelligible scales, so that the question of what the city looks like *between* scales – for example, *between* the neighbourhood unit and the housing unit, *between* the visual script of the flow of pages in this document – becomes an impossibility, a non-representational movement between representable typologies of the city.

It is important for Pani and his colleagues in the Taller de Urbanismo that Mexico City is produced as both a whole in and of itself, a thing that can be defined, has boundaries, exists, and as an assemblage of parts, all interconnected and related. This is important because then one could justify thinking about the layout of a home as central to the structure of a block or neighbourhood and base this on structural or demographic information about the city as a whole. The visual construction of a relationship of scale constructs the mobility of content. The requirements of the neighbourhood unit in terms of services, for example, could provide legitimation for potential changes to city-wide transport, sewage, water or other infrastructures. Equally, having defined a problem at the urban scale, one could consider a solution that intervenes in a part of it, with a desired effect scaling up to the whole. This is how the domestic is made monumental.

While the move from the very large of the city to the very small of the room is not in any way an innovation in this particular set of visual materials, they do suggest that the arbitrariness of the zoom should be considered. What is the next appropriate scale after one has produced a visualisation of the scale of 'the city'? Is it the 'neighbourhood'? How big is the neighbourhood unit, and why? How much peripheral context do we show, and what detail of the particular? We do not get the choice of asking this question in the document examined here as it is published. Rather it asserts that the five spatial scales are: the city; the cardinal zone; the neighbourhood unit; the unit (apartment or house); and the room. The confidence of this scalar flow as a visual argument masks the debate, the controversy and finally the decision or professional understanding that the 'neighbourhood unit' would be an agreed, legible and legitimate unit in planning the city. Equally, it presumes that the smallest scale is that of the single-family home – a modern invention at the time with its own contextually produced histories.[14]

In analysing the visual presentation of scale in Mexico City from the publications of the Taller de Urbanismo in preparation for the Pan American Congress of Architects in 1950, it seems that one of the many strategies of the visual is that it allows the representation of an assemblage as an object. That is to say, it is a strategy to flatten the complexity of a myriad assemblage like a city. Returning to the presentation of the Nonoalco-Tlatelolco project a decade later, the organisational structure is equivalent. It opens with the city, shifts to the neighbourhood unit, and ends with details of the apartment blocks themselves. Without the 'map' of the city, and without the scales of this entity which are such that work can be broken down, divided, and reassembled into a whole, the presumed objective methods of urban research could not function. A research method requires an object, and the visual method is research, in and of itself, as much as it is the technology that produces the object it is researching. Equally, the legitimacy of the specific architectural interventions of Nonoalco-Tlatelolco depends on the relationships of scale created through the visual narrative from part to whole, so that the two-bedroom floor plan becomes an intelligible solution to the rapid urban growth of Mexico City. This is how the domestic becomes monumental in the modernist city.

I began this chapter with a quote from Mario Pani about the failed monumentality of the monumental modernity at Nonoalco-Tlatelolco. I end here with a quote from the project's inauguration on 20 November 1964. The speaker was introduced by Guillermo H. Viramontes, the president of the financers of the project, the Banco Nacional Hipotecario Urbano y de Obras Públicas (today known as Banobras). President Adolfo López Mateos took the microphone and began:

> At a distance of 443 years, you have given new life to Tlatelolco by creating this impressive city inside the great capital, next to the same venerable stone of our ancestors, enhancing the dignity and heroism of our race. This monumental urban estate aspires to be a symbol of the greatness of Mexico.[15]

As I focused on the visual artefacts produced in urban research studios and the projects of Mario Pani and his Taller de Urbanismo, at times I lost sight of their materiality. This inaugural moment brings the materiality of Tlatelolco back to the foreground. It opens our thinking not only in thinking the monumentality of the project, nor the link to the materiality of antiquity (the venerable stone whose ambiguous reference could point to either the temples of the ancient Aztec city, or to the sixteenth-century cathedral built on their ruins), but also to the relationship between architecture and the materiality of the state. What's missing among the ruins of monumental temples and churches is, perhaps, a material gesture to the tiled floors, the upholstery on couches and chairs and the texture of house plants, the materiality of the modern domestic imaginary that fuelled the scalar urban monumentality of the revolutionary Mexican state.

Notes

1. 20 November in Mexico is *el día de la revolución* ('the day of the revolution'), commemorating 20 November 1910, regarded as the start of the Mexican Revolution.
2. Gallo, 2010, p. 57.
3. Notable projects include the first multi-family housing block, the Centro Urbano Presidente Alémen, completed in 1949, and the Centro Urbano Benito Juárez, completed in 1952.
4. Box 433/622, Folio Presidente Miguel Alemán Valdes, Archivo General de la Nación. The Mexican edition of the Pan American Congress of Architects in 1952 centred on previews of the newly constructed University City, and provoked the comment from the US-based architect Richard Neutra that 'The epoch of the prima donna is, perhaps forever, gone. If architects want to accomplish the mission they have claimed in our time they should do as the Mexican architects: work in teams and understand that a common mission can only be realized collectively' (quoted in Flaherty, 2013, p. 258).
5. It is interesting to note that on 16 March 1950, nine days before granting Zárraga permission to represent Mexico at the Congress, Rogerio de la Selva, the President's consul, received a letter from Mario Pani, in his capacity as *El Vocal Pro-Cultura* (representative for culture) at the Society of Mexican Architects, confirming the status of Guillermo Zárraga as president of both the Society of Mexican Architects and the Colegio Nacional de Arquitectos de México. Both letters from Box 433/622, Folio Presidente Miguel Alemán Valdes, Archivo General de la Nación.
6. Carlos Contreras is widely heralded as the most important urban planner in post-revolutionary Mexico, responsible for the 1933 'Plano Regulador del Distrito Federal' (Contreras, 2003).
7. Cuevas, 1950, p. 21. Translations by Adam Kaasa except where stated otherwise.
8. Box 433/622, Folio Presidente Miguel Alemán Valdes, Archivo General de la Nación.
9. Cuevas, 1950.
10. The study from the archives is authored by the architects Mario Pani, José Luis Cuevas, Dominguez García Ramos and H. Martinez de Hoyos and the engineer Victor Vila; the publication is twenty-seven pages long and primarily visual. Some of the images were subsequently published in *Arquitectura/México*: see, for example, Gomez Mayorga, 1949; Cuevas, 1950; García Ramos, 1959.
11. Latour, Jensen, Venturini, Grauwin and Boullier, 2012.
12. Certeau, 1984, p. 94.
13. For a history of the concept, including the argument that the 'neighbourhood unit' has its genesis not in an influential paper written by the US sociologist Clarence Perry ([1929]1998), but in earlier professional debates in Chicago between 1898 and 1916, see Johnson, 2002. For more on the neighbourhood unit in practice, see Mumford, 1954.
14. For a history of the home in Mexico, see Shipway and Shipway, 1960. For modernist ideals of the future of the home in Mexico, see Hannes, 1982. For a contemporary reading of the space of the home in Mexico, see Pader, 1993. For a history of modernity and changes to the single detached home in the US, see Clark, 1986, pp. 131–70.
15. Vivir en Tlatelolco, 2012.

Bibliography

Certeau, Michel de. *The Practice of Everyday Life*, translated by Steven Rendall. Berkeley: University of California Press, 1984.

Chapa, Rubén Cantú. *Tlatelolco: La autoadministración en unidades habitacionales: Gestión urbana y planificación*. Mexico City: Plaza y Valdés, 2001.

Clark, Clifford Edward. *The American Family Home, 1800–1960*. Chapel Hill: University of North Carolina Press, 1986.

Contreras, Carlos. 'El Plano Regulador del Distrito Federal'. In *Planificación y urbanismo visionarios de Carlos Contreras: Escritos de 1925 a 1938*, edited by Gerardo G. Sánchez Ruiz, 85–129. Mexico City: Universidad Nacional Autónoma de México, 2003.

Cuevas, José Luis. 'Raiz, contenido y alcance de una ponencia', *Arquitectura/México* 31 (1950): 20–5.

Flaherty, George F. 'Mario Pani's hospitality: Latin America through *Arquitectura/México*'. In *Latin American Modern Architectures: Ambiguous Territories*, edited by Patricio del Real and Helen Gyger, 251–69. New York: Routledge, 2013.

Gallo, Rubén. 'Tlatelolco: Mexico City's urban dystopia'. In *Noir Urbanisms: Dystopic Images of the Modern City*, edited by Gyan Prakash, 53–72. Princeton, NJ: Princeton University Press, 2010.

García Ramos, Domingo. 'Tesis sustentadas en los trabajos del Taller de Urbanismo del Arq. Pani', *Arquitectura/México* 67 (1959): 161–71.

Gómez Mayorga, Mauricio. 'El problema de la habitación en México: realidad de su solución. Una conversación con el arquitecto Mario Pani', *Arquitectura/México* 27 (1949): 67–74.

Johnson, Donald Leslie. 'Origin of the neighbourhood unit', *Planning Perspectives* 17, no. 3 (2002): 227–45.

Latour, Bruno, Pablo Jensen, Tommaso Venturini, Sébastian Grauwin and Dominique Boullier. '"The whole is always smaller than its parts": a digital test of Gabriel Tardes' monads', *British Journal of Sociology* 63, no. 4 (2012): 590–615.

Meyer, Hannes. 'El espacio vital de la familia'. In *Apuntes para la historia y crítica de la arquitectura mexicana del siglo XX, 1900–1980*, vol. 1, edited by Alexandrina Escudero, 165–71. Mexico City: Secretaría de Educación Pública/Instituto Nacional de Bellas Artes, 1982.

Mumford, Lewis. 'The neighborhood and the neighborhood unit', *Town Planning Review* 24, no. 4 (1954): 256–70.

Pader, Ellen-J. 'Spatiality and social change: domestic space use in Mexico and the United States', *American Ethnologist* 20, no. 1 (1993): 114–37.

Perry, Clarence. *The Neighbourhood Unit* (Early Urban Planning 7). London: Routledge/Thoemmes Press, [1929]1998.

Shipway, Verna Cook and Warren Shipway. *The Mexican House, Old and New*. New York: Architectural Book Publishing Company, 1960.

Vivir en Tlatelolco. 'Hoy cumple la Unidad Tlatelolco 48 años', *Vivir en Tlatelolco: Periodismo comunitario*, 21 November 2012. Accessed 28 July 2019. http://vivirtlatelolco.blogspot.co.uk/2012/11/hoy-cumple-la-unidad-tlatelolco-48-anos.html.

19
On an alleged thought of inflicting harm on a Lenin statue

Oleksiy Radynski

The following text is based on my intervention in the conference 'The Centre Cannot Hold', held in June 2016 at the Calvert 22 Gallery in London. As a response to an invitation by Michał Murawski to give a talk within the framework of 'New monumentality, neo-modernism and other zombie urban utopias', I suggested that the venue of this event itself should be put into question and reflected upon. Since the outbreak of war in Ukraine sparked by Russian military occupation of Crimea in March 2014, I've been staging interventions at various Russia-related institutions and events, calling for the release of Ukrainian political prisoners held in Russia. Calvert 22 Gallery is a project of Calvert 22 Foundation that was, following 2011, sponsored by VTB Capital, an investment company linked to Russia's VTB Bank, which was sanctioned in 2014 by the US, EU and Canada for its financial support of the Russian invasion of Ukraine. Initially, the partnership between Calvert 22 Foundation and VTB Capital was hailed by the latter as 'a key part of VTB Capital's soft power approach to changing perceptions of Russia'.[1] Even though the strategic partnership between Calvert 22 Foundation and the VTB was said to be over in 2015, the Foundation's Calvert Journal, *branding itself as 'a guide to the New East', has frequently been criticised for fostering a 'soft-power' neo-colonial approach to the region formerly known as the Soviet-dominated Eastern bloc.[2] This context has shaped the text of my intervention, which is reproduced below along with some updates and clarifications added in April 2019.*

My intervention aims to reflect on a certain interruption in the cultural exchange that occurs between Russia and so-called Central Eastern Europe. The interruption I'm talking about was caused in spring 2014 by the military occupation of the Crimean Peninsula by the Russian army, the subsequent annexation of Crimea, and the war in eastern Ukraine, which was ignited first of all in order to conceal and distract attention from the Crimean land grab.

At that point in time, my own research on internationalism and colonialism in Soviet Crimean architecture was interrupted as well, but this fact is of no importance compared to the scale of the social and cultural disaster that is taking place in Crimea at the moment. So, rather than presenting my interrupted research, I will focus on the interruption itself, and on the impact of this interruption on art, culture, new monumentality, zombie urbanism, and so on.

In May 2014, the Crimean film director Oleg Sentsov and the anti-fascist activist Aleksandr Kolchenko were kidnapped in Simferopol by the Russian secret services. They were smuggled into Russia, stripped of their Ukrainian citizenship, and put through a show trial that led to their imprisonment for twenty and ten years respectively. Sentsov and Kolchenko were accused of participation in a notorious nationalist group, the Right Sector. This shows, of course, a kind of gloomy irony on the part of the Russian judiciary, since Aleksandr Kolchenko is known to be a committed anarchist and anti-fascist. Sentsov and Kolchenko ended up in Russian prison solely because of their opposition to the Russian invasion of Crimea.

I regard the arrest and imprisonment of Sentsov and Kolchenko as acts of war committed by the Russian Federation with a particular purpose. This purpose is to create an unbridgeable gap between the cultural communities of Russia and Ukraine by jailing one of the most promising Ukrainian film directors, Oleg Sentsov. How to respond to this act of war? One way to elude this logic of division would be to continue the so-called cultural dialogue, to try to prevent politics from interfering with cultural life, and to go on with the other ways of cynical self-justification. Another option is a boycott, which is problematic not only because of Russia's size – much bigger than Israel – but also because the boycott would play into the hands of Russia's intentions to create an insoluble conflict between cultural actors in the two countries.

I would suggest a different response to a state of exception that is created by the ongoing imprisonment of Sentsov and Kolchenko. Rather than a boycott, what we need is an obsessive participation in the activities of cultural institutions related to Russia, but this participation should be limited to the topic of the imprisonment of Sentsov and Kolchenko, with the aim of creating the pressure necessary for their release or prisoner exchange. My point is that any event with Russian backing – be it state or private – may and should be hijacked in order to remind Russia that business as usual is not possible as long as Sentsov and Kolchenko remain in jail.[3] It seems that the Calvert Foundation is an appropriate place to do so.

For better or worse, in this context I cannot limit myself to a mere political statement totally unrelated to the conference topic, although that's what I would have preferred to do. The thing is that the trial of Sentsov and Kolchenko is deeply related to the issues of new monumentality, and it's certainly linked to a kind of a zombie utopia. In fact, Sentsov and Kolchenko were accused by the court of an alleged plan to blow up a Lenin statue in Simferopol as an act of terror that would plunge Crimea into chaos.[4] This is obviously a kind of symbolic overreaction to a wave of Leninoclasm that has swept through Ukraine since 2014.[5] But this accusation reveals an interesting paradox that underlies the Putin regime.

On the one hand, Lenin monuments have a kind of a sacred status in Russia: one can get an exorbitant prison term there merely for an alleged thought about inflicting harm on a Lenin statue. On the other hand, the current Russian regime is perhaps the most anti-Leninist in the since the Revolution of 1917. This is obvious, for instance, from regular public attacks by Putin on Lenin, whom he constantly accuses of ruining the might of the Russian empire. This is understandable, since Putin's rule reminds us more and more of the regime that was toppled by the Bolsheviks 100 years ago.

On 7 June 2016, one of the Lenin monuments in Moscow was toppled by unknown perpetrators – and his head went missing. This action most probably referred to the fact that many of the Lenin monuments in Soviet public space were actually the replacements of Stalin statues, erected in the late 1950s in a wave of de-Stalinisation. And it was rumoured that this particular Moscow monument had in the past actually been a Stalin figure, with Lenin's head attached to it later. This anecdote explains a great deal about the unfortunate case of Ukrainian Leninoclasm: the attacks on the Lenin statues in Ukraine are not really attacks on the Bolshevik leader himself. They are actually attacks against a certain historical period in which these monuments were erected, namely the 1960s to the 1980s, which was a period of a neo-colonial policy of the Russification of Ukraine and ruthless exploitation of its natural resources.

In the centre of Kyiv, there's a plinth of a toppled Lenin statue that now looks like a piece of minimalist sculpture.[6] On its side, there's an inscription that has miraculously survived the recent popular rage. This quote from Lenin says: 'The united activity of Russian and Ukrainian proletarians makes a free Ukraine possible. Without such a unity free Ukraine is unthinkable.' I would add that the same could be said about the conditions under which a free Russia is possible.

Notes

1. 'hecksinductionhour', 2013.
2. Shortly after my publication of an essay mentioning the connections between the Foundation and VTB Capital on a Russian website, Colta.ru, all mentions of VTB went missing from the Foundation's website.
3. On 7 September 2019, Oleg Sentsov and Oleksandr Kolchenko were released from Russian prison in a prisoner swap. Needless to say, this does not affect any of the positions expressed in this text, especially on the complicity of Russia-related institutions in this war crime of the five-year-long illegal detention of Sentsov and Kolchenko.
4. Apart from the alleged bombing attempt, the accusations against Sentsov and Kolchenko included the burning of an office of a pro-Russian political party in Crimea (which, unlike the monument bombing, actually took place; Sentsov and Kolchenko deny all charges against them). The case against Sentsov and Kolchenko was condemned as a political show trial by various international human rights organisations, and the evidence presented by the prosecutors in court was vague even by the standards of the Russian judiciary (it was largely based on the testimony of Gennadiy Afanasiev, another alleged plot member, who later claimed that this testimony was forced from him by torture).
5. The Maidan uprising that started in Kyiv in late 2013 was accompanied by the spontaneous demolition of Lenin monuments, which were largely untouched during the first wave of 'de-communisation' in the early 1990s, when Ukraine gained independence from the Soviet Union. In spring 2015, the Ukrainian parliament passed a series of laws on 'de-communisation' that ordered the removal of all statues of Lenin and many other Soviet-era monumental works from public space.
6. I'm indebted to Vasyl Cherepanyn for the ideas discussed in this paragraph.

Bibliography

'hecksinductionhour'. 'Marxism today (or, The Soft power approach to changing perceptions of Russia)', *Chtodelat News*, 27 April 2013. Accessed 21 July 2019. https://chtodelat.wordpress.com/2013/04/27/marxism-today/.

20

We're losing him! On monuments to Lenin, and the cult of demolition in present-day Ukraine[1]

Yevgenia Belorusets

In this photograph (Figure 20.1), the figure of Lenin is absent; instead we see a man standing guard over a pedestal, his arms thrust open, looking straight ahead.

Vandals are absent too. Just a man and a pedestal, each taking root within the other. Winter's cold interacts with the cold of the stone; just as the power of nature does with the inviolability of the pedestal, the poor quality of the picture renders its contents abstract and turns the human figure into an outline, an anonymous form.

The difference in scale is clear; the man – immeasurably more vulnerable, unable to stand whole before the statue, to cover it with his body.

Yet the man is able to adopt a pose reminiscent of crucifixion, no less expressive than the iconic gesture of a sculpted Lenin raising his right arm, demonstrating the correct path.

This photograph is among many untitled images to be found online, and which illustrate the process of the destruction of Lenin statues throughout Ukraine. Finding a high-resolution version, or discovering its true source, the photographer or the exact location where it was taken, has proved difficult. Most frequently, this image is attached to news stories about an unsuccessful attempt to topple a monument to Lenin which occurred in Slovyansk in the Donbas region in January 2015.

At that time, the war with Russia was in its 'hot phase': further seizures of towns and cities, to the accompaniment of artillery fire, still lay ahead.

Figure 20.1　A man guards the pedestal of a Lenin statue. Photographer unknown.

In those days, small towns in Donbas lived either in hope of being saved, or in fear of impending disaster. The root causes of disaster and salvation were constantly changing places. The war lumbered on threateningly, while for half a year the residents of Slovyansk resolutely defended their Lenin monument until, following several unsuccessful attempts, it was finally destroyed in June 2015.

It might seem that a monument to Lenin is a symbol of an era which is irrevocably past. After Ukraine gained its independence from the Soviet Union in 1991, these monuments were just utterly unremarkable objects which, with few exceptions, remained outside the sights of politics right up until 2013. Yet on 8 December, during a protest on Maidan, the first statue in Kyiv was brought down. Responsibility for the statue's destruction was claimed by the far-right 'Freedom' party.

The eighth of December can be considered one of the key turning points of Maidan. It was the third protest and, until that point, the largest recorded assembly of protesters. According to many estimates, participants numbered over 1 million. The protesters gathered not just on Independence Square, but also in neighbouring Institutskaya Street and in Kreschatik, Kyiv's principal thoroughfare. Participants in the gathering were calling for the punishment of all those responsible for the beating of protesters in Kyiv, the prosecution of the head of the police force, Vitaliy

Zaharchenko, the resignation of members of the government, and the announcement of parliamentary and presidential elections. When the protesters started to transfer their attention away from the declaration of demands to the planning of immediate actions, such as the occupation of the presidential administration building, an unknown group of masked protesters began to demolish the Lenin monument in Bessarabskaya Square. This collective destruction of a monument would have passed virtually unnoticed but for the fact that it changed the whole plot of the protest, becoming its denouement, its crowning achievement.

For the first time in the history of Maidan, an unplanned, symbolic and empty gesture outshone the goals of the protest, overshadowing the order of play, literally laying claim to its purpose and ideas. The demolition of this monument made from rare red granite was followed by the selling-off of its fragments and the theft of the large remaining lump of the shattered statue. Thus began a spontaneous process which later gained the name of 'Leninopad' – 'Leninfall' – the destruction of monuments to Lenin all over Ukraine. Almost every impromptu demolition was accompanied by ritual celebrations; many battles were fought to try to preserve monuments, as though the political future of Ukraine was to depend fully on their (non-)existence.

It seems to me that on 8 December, the Euromaidan movement, a social, political, human rights protest, was infected by populist action, an action that was senseless, and invoked to supplant essential practical and political decisions. Wherever poverty and desperation demanded immediate change or at least a programme of reforms which would be comprehensible to the masses, monuments were ruined and continue to be destroyed, and streets have been, and are being, renamed.

Lenin returns?

The space left after the toppling of the statue in Kyiv, and by others which were later demolished, was for some an unstable realm of long-suppressed hopes for a different future. For others it became a no longer relevant symbol of imperialism, oppression, totalitarianism, and a host of other ideas. And suddenly, unexpectedly, starting with events on Maidan, this empty space, like a hollow or a canal, was being filled up with the water of a new existence.

In this photo (Figure 20.2), taken by me during one of my trips to Donbas, Lenin has acquired an opinion, a view on reality and on politics, and finds his voice after many years' silence.

Figure 20.2 Dimitrov, a town in Luhansk region, October 2014. Graffiti on the monument: 'LENIN is FOR Dimitrov, FOR PEACE!' Source: Yevgenia Belorusets.

Who shares this voice with Lenin? Those who count themselves among the oppressed? Those who have no voice? Is this a voice from the past? Is this voice at least in some small way connected to the historical figure, Vladimir Ilyich Lenin?

The photo is from Dimitrov, a mining town in the Luhansk region where women from a workers' neighbourhood tried to defend the Lenin monument from destruction. Anti-Lenin activists were forced to resort to multiple small surgical amputations – at first, in August 2014, they cut off a hand; later they managed to take off a piece of his foot – until finally they succeeded in bringing the whole thing down.

An older resident of Dimitrov who joined protests in defence of the Lenin statue told me that since Lenin was not to blame for the war, she would, at least for that reason, have liked him not to be brought down. I started asking her questions about the statue, and she burst into tears: 'Let us keep our Lenin! If only because it's ours, not something that belongs to somebody else. We're protecting him, yet they're calling us "enemies". Is history really our enemy?'

And then I spoke to an activist from a Ukrainian battalion stationed near Dimitrov, who, until the passing of the anti-communist laws, had tried together with his friends to destroy all the statues and busts of Lenin within reach. He maintained: 'Lenin represents a past which is waging war on us. Lenin is post-Soviet power, the system which until now has been destroying our country. Lenin is Russian imperialism in its purest form and, at the end of the day, he's a symbol of separatism and corruption. If he stays standing, our country will also stand still, it'll go nowhere, it cannot become European so long as monuments to Lenin stand.'

From these conflicting utterances arises a 'Lenin-fragment', a living splinter of political projections, absolute evil, rising from the grave like the living dead or an innocent victim of the arbitrariness of a modern history which has decided to take revenge on those who conjured its beginnings. Those who have succeeded in appropriating and affirming one of the *meanings* of the figure of Lenin shall determine the fate of monuments to him.

Residents of central, eastern and western Ukrainian cities, those who defended Lenin statues and tried to save them from destruction, often told me that they see history itself in these typical Soviet sculptures. It's a history which they say 'doesn't bother them' and should, therefore, stay in their towns.

'Doesn't bother.' Does that mean it helps in some way, or serves some purpose? Paraphrasing the pre- and post-revolutionary Russian

Figure 20.3 Cover from *Red Neva* magazine, No. 3, dedicated to 'A year without Lenin', 18 January 1925 (the year after his death). Source: Yevgenia Belorusets.

poet Osip Mandelstam, I think the time has come to discuss a process of forced separation from history and continuity, and the fact that history without debate and discussion once again finds itself under the control of a marginal political ideology which attempts to usurp its quality, its sense, on behalf of everyone.

After a long absence, Lenin appears before us anew, as a frightening or perhaps long-awaited personification of history, a history-she-wolf who appeared, just as at the founding of Rome, intending to suckle children abandoned by their mother. But the children were dragged away from the she-wolf too soon, and now they cry with hunger.

And, if history can conceal danger within itself, if it can become a shadow chasing after society, then deliverance from history, as it turns out, can have a ritualistic nature.

A ritual with fragments

In February 2015, the head of a local Lenin statue was taken from the village of Taynitsa in the Kyiv region. It had been erected in the 1950s and had played the part of the sole cultural object or work of art in this tiny community. It's not known who was behind the act.

Earlier that evening, they had wrapped the monument in ropes, shouting over and over, 'Glory to the nation, death to enemies!' and 'Glory

Figure 20.4 The head of a Lenin statue from the village of Taynitsa. https://twitter.com/HromadskeUA/status/565627298683301890.

to Ukraine, glory to the heroes!' They brought Lenin down and, continuing to shout, took to smashing the statue into smithereens. Somehow, the head remained intact.

The head is a standard trophy. Since the demolitions began in 2013, it falls into the victors' hands, to the destroyers of monuments, and they carry it off. As for Lenin's body, they break it up into tiny pieces, which are commonly discarded, left to lie around the plinth.

A year earlier, in February 2014, in Pereyaslav-Khmel'nitskiy, to the east of Kyiv, another statue of Lenin had been removed in the spirit of the early Christian wars on paganism. Activists wanted to drown it in one of the local rivers, like an idol. Having first destroyed it, they gave a salute.

That same month, during the destruction of a Lenin monument in the regional centre of Khmel'nitskiy, an act of revenge took place. Activists first tried to cut off its head, but when that failed, they sawed off an ear. In such a way, the activists carried out vengeance for a well-known Maidan activist, who had been abducted and subjected to torture a month earlier.

This ritual arises unexpectedly, as if bursting up out of the ground, and becomes a part of the sudden rebellion against Lenin, ready to embody the strength of the anti-Maidan, of Ukraine's colonial past, of the reign of (the toppled Ukrainian president) Yanukovych.

Figure 20.5 'The heart of Lenin' from fragments from the village of Taynitsa. 'Let's put Lenin's head back together again!' exhibition at Pinchuk Art Centre, Kyiv, October 2015–April 2016. Source: Yevgenia Belorusets.

Figure 20.6 An ear of Lenin from Odessa Region. 'Let's put Lenin's head back together again!' exhibition at Pinchuk Art Centre, Kyiv, October 2015–April 2016. Source: Yevgenia Belorusets.

De-communisation, monuments to Lenin and the rituals of their destruction should it seems be the source material for building a new Ukrainian political myth. And yet there still does not exist an overarching objective, a programme which could unite these separate and chaotic actions. Demolition of monuments, of mosaics, of frescoes, of bas-reliefs has been going on since 2013, but these acts continue to resemble senseless vandalism, chaotic, nervy demonstrations of power, which, apart from political symbols, has almost nothing to offer society.

As it turned out, it has proved impossible to fashion a new national myth from these fragments of Soviet monuments, nor even an image of an enemy which is in the least bit convincing. They also fail to constitute justification for appropriation by the new regime of the legacy of Maidan. The destruction of monuments, and de-communisation, was never a goal or even a part of this protest.

Fragment/fetish

Even so, monuments to Lenin have, since 2013, returned to the sphere of politics. They have become a part of the protest movement, fulfilling the role of a ritual object; they are destroyed and defended.

Following the destruction of a monument, the empty pedestal is usually painted in the colours of the Ukrainian flag, an act which cannot but recall an Orthodox Christian ritual of consecration, and reclamation of space. As for the sculpture itself, if it was significant or presented a certain 'cultural value', it would usually disappear without a trace, its fragments turning with great speed into trophies or fetishes.

A search which I undertook, lasting several months, proved fruitless in that it failed to unearthing even a few pieces of the 3.5-metre-tall granite statue in Kyiv. All the fragments disappeared without trace into private, secret collections.

A similar thing happened to the massive bronze figure of Lenin from the second-largest city in Ukraine, Kharkiv, which stood 8.5 metres tall. Somehow, journalists from the city's public TV station were able to acquire Lenin's nose.

Lenin's nose turned out to be the only intact piece of the giant monument. It completed the journey to Kyiv and now, following its exhibition at the Pinchuk Art Centre, it is available for hire.

Trying to assemble not even an entire figure, but just the head, of a Lenin, is an undertaking doomed to fail.

Figure 20.7 The nose of Lenin from Kharkov. 'Let's put Lenin's head back together again!' exhibition at Pinchuk Art Centre, Kyiv, October 2015–April 2016. Source: Yevgenia Belorusets.

Figure 20.8 'Let's put Lenin's head back together again!' exhibition at Pinchuk Art Centre, Kyiv, October 2015–April 2016. Source: Yevgenia Belorusets.

The pieces are scattering in all directions. The meaning of the present is slipping away. Imagination, action, politics, tears, hands extended in a dramatic gesture – I have to cut short my reading of the events connected to the destruction of monuments to Lenin. We can freely arrange them into any narrative, but in this particular work, it seemed better to me to present fragments which resist attempts to build something from them.

Note

1.   Translated by Rahim Rahemtulla and Patrick Evans.

Bibliography

Collier, Stephen J. *Post-Soviet Social: Neoliberalism, Social Modernity, Biopolitics*. Princeton, NJ: Princeton University Press, 2011.
Cover and illustrations, *Yunye Stroiteli* [Young Builders]. Moskau 3 (1924).
Cover and illustrations, *Krasnaia niva* [Red Cornfield]. Moskau 3 (1925).

Geertz, Clifford. *The Interpretation of Cultures: Selected Essays*. New York: Basic Books, 1973.

Merridale, Catherine. *Night of Stone: Death and Memory in Twentieth-Century Russia*. New York: Viking, 2001.

Plamper, Jan. *The Stalin Cult: A Study in the Alchemy of Power*. New Haven, CT: Yale University Press, 2012.

Rancière, Jacques. *Disagreement: Politics and Philosophy*, translated by Julie Rose. Minneapolis: University of Minnesota Press, 2004.

Tumarkin, Nina. *Lenin Lives! The Lenin Cult in Soviet Russia*. Cambridge, MA: Harvard University Press, 1983.

Verdery, Katherine. *The Political Lives of Dead Bodies: Reburial and Postsocialist Change*. New York: Columbia University Press, 1999.

Index

Lightning Source UK Ltd.
Milton Keynes UK
UKHW052206070722
405523UK00024B/419